DAMN GLAD
TO MEET YOU

DAMN GLAD TO MEET YOU

MY SEVEN DECADES IN THE HOLLYWOOD TRENCHES

TIM MATHESON

New York

Hachette Books
Hachette Book Group
1290 Avenue of the Americas
New York, NY 10104
HachetteBooks.com
Twitter.com/HachetteBooks
Instagram.com/HachetteBooks

First Edition: November 2024

Published by Hachette Books, an imprint of Hachette Book Group, Inc. The Hachette Books name and logo are trademarks of the Hachette Book Group.

The Hachette Speakers Bureau provides a wide range of authors for speaking events. To find out more, go to hachettespeakersbureau.com or email HachetteSpeakers@hbgusa.com.

Books by Hachette Books may be purchased in bulk for business, educational, or promotional use. For information, please contact your local bookseller or email the Hachette Book Group Special Markets Department at Special.Markets@hbgusa.com.

The publisher is not responsible for websites (or their content) that are not owned by the publisher.

Print book interior design by Amy Quinn

Library of Congress Cataloging-in-Publication Data

Name: Matheson, Tim, 1947– author.
Title: Damn glad to meet you: my seven decades in the Hollywood trenches / Tim Matheson.
Description: New York: Hachette Books, 2024.
Identifiers: LCCN 2024016273 | ISBN 9780306832932 (hardcover) | ISBN 9780306832949 (trade paperback) | ISBN 9780306832956 (ebook)
Subjects: LCSH: Matheson, Tim, 1947– | Actors—United States—Biography.
Classification: LCC PN2287.M54283 A3 2024 | DDC 792.02/8092
  [B]—dc23/eng/20240708
LC record available at https://lccn.loc.gov/2024016273

ISBNs: 9780306832932 (hardcover); 9780306832956 (ebook); 9780306837081 (B&N.com signed edition); 9780306837562 (B&N Black Friday Signed Edition); 9780306837074 (signed edition)

Printed in the United States of America

LSC-C

Printing 1, 2024

To Lizzie
My beloved wife. Without whom there would be no passion or
Third Act in my life. You accepted my proposal over tacos, shared a
honeymoon amidst the Japanese cherry blossoms, and bring joy and love
to my heart every day I awake to find you next to me.

Contents

Fade In

I CAN BARELY BREATHE.

My chest is clenched like an angry fist. Small gasps of air only. *Last* gasps, I'm certain. The exam room spirals. My hold on reality waning—*Will my children know where to find the will?*—I reach for a pallid wall to steady myself as the doctor sullenly reenters the room. Test results in his hands, he may as well be carrying a scythe or a guillotine.

"I'm not surprised," the doctor confirms.

I knew it! The big one. I probably have an hour, tops. I focus on the stark walls again softened only by a few framed diplomas and medical charts. My own story soon to be told only as a cold statistic on that same wall the color of a sun-bleached skull. I calculate who, if anyone, will visit me before my Shakespearean "mortal coil is shuffled."

My wife of twenty-five years has recently left me. My kids have chosen sides, and somehow, I've become the bad guy. *Bonanza* and *Animal House* and *The West Wing* are all now ancient history, like I'm about to be. My last feature movie role was as "Eli's Dad #2."

And the two TV networks I'm currently working for are suing me. *No wonder it's the end . . .*

"Is there anything we can do now, doctor?" I ask terrified.

"Nothing much really," he confirms.

Dear God. "I can't believe it." I'm gripping my heart. (Or where I thought it was.) "So, now what? I just wait while my heart stops working or—"

"No," he says. "*This* . . ." He indicates me. "Your heart's fine, I'd say. It's just nerves or maybe even a little panic attack."

Huh . . . ? I cock my head like a dog watching Chris Farley get out of a bathtub.

"If this were a heart attack . . ." He waves the test printouts at me. "You'd know it, pal. This is more like heart *burn*. Indigestion."

With the unmistakable crunch of crisp, disposable paper, I collapse back onto the examination table.

"Some good old Pepto-Bismol will probably do the trick," the doctor says. "And relax more. You *do* seem a little stressed. Just take it easy for a while, okay?"

"Sure, sure." I fumble out the words.

"What is it that you do for a living, Mr. Matheson?" he asks.

And then I laugh.

Third Kid Through the Door

A TYPICAL *LEAVE IT TO BEAVER* SCRIPT:

INT. BEAVER'S HOUSE—DAY

After school, BEAVER and his two pals enter his front door into a perfect living room. The fresh scent of domesticity and oatmeal cookies pervades the Cleaver household. No one is drunk on stingers.

> BEAVER CLEAVER
> Boy, Mrs. Obreza was sure weird in class today.
> She asked me to name two pronouns.

> LARRY, BEAVER'S FRIEND
> I never know what she's talking about. What'd
> you do, Beave?

> BEAVER CLEAVER
> Nothin'. I just said, "Who, me?" And she gave
> me a gold star anyways.

> BEAVER'S OTHER FRIEND
> That *is* weird.

Beaver, the star, was always the first guy through the door, then Larry, his best pal. Then Beave's *other* friend—if needed for a scene and rarely at that—pushed through behind them.

That was me. The *third* kid. And the next seven decades of a career in show business probably came from the saving grace that I wasn't ever number one or a child star or a teen star. I was merely a guy daydreaming about a future with Hayley Mills—the spunky, cute, lead of 1961's *The Parent Trap*. The girl whose face was now on billboards all over Hollywood. Now, *she* was a star!

Others included guys like Jerry Mathers (*Leave It to Beaver*) and Jay North (*Dennis the Menace*), and Billy Mumy (*Lost in Space*). They were on lunch boxes and talk shows, and people were futzing with them 24-7, all before they hit puberty.

Jay North was an enormous star actually, a king of kings in our circle, making $3,500 (the equivalent of nearly $40,000 today) an episode. At eleven, he was on the cover of *TV Guide*. But at twelve, he was back again sitting in an audition chair across from me and a bunch of other Joes for a guest role in a single episode. And he looked absolutely miserable. Worse, directors and producers had settled on what kind of roles he *would* be getting. He'd been typecast, the dreaded trap when an actor becomes too strongly identified with a specific character.

Meanwhile, I was still a walk-on actor with a couple of lines who could sit back in the shadows and slowly learn a craft. For years.

I had only one rule I would try to live by: *Don't make the same mistake twice.* Simple enough. All I had to do was watch what the professionals were doing and try to copy that.

And in my world, the *first* kid through the door was a professional.

Jerry Mathers ("Beaver") had his own TV show. He had his face on a board game called Leave It to Beaver: Rocket to the Moon Space Game ("Thrills with Beaver on a race to the moon"). He had pool parties. To me, he was Laurence Olivier and Richard Burbage and Charlie Chaplin all rolled into one.

Jerry Mathers invited me to one of the pool parties at his home, the preteen Hollywood version of the Playboy Mansion. Everyone wanted to be invited, and only the cool kids got in. The adults had the grotto; the Beaver had pool floats. The adults had coke; the Beaver had Coca-Cola and unlimited ice cream. They had starlets and boobs; well, the Beaver had magicians who could make coins vanish.

Clearly, I'd arrived.

Handing my towel to the nearest mom, I began searching for Hayley Mills.

I was born on New Year's Eve 1947 to Sarah (Sally) and Cliff Matthieson, joining my sister Sue in what was never a traditionally happy household. The Great Depression and alcoholism were the other two members of our family.

My parents had been affected in completely opposite ways growing up during the Depression. My dad was convinced the next collapse was always right around the corner: "What's the point? You can't fight City Hall!" kind of mindset. Mom, however, was ready to take all comers head-on. Always building for the future. So, without telling Dad, she'd bought our first house. (She had a good job then, and good credit, and so she took out a loan, paying less for the mortgage than the rent would have been.) Dad would never have allowed or understood this kind of optimistic thinking. This difference was a simple anecdote for how these two would never last.

When my parents first began their life together in Los Angeles, Dad would always say L.A. was paradise—orange groves, walnut groves, and pristine mountains and beaches as far as the eye could see. He was a pilot and flight instructor with Lockheed, and Mom worked for Bell Telephone. But after the war, when returning GIs also found out how great it was here, the farmland was soon stripped away for housing, and the city was transformed from a sleepy little place where they made movies into an ever-expanding suburb for the booming postwar economy.

Here, every day seemed to bring new arguments, new tears. I never had any idea what tomorrow would bring for me or my family.

So I, like many, escaped to movies and TV shows. I *loved* TV. *Dragnet. The Lone Ranger. I Love Lucy. Alfred Hitchcock Presents. Beany and Cecil, the Seasick Sea Serpent.* And my favorites: Adventure serials and the newest kids' movies at the Saturday Matinees. In our house was this enormous mahogany entertainment cabinet with a black-and-white television on one side and a turntable system on the other for my parents' collection of 78 RPM records. (Remember those . . .)

In 1952, when the TV broke, you didn't just go buy a new one. (Heck, it took three people to lift it.) Back then, an appliance guy came to your home and took the TV tubes and all the guts back to his shop. Now our home had just a half-empty cabinet and the frame of a television set.

For two weeks, I'd crawl into the back of the emptied TV cabinet and play like I was *on* TV. I could sneak up on the gold bandits beside Tonto in *The Lone Ranger*, push the rattler aside, and then shout "Hi-yo, Silver! Away!" with the best of them. My older sister was not amused, but these were two of the "funnest" weeks I'd ever had. And I needed more fun.

My parents were fighting more. Lots of name-calling and doors slamming.

Then, somewhat thankfully but still a surprise, they separated.

Dad was gone.

LONG BEFORE THE IPAD, THE TELEVISION PROVED TO BE MY TRUSTY babysitter when Mom would head off to work or when I had to visit Dad for the weekend and he was at *his* new job all day. My sister and I were latchkey kids decades before the term became popular.

And the summer before first grade was filled with watching a local Los Angeles program called *Sheriff John's Lunch Brigade*. John Rovick played Sheriff John. He'd show cartoons and talk to the kids and he dressed like a sheriff—what else did a first-grade boy need? Then it got better: Sheriff John was "Coming to a Supermarket Near Me."

"We gotta go!" I begged my mom. "Can we?! Can we?! We gotta go say hi. We gotta!" God bless her, we went down and stood in a pretty long line. And then I finally stood before him. My whole body was shaking.

Sheriff John stretched his hand out to shake mine. "Hello, son," he says.

"Hello, son??"

Right then and there, I finally realized, *He doesn't know me.* This guy doesn't know my name and has clearly never seen me before. I could tell he was looking at a total stranger. *Oh my God! When watching TV, he can't see me. I can only see him.* It was the first time I recognized what television was, and I was a little hurt. Some of the magic was lost forever. But I was still there in front of the TV set, laid out on the shag carpet, tuned in every day.

But other concerns were coming.

———

IN 1954, MY PARENTS FINALLY ENDED THEIR MARRIAGE.

They never did get divorced, however, as a divorce cost too much in those days. My dad simply left for good, and my mom, older sister, and I moved to Sherman Oaks, California, to a one-bedroom apartment, Mom claiming the couch every night so that Sue and I could share the bedroom.

Dad, meanwhile, opened an upholstery business in Laguna Beach (about an hour away), which soon closed. Then he was off to Yuma, Arizona, to manage a sports arena and drive-through liquor store. I saw him sporadically as most children of divorce did then and many still do now. And the years trickled by.

My mom was older than most of the other moms (she'd been 36 when she had my sister and 37 when she had me; Sue and I were barely thirteen months apart). And after bouncing from secretarial job to secretarial job, she had finally figured out a truth: Nobody wanted a 45-plus-year-old secretary.

Mom drank more; her new boyfriends also drank.

Meanwhile, in the La Reina Movie Theater, I took in another viewing of *Witness for the Prosecution*. I am now nine and have already seen the movie three times. Charles Laughton—Quasimodo, Captain Bligh, Rembrandt, and now as a lawyer named Sir Wilfrid Robarts—fills the screen again. I scoop another handful of popcorn as the film's light enfolds me. Here, Charles Laughton awakens in me a yearning and a dream: I want to be like him. I want to do what he's doing.

Not to be a lawyer. Or even, yet, a director or an actor. I want to escape this world and live inside a fantasy world.

A world with happy endings.

A world that stays exactly the same with every viewing.

By the fifth grade, I was consumed by the unfairness of it all: visiting Dad here and there, Mom never being home. I truly hoped and believed they'd get back together. But as each day went by that they didn't, the rage inside me grew.

I was sent home from school after a kickball game when a kid on my team, whose name I don't remember, missed the ball and I lost control. I screamed at him, and I probably hit him. He had a happy family, because I assumed everybody else did, and I was angry that I didn't. I was losing friends and alienating people. And I couldn't control my anger. I didn't even know where to begin. It was horrible.

Then, from a certain point of view, a miracle.

Now fifty, my mom had just gotten laid off again. The terms *ageism* and *sexism* hadn't entered the discourse yet, but Mom's latest executive secretary position had evaporated so that someone younger and prettier could take the job. No matter how hard she tried, now she couldn't find work. And she just couldn't handle it anymore. She started drinking more, if that was possible. As much as I liked her new boyfriend Dick Weevil, who sold Studebakers, everything they did was about having a good time. We called them "Valley drunks" back then.

This Valley drunk, my mother, decided she needed a break and asked her sister in San Bernardino, California, for a favor. The answer was yes.

My sister and I were both shipped east.

AUNT ESTELLE AND HER HUSBAND JOE MARTIN WERE LIKE ONE OF those families I watched on TV. Straight out of *Father Knows Best* or *The Adventures of Ozzie and Harriet*. They *were* the Cleavers before we knew what that meant. They had a grown son named Harlan who still lived at home and who everyone called Curly because he was already bald in his twenties. Curly and Uncle Joe would come home for lunch where my aunt cooked three meals a day (Aunt Estelle was a great chef who created incredible pastries and cakes and other desserts). She was a flesh-and-blood 1950s TV mom, and our stint with her was the only time I had a normal home life.

Baking skills notwithstanding, my sister and I still gave hell to my aunt and uncle, because life in San Bernardino was so different from being a latchkey kid in Los Angeles. In L.A., I did whatever I wanted; I came and went as I pleased—there was no adult supervision. Here, we couldn't have sleepovers, nobody could ever come over to play, and we could rarely go over to anybody's house. And if we weren't where we were supposed to be, we got a severe earful.

An adjustment to say the least, but it also gave me the chance to start over. I resolved to change, to re-create, refind myself, and to leave all that anger behind in Los Angeles. It was such a relief.

One of my favorite Friday night adventures was going to the local hospital just up the street with the local kids. The hospital had a multifloor circular metal slide outside the rear of the building for immobile patients from the upper floors to slide down to safety in case of a fire. I don't know if this slide ever saved anyone from a fire—but it saved us from boring Friday nights! We would stealthily sneak up the slide, past various nurses' windows, to the top floor. There, we'd hand out wax paper to sit on so we could slide faster than lightning. We all had to go at the same time, because if the nurses heard us, they'd throw buckets of water down the slide trying to soak us. Sometimes we'd get two or three rides in before they'd yell for us to get away and stop. If we dared try one more run, we'd have to explain why we were soaked when we came home.

Everything in our new "home" wasn't as fun.

Part of Aunt Estelle and Uncle Joe's requirements was that Sue and I attend Sunday school at their church. It just so happened they were putting on a talent show and—since most of the other kids were already in a band together—the Sunday school teacher asked me to be the conductor for the band. He asked my aunt and uncle if I could stay for the rehearsal after church and told them he'd drop me off at home after.

This was a time when kids, and adults, trusted adults more. In 1950s San Bernardino, if an adult told you to do something, you did it—why wouldn't you? But this guy seemed a bit weird from the start. First, he was standing—in retrospect—way too close and kept grabbing my arm that held the baton. Moving my arm to show me what to do while I kept telling him, "I've got this, it's okay," and did a passable job leading this motley band of kid musicians.

Driving me back home, this Sunday school teacher asked if my dad ever let me sit in his lap and "drive" the car. Odd question, it seemed to me, but I said, "Yeah, sure . . ."

"Well, I'll let you drive too. Just jump on my lap and grab the wheel."

Given the chance to drive a car, I went along and slowly moved over behind the wheel. An easy target I must have seemed, so many miles from my real home or parents. I sat on this guy's lap for all of about thirty seconds. "I don't want to drive anymore," I said and slid back across the front seat all the way until I was up against the passenger door.

"Why you sitting so far away?" he asked.

"I like looking back out the side rearview mirror," I lied. "And watching cars behind us." I couldn't wait to get home; I'd never felt so uncomfortable and confused around any adult in my whole life. Everything about this man and situation felt wrong, ugly, and uncomfortable.

When we got to Joe and Estelle's house, I jumped out and sprinted inside, relieved to get away. Once I was safely inside, my aunt and uncle asked about the talent rehearsal and I just told them I didn't like it and didn't want to be in it. Disappointed as they were, they were also fine with my decision.

That same night, I talked with my sister as we lay in our bunkbeds about this creepy guy and everything that had happened. She listened carefully before we fell asleep.

A couple of days later, Joe and Estelle went out for an evening event at the church. Not more than three minutes after they drove off, there was a knock at the door. This was extra scary since we were home alone and no one ever came over to the house in the evenings.

I peeked out the curtain and saw the Sunday school teacher, who must have been lurking and watching for them to leave. "No, no!" I turned to my sister and shook my head. "I don't want to see him. Don't let him in!"

Sue came to the door. "Who is it?" she asked, and he gave his name and asked if I was home. "I just want to talk with Tim," he said. I kept shaking my head *no*. He knocked again and again.

Then my sister did something . . . remarkable. She said, "Just a minute," and turned and went straight for Joe and Estelle's bedroom. Sue returned seconds later with Joe's bedside pistol, which he kept in a nightstand drawer—this was long before responsible people locked up their guns when kids were around.

Sue held the pistol down at her side as she approached the door. This man was still knocking and asking to see me as she carefully lifted the pistol chest high, pointed it at the door, and slowly opened the door as far as the chain would allow. All this guy could see was my thirteen-year-old sister and a big gun in her hand pointed in his direction, finger on the trigger.

"Go away," she said in a voice so calm I can still hear it. "Leave us alone. Don't ever come back!"

As Sue evenly closed the door, all I heard next was a quick patter of feet, a car door slam, and the screech of tires as he fled. My sister had already locked the door again and returned the gun to the bedside drawer. She came back to the living room and we both stared at each other in wonder.

We never did go back to Sunday school. When I shared this memory as an adult with Sue, she remembered it clearly and always thought that I just didn't want to ever talk about it again. We both regretted that we never had the courage to tell Aunt Estelle and Uncle Joe what had happened. I wished we had.

During all my later years as a kid in Hollywood, not one person in the film business ever made advances toward me as this Sunday school teacher had. I know others have been mistreated, but for some reason, I was lucky enough to never have it happen to me.

Meanwhile, Elizabeth Bradley Elementary School in San Bernardino, in all the best ways, changed my life. The school had a weekly little morning play, a kid's *Today Show* with invented commercials and everything. I was intolerably shy, but if you gave me a character to play, I could shine. I didn't want to be Tim Matthieson. That guy was angry, short, and hardly ever talked. Bradley Elementary gave me the chance to be "Gus, the farm boy," or "Walter, the guy who just saw a ghost." Hiding behind these characters gave me the freedom to try on behaviors. All of a sudden, I'd become fairly popular. One of the prettiest girls in the school, Linda Butterfield, said that I made her laugh. *Oh yeah,* I thought, *this is working great. I like the new, old, me.*

Not surprisingly, I now began dreaming of a life in show business.

———

AFTER I FINISHED SIXTH GRADE, MOM PULLED HERSELF FREE from wherever she'd gone and finally called us back home to Burbank. I said goodbye to all my new friends, and we began again, in a small one-room apartment with two sofas that moonlighted as beds.

I watched TV even more incessantly now. Without Aunt Estelle watching me like a Betty Crocker hawk, I'd cut school to stay home to take in the old classic movies on Channel 9. And I went to the movie theater whenever I could. I'd even started to believe that I could make some money if I somehow got into that world. Beyond the escape it would provide, I could afford to help my mom. With money, I could get us *another* one-room apartment and then there'd be enough space for us all to have our own room. (This renting logic made perfect sense to eleven-year-old me.)

And so actors—in addition to Sandy Koufax and John F. Kennedy and Neil Armstrong—became my heroes. Of course, Charles Laughton (*The Hunchback of Notre Dame* and *Witness for the Prosecution*) but now also Richard Boone (*Have Gun—Will Travel*), Steve McQueen (*Wanted Dead or Alive*), James Garner (*Maverick*), and Humphrey Bogart, Cary Grant, Katharine Hepburn, Jimmy Stewart, and Bette Davis. Reruns of *The Honeymooners* and *The Jackie Gleason Show* from Miami, with the June Taylor Dancers, Joe the Bartender, Reginald Van Gleason III, Rum Dum, and Fenwick Babbitt. I spent hours at the movies and always stayed to watch the credits, learning and fascinated that it took many more people to make a movie than just the actors on the screen and understanding that each movie or TV show was its own family.

I'd also started reading all the autobiographies of random classic actors and directors I could find—guys like Laurence Olivier or George Arliss, the first British actor to win an Oscar. My pals were reading *Justice League of America* and *Tales from the Crypt* and *Mad* magazine as I worked through *Up the Years from Bloomsbury* to fully appreciate Arliss's earlier Broadway experiences. *(How did he do it? Should I go into theatre?)*

I'd become enraptured with Hollywood. Convenient, then, that some of the back lots were only a short bike ride away. Disney, Paramount, Universal, Warner Bros., RKO. I would climb a fence or slip through a broken plank and wander the back lots pretending to be Zorro or cowboy Bret Maverick until it got too late or security chased me away.

"I want to be an actor," I finally confessed to my mom.

"Fine," she said as if I'd asked to be a Boy Scout or play Little League. (To her, it was just a hobby of mine well into my twenties.) "If you ever change your mind," she said, "you can always do something else."

WITH DAD GONE, MONEY WAS ALWAYS TIGHT FOR THE THREE remaining Matthiesons. Mom worked two full-time jobs again, doing her best to climb out of the financial hole she'd dug during her "lost year."

She'd since taken the civil service exam and got the top score in her class—an achievement that led to a coveted job as a dispatcher for the Los Angeles Police Department. She was also working as a bookkeeper for some construction company. Every week, she'd trade away her LAPD day hours to coworkers to take on the night shift. This way, she'd go into the construction company from 8:00 a.m. until 5:00 p.m. and then head to the dispatcher job from 7:00 p.m. until 3:00 a.m. She rode buses for hours. Four hours of sleep, and she'd do it all again. She worked eighty hours a week, enough to keep us afloat while she paid back the people she owed from her party phase. Her schedule must have been excruciating. She worked so hard and was always an inspiration.

Every time I didn't get the job or do as well as I'd hoped throughout my life, I mirrored my mom. *Bad performance in a play?* Mom would have gotten back on stage the next day, and so did I. *Marriage falls apart?* Pick yourself back up. *There's no work for Cowboy Tim?* Reinvent yourself and start auditioning again.

But as a kid, I still couldn't get over the fact we were still so damn poor, stuck in a tiny apartment. The bare necessities were all we had.

My sister and I were the only children in the entire complex. Most of the residents were single guys who were full-blown alcoholics. One man proudly drank *sixteen* stingers in one day. I had no idea what that meant—eventually, I discovered it's brandy and crème de menthe—but he knew this was his greatest accomplishment and I knew that I should live somewhere else.

We didn't have a car like all my friends' parents did—Mom was taking the damn bus between downtown L.A. and Burbank, two hours, every day.

I saw an ad in the newspaper that claimed "For $7 down and $7 a month," you could buy a car. A used car, sure, but a car. Now in the seventh grade, I thought, *Who can't do that? Who doesn't have $7? Hell, even I can get $7.* So I convinced my mother to buy a used car. A 1957 Ford Fairlane. In Burbank, it seemed like all the kids around me had a mom and dad and lived in a house with cars and other nice things. Getting that hideous Fairlane felt like a step toward normalcy.

I grew more determined than ever to get into show business. Not from some great passion to play Hamlet or even to meet Hayley Mills. I really believed this might be the best path to what I saw as having the normal things that other people around me had.

MOM TRIED TO HELP ME FIGURE ALL THIS OUT BUT WAS ALSO WORKING on about four hours' sleep. I found this group called the Screen Children's Guild, which posed as a way into show business but proved to be a total con. They'd send kids to the John E. Reed Photography Studios for actor headshots and pretend to be your agent. Mostly, this so-called guild was making money off the portraits; they certainly weren't sending us out for auditions. They *would* put on some talent shows that you paid to be featured in, but the audience was entirely parents, and it proved a waste of time, energy, and worst of all, money. I'd researched enough to know that without an actual agent, this wasn't going to work.

The construction company that my mother was doing bookkeeping for was developing a patch of Anaheim orange groves that would soon become Disneyland. As fate would have it, her boss had a son my age, and *this* kid had an agent and he'd just gone up for some parts. "Well," I pressed. "Maybe ask your boss if they'll set me up." I already had these awful, corny pictures from John E. Reed Photography Studios I could use. She agreed to give it a shot.

The irony being that mom, our family, had gone through that horrible year and because of the way she came out, working two jobs, she'd found her son an honest-to-God agent.

NANCY BINDA, THE WOMAN WHO REPRESENTED THE BOSS'S KID, had only four other clients and worked solo out of her kitchen. But she took me on and represented me for the first several years of what would become my career. Now, I was going out on actual auditions for commercials and television parts.

While waiting to land my first paying job, I did a little theatre production of *Auntie Mame* in Burbank. It was only a couple of scenes, and I played Beauregard Jackson Pickett Burnside. This guy was funny and got all the laughs; he had nothing to do with Tim Matthieson. Pulling out a Southern accent felt natural because my mother was from Nashville, Tennessee, and my grandmother was from Richmond, Virginia. That Southern flavor was all around me, which I credit for the positive reviews I got in the local Burbank paper.

I also started to take more acting classes, and during a showcase (the right kind that I didn't have to pay extra to be in), I was noticed by a casting agent who set up an audition for me for a starring role in a new CBS series called *Window on Main Street*. After numerous auditions, I wasn't chosen for the lead but landed a walk-on part with a couple of lines. The program starred Robert Young (of *Father Knows Best* fame) as an author who moves back to his small hometown and falls in love with a young widow. This was my first role in front of the camera.

Weeks earlier, I'd had to climb a fence and sneak onto studios to run around the back lots. This time, I'd been invited to Desilu Studios—the place where they shot *I Love Lucy* and dozens of the other shows I watched religiously. They even sat me down and put makeup on me. I was on a real Hollywood set for the first time in my life, and I stumbled onto the soundstage like Dorothy first stepping out into Oz.

My brief scene was in a lavish hotel suite. I'd never seen such opulence, such beauty. I passed the enormous camera ready for the day's shooting and explored the room. The set was amazing. Chandelier, grand marble fireplace, fancy rugs, antique chairs, the wallpaper, and the paintings. A beautiful world so different than anywhere I'd ever been, so different from the Burbank apartment where I lived with my mother and sister: one room, a kitchen with a little table, and a closet you had to walk through to get to the bathroom.

This, however, I thought to my twelve-year-old self, *THIS is where I want to live*. I had never been in a room so nice. And I found myself drawn to the stunning marble fireplace. I looked around to confirm no one was looking, certain I would get in trouble, and then carefully brought my hand up to touch it.

My hand jerked back.

It wasn't marble. Not even close. It was paper, contact paper that *looked* like marble stuck to plywood underneath.

It finally hit me: *My God, it's all fake.* Every movie or TV show I've ever seen. My old pal, Sheriff John, was just a glimpse of the great lie. This world I so desperately wanted to fall into and be part of is a fake world. The realization might have crushed other idealistic dreamers.

My immediate thought was, *THAT'S FUCKING GREAT!*

That fireplace seduced me. I got it now: It just has to look real for as long as it's on screen. After or before that, it doesn't matter. Anything else is the magic and illusion of special effects and props, acting, editing, crew, and camera placement. All these entertainment trickeries to make fake seem real.

It made perfect sense.

Real-world Tim slept on a pullout couch and first had to walk through a closet to brush his teeth. Fake-world Tim now had a cool marble fireplace.

———

ON *WINDOW ON MAIN STREET*, I HAD MY ONE OR TWO LINES, AND I barely knew what I was doing. Everyone else worked like the parts of a Swiss watch: quiet, calm, and precise. Meanwhile, I just played those lines when the time came and tried to be as natural as I could—like a real kid. Other than being a ham, which had worked in the play I'd just done, I wasn't sure what else to do. But my performance must have been okay, because they asked me to come back and do a two-day part the following week. My $100 for a day's work had already become $200. And my good fortune was just getting started!

By midseason, *Window on Main Street* was struggling in the ratings. To help, they made some changes to the plot and expanded the cast, adding me as a featured kid in town. I was suddenly a regular, working all five days and making $400 a week and—

Hold on! This was incredible money for us, but I still knew math well enough to know I'd just been screwed somehow. They paid me $100 for one day, $200 for two days and $400 for five days. *It's five days! I don't get it.*

"That's the guild," I was told. "There's a weekly rate and there's a daily rate."

"Well, maybe I should only work four days next time?" I offered hopefully.

A look of abject pity was the only response I got to my ingenuous idea.

The guild, from all I could tell, had just cost me $100.

The Screen Actors Guild also made me sign a "loyalty oath to the United States of America" to be admitted. I had to swear to never do anything treasonous; this was the McCarthy era, after all, and the oath was something Ronald Reagan had instituted when he'd been president of the guild. Even as a kid, I knew making a twelve-year-old sign a loyalty oath was wrong. I'd grown up in a very First Amendment family, and my grandmother, in particular, would have gone ballistic if I'd ever told her I'd signed it. I never did tell her.

Whatever. I'd have signed a murder confession. I had my $400 check ($4,000 today) and marched into the bank opposite Warner Bros. Studios. It was only another half mile to my house, and I soon had a giant wad of cash in my pocket to bring back home. In the bedroom, I closed the door, took out the cash, and just tossed it up in the air like they do in the movies. It fluttered down on top of me—not in the slow motion I'd hoped for, but the moment was still the happiest I'd ever been. Here was a way of helping. It was really all about getting out of that pit; I just thought, *We deserve better than this.* And I could make that happen. I started by taking Mom and Sue out to dinner.

But with my expanded role on the show, I was now called on to do more heavy lifting as a child actor: a scene I could not just clown my way through. On the same street set they had recently used for

The Untouchables with Robert Stack and Walter Winchell, I was expected to cry in front of a hundred people on cue. I was expected to . . . act.

So I urgently needed to find that emotion. And I found one, accidentally, in the music from a popular musical currently capturing the zeitgeist.

In 1960, *Camelot* premiered on Broadway with Richard Burton, Julie Andrews, and Robert Goulet. The idea of Camelot was projected by Americans onto the Kennedys in the White House, and it seemed like everyone had the soundtrack album. Yet for me, the shattering of the dream of Camelot in the show reminded me of my own broken home. I listened to that album over and over again, especially the heartbreaking song Richard Burton sings at the end, when his love has been lost to another and his family ideal has been shattered. It brought tears to my eyes, every time. Rehearsing my scenes at home, I would have the record playing on my portable RCA player. And when I needed to cry, all I had to do was hum to myself, "Don't let it be forgot / That once there was a spot / For one brief shining moment that was known / As Camelot."

Still lacking any real training, I'd accidentally uncovered a technique taught in acting classes for decades, and it's one I still use to this day.

Film School Boot Camp

An Actor Prepares . . .

Konstantin Stanislavski wrote *An Actor Prepares* in 1936. Stanislavsky was perhaps the first person to write about an actor's technique. To do so, he went to the most successful and best actors working on stage at the time and asked each of them how they worked and what their methods were in approaching a role. The Stanislavski technique became the compilation and distillation of these lessons he took from these great actors. For nearly ninety years, *An Actor Prepares* has been the actors' bible of how to act—for creating real, honest, and true character and performance. But while his book is the bible, an actor should study as many different techniques as they can. Find the ones that speak to your heart, but also mix it up! Study the many techniques developed by the masters of the craft—Stella Adler, Sanford Meisner, Michael Chekhov, Viola Spolin's improv, classical theatre, Shakespeare, and Lee Strasberg to name a few. This is the lesson that I want to share with you: *Never ignore your inner voice.* Use what works best for you when creating a character.

———

BACK ON *MAIN STREET* IN 1962, I WAS FILLED WITH EMOTION, thinking of *Camelot* and dredging up emotions from my own life. It proved a convincing performance; the adults were thrilled.

This is gonna start my career, I thought. *I really am an actor.*

Two weeks later, the show got canceled.

———

STILL, THE JACK WORMSER AGENCY WANTED TO REPRESENT ME. IN the 1960s, leaving Nancy Binda and moving to Jack Wormser's agency was like being called up from Single-A Ball to the Dodgers. They had a whole kids department run by a woman named Pat Domigan, who took me on.

Now I was going to lots of auditions. Lots.

And the hardest things for me were the auditions.

I'd soon come to realize there were two parts to this job: getting the role and then the actual acting. I'd sit out in some lobby for an audition with forty other kids, most of whom had their stage mothers running lines with them. I didn't quite come from that same situation. Kids' auditions were between 4:00 and 6:00 p.m., the same break my mom had between her jobs, and she would wait outside for me to finish and then race back to work.

In some auditions, I'd be awful. I couldn't get outta my head, or I was embarrassed by all the people in the room. Or, worse, I didn't have a single clue about how to approach the part. I hadn't gotten much training yet, but I already knew there was no quarter given just because you're twelve. My only goal was to convince the adults that I wasn't gonna screw it up if they gave me the part—that I could handle it and do the work. The acting was secondary to that.

Somehow, the parts came anyway. And with parts, came checks. *Terrific!* Money to help the family. *I just don't wanna live that life anymore*, I thought. *We can do better than this.* We should live like Aunt Estelle and Uncle Joe and Curly in San Bernardino. We should be normal.

And we were about to get our chance.

I'd landed recurring parts on *My Three Sons* and *Leave It to Beaver*.

The work wasn't steady enough to count on. But still, I threw money into the family pot whenever I could. For a day's work, I'd bring home about $50 after the agency, the guild, and Uncle Sam took their cuts.

The biggest purchase of my life was, no surprise, a color TV.

Almost no one had a color set yet. My mom and sister and I used to go over to other people's homes to watch color TV, and on Sunday night, we'd watch *Bonanza*, one of the few shows shot "in living color." The NBC peacock would blossom brightly and fan vivid hues more vibrant than real life, giving way to a colored map of Nevada with Reno and Virginia City and the Ponderosa, and then the title *Bonanza* would explode into multicolored flame. It seems absurd to think of that as exciting today, but in 1959, when *Bonanza* started, the world shook. I know mine did.

Thirteen and determined, I borrowed money for my very own color TV: $50 down and then $5 each week. Acting roles or not, I could always get $5 a week for the required payments. I cleaned the lady's house next door. I washed cars. I walked dogs. But not all my schemes were winners. In Yuma, while visiting Dad, I tried selling popcorn at a wrestling match at the sports arena he managed. The other guys were shouting, "Get your popcorn heeeere! *Pop-pop-pop!*" Instead, I approached people who looked nice and bashfully asked, "Would you like some popcorn?" By the end of the night, I somehow *owed* the arena money. Still, I never missed a TV payment. Although it cost $500 (over $5,000 today), I kept chipping away at it. Eventually it was mine.

This sucker was outrageously enormous, and we put it in our apartment living room where all three of us could watch.

Almost like in a real home.

All-American Boy

M<small>Y</small> <small>MOTHER DROPPED ME OFF, WISHED ME GOOD LUCK, AND THEN</small> ran to the store to take care of errands. "I'll be back in half an hour . . ."

I was fifteen. It was 1963 and this wasn't just another audition. Many of the shows all my friends and I watched were made by two men: William Hanna and Joe Barbera. Other than maybe Walt Disney, Hanna-Barbera were, to us, the most influential people in the world. These two guys created *Tom and Jerry*, *The Flintstones*, *Scooby-Doo, Where Are You!*, *Yogi Bear*, and *The Jetsons* and were now casting a new show. While my chance of getting the part, as with most auditions, was slim to none—I'd never done work as a voice actor—that didn't mean I wasn't going to enjoy the next few hours.

Joe Barbera himself met me at the door. He was stocky with really big eyebrows and right away one of the most friendly adults I'd ever met. Mr. Barbera—"Joe," he assured me—first showed me around the recording studio and then shared drawings of characters named Jonny and Hadji and various lizard men. These drawings looked different from anything else on TV and blew my mind; the characters looked and felt like the art I'd fallen in love with in comic books. Joe told me about the show, an idea they'd borrowed from a once-popular radio program called *Jack Armstrong, the All-American Boy* but couldn't get the rights to. Then we recorded an audition, and Mom picked me up. Done.

This was the last I thought about *Jonny Quest* or *Quest File* or whatever it was going to be finally called. It was cool to see how they made cartoons, but it was also one of ten auditions I'd done that same week and, I assumed, one of the ten "no thanks" or "never heard backs" I'd get.

Three months later, Hanna-Barbera Productions was making *Jonny Quest*, and they had decided I was their Jonny. This was, to a sixteen-year-old, the most monumental thing that had yet happened in my life.

Film School Boot Camp

More than Acting—Acting Is Your Business

As my career grew and developed, I'd set my sights on larger and better agents, and I'd study and appraise how they worked for their clients. I was constantly scanning the horizon and investigating other agencies to see if I could do better. Today, you can simply punch in names on IMDb. But when I was coming up, I'd spend hours researching actors of my "type" whose work I admired or whose career path I wanted to emulate. I'd get this information from something called *The Academy Players Directory*. This was an annual big fat photo book where all actors were listed for casting directors to look at. It was where you (as an actor) annually posted your photos, agency contact, and category to remind the industry you were still working. This is how I chose the Wormser Agency when I was a kid. It was a proven place that cared about young beginning actors. It was a very effective smaller agency compared to the William Morris Agency, which was the king of all agencies at the time, or ICM (International Creative Management). Neither of them would even return my calls or represent a beginning actor.

Over my career, I have been represented at various times by Wormser, Creative Artists Agency, William Morris, Agency for the Performing Arts, Generate, Gersh, and several managers. While access to material is a factor, the most important thing is to choose as guides and representatives people whose belief in you is real and tangible. Someone—or a whole team of someones—honest and creative, willing to work hard for you, regardless of where they work.

Most everyone else cast for *Jonny Quest* was a Hall of Fame first-ballot voice pro—Don Messick (Astro, Scooby-Doo); Mel Blanc (Bugs Bunny, Daffy Duck, and fifty more); and June Foray (Rocky the Flying Squirrel, the Smurfs). Meanwhile, I was on my first-ever voice acting job.

I worked hard to make Jonny as real as I could. No corny stuff. Joe Barbera, who directed the episodes and handled the creative side of Hanna-Barbera, was always incredible with me. Patient. Encouraging. Always kept the recording sessions light and positive. My luck in this regard was immeasurable. And it only got better.

Only a teen, I still had to "go to school," and whenever I did an episode of *Jonny Quest*, I was required to go into Hanna-Barbera three hours early to do my schoolwork with some fill-in teacher *before* recording: union rules.

(On other programs and movie sets, Mom would often take me the first day of production and find another kid with a mom to claim me. "Tell the teacher you've got Tim also," she'd ask, and then head off to work. She'd always find somebody to say okay, and the schoolteachers were fine about it.)

Three hours of schoolwork? I'd always finish mine in maybe twenty minutes and spend the next two-plus hours wandering Hanna-Barbera studios. Carte blanche to sneak around and see all the other shows they were working on. I'd pester the animators while they worked on cels and then sit in while *The Flintstones* and *The Magilla Gorilla Show* teams did their recordings.

This is where I really first learned about the craft of acting. Watching Alan Reed (Fred Flintstone), June Foray (Betty Rubble), and Janet Waldo (Judy Jetson, Penelope Pitstop) became the advanced acting classes I hadn't yet taken. Then there was Mel Blanc—Bugs Bunny, Porky Pig, Pepé Le Pew, Barney Rubble, and a hundred more. Mel could do a scene entirely by himself, playing *two* characters. He'd do a dog impression and then do another dog, even giving it a personality, different from any other dog he'd done before. I was still figuring out how to give Jonny Quest a personality, and this guy could do it for dozens of characters *on the fly*.

For *Jonny Quest*, all the actors would gather with script in hand in front of a bank of microphones before a glass window where Joe Barbera, who directed everything, and the technicians sat. We played it like a stage play or an old-school live radio recording. There was none of the "record the line twenty different ways and we'll mix it all together later" stuff. I had to act in real time with the adults who I'd listened to each morning in my living room.

But they worked together in a way that I recognized as a sports team. Most of them had come out of an earlier career in radio plays. There was a rhythm I'd begun to hear: It wasn't just waiting to get your own lines out. For the first time, I could see how actors worked off, and really listened to, each other.

Sometimes, Joe Barbera would ask me to play the voice of another part for a few lines, and I often had a hard time remembering what *that* other kid sounded like. Jonny Quest was me; that one was easy. Joe would just wave it off. "No problem," he'd say. "Let's just play it back." I'd hear the other kid's voice again and get back to work. It was a great education.

One day, with trembling voice, I even told Joe, "I'm gonna write an episode."

Ninety-nine of a hundred producers would have laughed me out of the room.

"That's great," Joe said. "Bring it in, or pitch me a bunch of ideas. If we like any ideas, we'll let you write one." I wrote three episodes, and he couldn't have been more gracious about my attempts or more helpful with revisions and suggestions.

If I was seeking parental guidance—and I no doubt was—the guy who'd given the world *Tom and Jerry* was a good start.

———

BETWEEN ACTING GIGS, I TOOK MY MOTHER'S EXAMPLE AND FOUND other work where I could. In high school, I picked up cash working league nights at Grand Central Bowling Alley, where they paid guys to keep the scores by hand. (These days, a computer keeps track of the byzantine sorcery of spare and strike bonuses and the extra balls on the tenth, and so forth. Until the 1980s, bowlers did all this by hand or paid someone like me.) All my coworkers were the neighborhood drunks and drifters, but scoring two teams at the same time, you could pull in $10 in about four hours, which was twice the minimum wage—pretty good.

I had other jobs as well. A buddy of mine told me about a "shitty job" at the *Los Angeles Times* that could make me some easy money. Sign me up! For the next six months, I'd go to the *Times* at 2:00 a.m. on Sunday to assemble and stack the day's newspapers and then help load them on the trucks for $20. Great money, but it killed your social life; it took hours to wash the black newsprint off your hands and you smelled like wet newspaper. I also flipped hamburgers at the Bel-Air Bay Club and fried the Colonel's chicken.

Meanwhile, *Jonny Quest* paid $135 a show.

I knew which career I wanted to focus on.

STILL, I'D ALREADY LEARNED IT'S AN INDUSTRY DESIGNED TO KEEP you humble. (Sometimes it feels like this place, and everyone in it, is working 24-7 to get rid of you. To replace you, to forget you. To break you.)

I thought I was a big deal when they booked Mom and me into first class for a flight to Kansas City and a promotional appearance. There, a helicopter flew over the Midwestern plains to some shopping mall. I was, after all, the voice of Jonny Quest! And hundreds of people stood in line for hours to get my signature on these little *Jonny Quest* cards the studio had given us. Now I was in the role of my old TV pal Sheriff John. I grinned and signed my name and probably imagined a future with Hayley Mills. And hours later, when it was time to head back to my "private helicopter," I noticed the white trash fluttering around the parking lot like snow caught in a winter wind. Dozens of little slips of paper.

Each one with my signature.

———

I WAS DOING *JONNY QUEST* EPISODES AND A FEW COMMERCIALS here and there. But nobody at my high school really knew about any of it. *Leave It to Beaver* and *My Three Sons* were too "straight" or "square" for most high schoolers, so my episodes there went unnoticed. (Today, however, decades later, people still ask me to sign autographs as Jonny Quest—the biggest reward for that work *and* the power of syndication and nostalgia.) And even though I was absent a lot from school, none of my friends really watched any of those shows.

Teenagers are focused on their own trials, so I was not a celebrity by any stretch. Then I did a live Stridex acne-pad commercial on *Shindig!*, the popular musical variety series. This acne ad became my big claim to fame. Not performing with Mickey Rooney and Burl Ives and Mel Blanc . . .

Instead, my peers were saying, "You talked about zits on *Shindig!* That's soooo cool!"

It was time to finally make my move on Janelle Penny, the prettiest girl in John Burroughs High School. She was the Little Red-Haired Girl to my Charlie Brown. The Roxane to my Cyrano. I wasn't a varsity letterman or on the student council, so my angle was humor. I finally took my shot, as they say, with some clever lines. She laughed; her friends laughed. Things were looking up.

"You're so funny and cute," Janelle said. Then she added with painful sincerity, "If you were six feet tall, I'd go out with you."

At the time, I was five foot three.

SINCE I WAS OFTEN AWAY SHOOTING COMMERCIALS, *JONNY QUEST*, or other TV episodes, nobody—especially me—ever really knew which social group I was in. Not with the Jocks (only lettering in varsity tennis), and not the academic or cool kids, either. Rather, I was the solo nerd who didn't fit in anywhere. The summer between my junior and senior years became my toughest time in high school. Yet, I pulled off dating a girl named Nancy Montgomery—a girl who didn't have height constraints—pretty steadily all summer. But I still didn't have any moves. Nancy drew the line: "Nothing below the neck or above the knee" if I ever got too frisky.

During that same summer, I took some extension courses at UCLA to dig deeper into filmmaking. Of course, I was the smallest and youngest person attending the film editing and film history classes *and* I was the only high school student, a detail I kept to myself.

But there, something totally new happened: a computer dating program called, I think, Operation Match. Nothing like it had ever existed before, because no one other than universities and IBM even had computers yet. (We were about to get the first peek at online dating apps!) I somehow believed this program might be a way to meet some cool young women with similar interests, and who knew where that could lead? College girls, I fancied, didn't have the same "nothing below the neck or above the knee" rule. Yay, science!

Operation Match charged participants $3 for the service, and you had to fill out a ten-page, 135-question form about your interests (Folk Music, Rock & Roll, French language); personal information (race, religion, class in school); attitudes (Do you believe in a God who answers prayers? Is extensive sexual activity in preparation for marriage part of "growing up"?); absolutes (religious background; my date's race should be X); and so forth. At this point, computers were still something from a sci-fi movie, but the idea that this computer could help you find your ideal soulmate was sure intriguing. I paid the $3 and took the application very seriously. Spent hours musing over my answers to get them just right. I must have redone it ten times to help these computers find my perfect match.

It took almost two weeks for the survey to be processed and the matches generated, but Results Day finally arrived. I went immediately to the office of the dating program to pick up my results rather than wait for them to be mailed out. The results came on an IBM computer primitive dot-matrix printout listing the names and telephone numbers of all your matches. These were placed in an envelope and handed over to me. I walked outside with exhilaration and anticipation. *My perfect match!!* I ran over to a grassy area under some trees for privacy and opened the envelope slowly.

Poor Nancy Montgomery, I thought, *how will she take the news when I leave her for some anthropology major?*

The contents were only two pages. Page one, a form letter describing the program, how many thousands of people had enrolled, how information was sorted and cross-referenced, and how then the computers matched up the participants. I read through the boilerplate leisurely, knowing my fate would be revealed on page two. Slowly I turned the page.

There were very few words on page two, and I was confused. I read on.

Participants: 20,000+ students

Females: 51%

Males: 49%

Matches to your profile: 0

ZERO?

Out of 10,000+ UCLA women, there were "0" who wanted to be with someone like me? I was shocked. Devastated. Heartsick. Humiliated. Now it was official—even a computer said so—I was a total loser.

I'd clearly die alone, and there was no way I'd ever—

Wait a second! I dashed back frantically to the dating program office and breathlessly asked to see my submission. The staff stared back at me in irritation. "Those aren't here," an older guy explained. "What's the problem?"

"I think . . . I think . . ." I said, looking around wildly. "Do you have one of those forms? A blank one, even?"

The guy grunted and then toddled over to another desk. He finally brought over a blank submission form like I'd filled out before. "Knock yourself out, kid," he said, and the woman next to him laughed as I scanned furiously.

I didn't have to scan long. The *first* question asked the respondent what year of college he or she was in. I'd answered honestly: high school.

Idiot! An honest idiot, but still. And forever after, I convinced myself the IBM computers had hastily discounted the high schooler as a viable option for college girls. What other reason could there be?

MERCIFULLY, THERE WAS STILL NANCY MONTGOMERY AND OUR young steadfast love to count on. Of course, as senior year began, she dumped me for a varsity basketball star. (Maybe she'd suffered too many arthouse film dates beside me, or maybe she simply had a height requirement after all.)

I was crushed. And again alone.

MY ONLY TWO FRIENDS WERE STUDY PALS: DOROTHY TANOUS AND Cliff Bochstaller. We'd meet up at Dorothy's house on many nights, musing about deep subjects—life, death, philosophy, why IBM hates high schoolers. Of course, we also studied for our school quizzes and finals.

Dorothy's parents would always gather everyone in the evening to cook dinner together. I'd never done anything like this in my own home, so it was a fantastic experience and one that I'd only thought existed in my aunt and uncle's home in San Bernardino. Also, because her parents were both artists and "intellectuals," this was the only family I knew that had no televisions. In their entire house. Nowhere. I couldn't believe this. Instead of watching TV every night, the Tanous family would cook together and have discussions about the news, art, and literature.

When I first met Dorothy's dad, he looked familiar. I'd definitely seen him somewhere before but couldn't—despite all the hours and dinners at her house—figure out where. Once I felt comfortable enough with the family, I mentioned this one night at dinner.

Mr. Tanous smiled and the whole table seemed amused. "I think I know where you've seen me before." Her dad, I already knew, had worked at Walt Disney Studios for many years as an animation artist. "We always based our cartoon characters on real-life models or people," he explained.

Slowly his face became a little more familiar, but I still couldn't place him. "Which character?" I asked carefully.

"Ha-ha-ha! You wouldn't dare fight old Hook . . . '" he said, and grinned playfully.

That was it! Dorothy's dad, Henry Tanous, was Captain Hook from *Peter Pan*. My God, I was having dinner with the pirate captain of the notorious *Jolly Roger*.

This, at times, really was life in Hollywood.

———

SANS NANCY MONTGOMERY OR HEIGHT-SNOB JANELLE PENNY OR any wistful UCLA English majors, I'd landed a commercial and now had a crush on the actress cast opposite me. The scene was a picnic with this cute girl alongside the Hollywood Reservoir in the Hills. Still terminally shy, I didn't have the guts or know-how to make my interests known. There was, I assumed, a pretty good chance I'd screw up the 135-point questionnaire, or she'd tell me I needed to be taller.

Not an issue for the *adults* on the scene that afternoon. The lecherous director—and all the agency people—kept hitting on this girl. She was seventeen. The director incessantly rubbing her shoulders and joking with her, calling her "baby" and "darling" and "hot stuff." He called me "you."

Raised in a house full of women, I was constitutionally uncomfortable with how she was being treated. It was all unsettling. I was taken aback by this smarmy guy and disappointed by my own weakness; I wanted to say something, but I didn't dare. And for the first time ever, I couldn't remember my fucking lines.

We had to do take after take. The director would groan and she'd giggle. I'd somehow driven them closer together. The entire shoot was a nightmare.

But my big takeaway had nothing to do with flirting first or better. Or how creepy Hollywood can be. Rather, I vowed that I would never get distracted from a job like that ever again. Anything that sidetracks you from the work is not your friend. Doing a job well meant more jobs and more money; I couldn't allow stuff to upset the apple cart. My family had begun to feel normal, and I *couldn't* mess that up.

The second insight was that I was going to speak up next time. Whatever the next offense, I would need to be braver and to protest. In Hollywood, you don't have to wait long for such an opportunity.

MONTHS LATER, DOING AN EPISODE ON THE SHOW *ROOM 222*, I'D landed a great part playing a kid whose parents had run off—something I could certainly work with—and this kid was living by himself, pretending he still had a family. Lots for me to work with, actually. And lots of lines and a great character—but I could never find a way to connect to it like I should have.

"Next time," the director told me afterward, "maybe, you know, we'll just give you a smaller part."

Ouch. Brutal. It hurt so bad that by the time I got home, I was no longer the same kid from the lake. I picked up the phone and called the director.

"That was really painful to hear you say that," I told him, voice shaking. "I gave you my all. You can't talk to actors like that." I wasn't sure at all whether this was true, but at sixteen, it made sense. "If you didn't like it," I told him, "you could have directed me more."

"I'm sorry," he said.

I wasn't sure where to go next with that. I'd assumed he'd tell me to quit acting or pound sand or something.

"Well, okay . . . Thanks, Mr. Becker," I said. "Bye."

Achievement unlocked. Young Tim had stood up for himself in Hollywood. An essential ability, I'd confirm a hundred times over, for any career in entertainment lasting more than four months.

Not a year later, I was screen-testing for a planned *Hardy Boys* series and sat waiting for hours behind all the other guys—Jeff Bridges was there; Jan-Michael Vincent (of *Airwolf*). Everyone was trying out. It was getting late when I overheard the casting agent say to the director, "Yeah, we're done here." They had completely forgotten about me or had already made their decision. Both reasons pissed me off. "Excuse me," I said, marching straight up to them. "I haven't tested yet. . . . My name's Tim Matthieson." They stared at me. "I'm Joe Hardy," I clarified. The director smiled and they gave me a "sure, sure."

An hour later, I was Joe Hardy.

—

I WENT TO VISIT MY FATHER WHO'D GRADUATED FROM YUMA TO Phoenix. I wanted to share the good news of Joe Hardy and all I'd been working for. I guess part of me wanted to show him all of the things I was doing that I thought *he* should be doing—taking care of my mom, my sister, and me. I was eating cereal alone when he padded into the small kitchen. He was groggy, still in his underwear and a tank top. He grunted hello, filled a cup with warm water from the tap, dumped in a couple spoonfuls of instant coffee, stirred, and then took a big sip. He sighed deeply, smiled, and slogged back out of the room.

His greatest joy in life was this sip of shitty coffee. He was content with that—worse, happy about it. For the first time ever, even though I loved my father, I felt sad for him. He seemed . . . somewhat tragic to me.

Shallow of me, perhaps. But it's how I felt.

My mother had come out of the Depression a fighter, willing to work 24-7 to never face that world again, to never let others dictate her life. He'd come out a victim, shrugging with a "What can you do?" attitude that blamed life or the world for his problems and accepted his lot in life.

I couldn't wait to get back to L.A.

———

MY MUCH-NEEDED CONFIDENCE WAS CLEARLY GROWING, A FEW commercials were coming in, and now Hanna-Barbera had asked me to record new characters for both *Sinbad Jr. and His Magic Belt* and *Space Ghost*—two new syndicated shows the company sold to local UHF channels. The money plan was working. I was now a senior in high school making $10,000 to $14,000 a year (over $120,000 a year today), very real money. My mother and sister had begun leaning on me to support the family. Finally, I cracked. "You can't rely on me so much!" I said. "There's some things *I* wanna do with this money. I'm not the father here!" I wanted to buy scuba gear and a car I could drive up to San Francisco whenever I wanted. I wanted money for college and more-serious acting lessons. I wanted some savings as a cushion for the next time I didn't get the job. I wanted freedom. The burden of having to be the "dad" was too much.

Unbeknownst to my mother, I'd rented my own tiny space in Manhattan Beach, about an hour's drive from where we lived.

One day after I graduated from high school, I moved out.

———

IT WOULD BE DRAMATIC TO END THE CHAPTER WITH THAT LINE about my tiny little apartment, but the truth is, just a few months later, I bought a house in Van Nuys with all my savings. It had two bedrooms with a den and a pool. I'd bought it so my sister and mom could live there with me, and they stayed with me until I got married.

Also, I'd sprung to six foot two by the end of my freshman year of college.

Janelle Penny got a phone call; she was interested now.

I Love Lucy

(Also Jackie, Dick, Henry and . . .)

I COULD TELL THE WHOLE SET WAS ON EDGE. DESPITE THEIR BEST efforts, the anxious energy of the producer and director had trickled out. We all knew what today meant. Lucille Ball was the most powerful, and popular, comedy TV star in history but was now trying to make a big return into motion pictures—a leap most fail magnificently.

This is a Hollywood truth I was extra aware of as I was also a TV actor in 1967 with his own first big part in a film. If Lucy couldn't pull it off, what chance in hell did I have?

The stakes were high, and today's scene was likely make-or-break stuff. The shot was built around Lucy doing what she was already a legend for: physical comedy. Inspired by what she had done in scenes like the iconic "Vitameatavegamin" scene she'd already done on TV, the writers were taking it up a notch from what was okay for America's most beloved star on TV—in the movies, she was going to play drunk. Glassy-eyed, tongue-tied, and all that. The original script—it had been rewritten a dozen times—had included this one scene to let Lucy let her physical-comedy genius run wild. For this film, it was Lucy's comedic money shot. But it was also trying to catch lightning or magic, or maybe Gordon's London Dry, in a bottle twice.

My specific role in the scene was to hand over a triple pour of scotch and gin and then sit back to appreciate the chaos while she went for it. I was curious what she'd do with the scene. Sure, it was funny stuff the *first* time around. Still new to comedy myself, I wondered if Lucy would actually show up a little drunk for the shoot; actors were known to do that.

Nope, Lucille Ball was stone-cold sober. Ready for business. She even casually moved another actor's glass half an inch left, getting it ready for some action she was planning twenty-plus moves from now. I sat spellbound.

"Action!"

The enormous cast began moving about as one, starting a burst of half a dozen side conversations, spinning the lazy Susan, reaching for drinks and food, playing the rambunctious party scene as a foundation for the actor to work from.

Then the classic comedy queen, Lucy, emerges. The raised eyebrow. A couple of understated hiccups. The subtle wobble of the head. Her lines came next, slurred just enough. Not overplaying it. Fumbling with a napkin. Purposely overpouring another actor's drink, liquid sloshing. Flinging food. Different from what the world had seen on TV but with enough familiar notes for fans. She reached out, "accidentally" spilling that glass she'd moved half an inch into the perfect spot, like it was the most natural thing in the world. As if she'd both practiced the move a hundred times . . . or never even once.

She was a monumental star for a reason. And I had the advantage of being allowed, directed, to smile and even laugh throughout. Thank God.

"Cut!" the director called.

The rest of the cast and crew were now able to laugh. And we did. Everyone cracked up. The scene had been perfect. A master class in physical comedy. One take, and Lucille Ball killed it. There was real applause, and the energy on set was now charged. This goofy comedy movie, I thought, could become an actual hit.

"Print it?" the director asked.

Lucille Ball scratched her chin, thinking, mashed potatoes still smeared in her fingers. I'd stayed in my chair, watching with genuine interest.

"Lucy?" the director prodded.

It is a moment frozen in my mind. She winked at me and then turned to the director.

"Let's run it again," she said. "I can do it better."

———

Lucille Ball, Bob Hope, Jackie Gleason, Debbie Reynolds, Dick Van Dyke.

First-ballot Hall of Famers, all. And, unbelievably, the stars of my first three films. Like *Leave It to Beaver* and *Jonny Quest* before, I just needed to keep my head down, pay attention, and learn from the pros.

They'd all perfected their craft performing in vaudeville and on live shows, twenty shows a week, in front of real audiences. Not a world that tolerated missed entrances or line flubs. So they could improv with the best of them but also showed up on set with their work done, lines ready to go, focused.

While I certainly recognized how big a deal all of these stars were (my mom was particularly impressed that I was working with Debbie Reynolds), their fame never really shook or impacted me. I was always too concerned about not screwing up to think about the fact I was now trading lines with Jackie Gleason. And, with the fame issue out of the way, each adult I encountered had something new to teach me by example.

Still in high school, I was about to get a PhD in acting.

When *Yours, Mine and Ours* was being filmed, Lucille Ball was the most powerful woman in Hollywood. She'd founded Desilu Productions with her husband Desi Arnaz and produced *I Love Lucy* (the most popular show in America for years), *Mission: Impossible*, *The Untouchables*, *The Dick Van Dyke Show*, and *Star Trek*. In 1962, she bought out Desi's half and was now the only, and first, woman to preside over a Hollywood studio. She was the talent of Tina Fey, the beauty of Nicole Kidman, and the cultural influence of the Kardashians all rolled into one.

Yet she still made time for seventeen-year-old me. I wasn't just one of the eighteen kid actors chosen to play in *her* movie. She took genuine interest in helping me as a young actor. Imagine Cy Young, Nolan Ryan, or Clayton Kershaw showing a Little Leaguer how to throw a curve ball. I'd sit in her trailer, where she'd talk about everything from how she prepared for scenes to how to fire an agent. She'd say things like "Tim, if you really want to be a star, you have to *act* like a star." Whatever the hell that meant. But I clung to every word like holy writ—because it was. (It took me years to understand what she meant: If you treat *yourself* as a successful actor, a star, a skilled performer, then that's how others will see you, and that's what Hollywood will let you be. You have to believe and behave like a pro 24-7 to make others believe the same . . . and respect you. A decade later, I was asked to basically audition *for* an audition. I acted like a star and said, "No way; I'm past that," and was offered the role the next day.)

Shooting one day, the entire *Yours, Mine and Ours* cast was doing a frenzied breakfast scene. Two dozen moving parts, including all the actors (mostly little kids) and one prop man wedged under the kitchen sink to shoot toasted prop bread up from the toaster on cue. Not an easy day's work. In the middle of it, Lucy stopped the scene and shouted at all of us, "Always rehearse with your props!"

It was an admonition from a world-famous pro who knew why the shot was taking longer than it should. It didn't matter that some of the guilty culprits were six years old. Lucy didn't give a shit. She wanted every actor in the room to know how to do it better next time. One of many lessons from this master of comedy.

Film School Boot Camp

A Master Class from Lucille Ball

Lucy was a genius. I don't know if she was a fan of Thomas Edison, but Lucille Ball could have easily coined the phrase "Genius is 99 percent perspiration." She drilled into all of us that to make comedy work, you had to practice and rehearse, and practice and rehearse, and then practice and rehearse to find the precise comedic elements that would work best in a scene. Then once you found those elements, you had to practice and rehearse, and practice and rehearse, and practice and rehearse to hone those elements and set it up so that everything would seem to happen by accident exactly when it was supposed to.

If you have to eat in a scene, you eat in rehearsals. If you have to smoke in a scene, you smoke in rehearsals. If you have to drink in a scene, you drink in rehearsals. This way, Lucy would preach to us, you would always do it the same way in every take in every angle of coverage of that scene. Because if you didn't properly rehearse it, then you'd be distracted by "When am I supposed to sip the drink? Or take the bite? Or drop the napkin?" As an actor, if you divert your attention to technical things, it always takes you out of the natural moment of a scene and takes the focus off what your character wants and how they want to get it. Lucy taught me to work out every scene in advance and to have a performance ready to deliver. Then, if there are some happy accidents or spontaneous alterations in the scene, you can just go with them.

In *Animal House*, when I had Dean Wormer's wife up in Otter's bedroom and was mixing her a drink, I knew the beats of the moment. Beat 1: Show her my room. Beat 2: Remove her jacket. Beat 3: Put some ice in a glass and fix her a drink. Those beats were great as we rehearsed, but then some accidents happened and I could imagine Lucy whispering in my ear. When I went to

> hang up Mrs. Wormer's coat, it missed the rack and fell to the floor. ("Go with it," Lucy whispered.) Then I felt that a cool guy like Otter would loosen his tie—a move that was made ludicrous by his wearing of a toga. ("Try it," Lucy whispered.) When I went to put the ice in the glass, the first and second cubes bounced out of the glass by accident. (Lucy was laughing in my ear at this point.) Just a little silly good luck on the first take. But because we had worked on the beats in advance, it was possible to keep going on with the scene when the little accidents happened.

A day later, Van Johnson was even less forgiving. I'd seen Van in a bunch of films (*Brigadoon, The Last Time I Saw Paris, The Caine Mutiny*) and I was a fan, but the feeling wasn't mutual. He had a plane to catch and somebody had missed their line in a scene. "Come ONNNN!!! Jeeesus!!" he yelled. He set to berating a bunch of kids in front of the whole crew. "Learn your damn lines!" We kids were glancing at Lucy for support, figuring she'd tell him to tone it down—she didn't. She let the scolding and the tantrum continue. Young actors were being taught a lesson. Someone *had* blown the line, and it had cost a hundred-plus people, especially Van, an extra fifteen minutes.

Henry Fonda, who played my father in the film, brought a whole other vibe to the set. First, he'd sit quietly between takes and do needlepoint. Legs crossed, squinting restfully at the canvas, busying his hands, trying to quit smoking, long before anyone was quitting smoking. Where Lucy was energy and had a type A focus, Fonda was all about staying calm and relaxed. In the first scene I had with him, I was curious how he'd play the scene. The movie had been custom-scripted for Lucy by her writers; Henry Fonda, not so much. So there were a dozen ways he could do this scene. But when the director called action, Fonda just became Henry Fonda. He spoke gently and calmly, and it sounded like the most natural thing in the world. It was simply a movie star talking like a father to his family.

There was no need for grand gestures or hamming it up. Henry Fonda's gift was his ability to be real, simple, and honest. His example was perhaps the most important takeaway any actor had given me up to that point in my career, and it prepared me perfectly for Clint Eastwood just five years later.

———

I WAS TESTING FOR A ROLE IN THE TV SERIES *JIGSAW JOHN*, starring Jack Warden (*Heaven Can Wait, 12 Angry Men*). Having problems with a transition in emotions during the scene, I asked Jack for some help. "I'm not telling you what to do," he said. "But you don't need to take a beat to have the idea right before your line. Play it like you've had that conclusion earlier in the scene. That will smooth out your transition." Boy was he right. (But just not enough help for me to win the part in the show.) He'd given me permission to play more natural, to trust my instincts as young as they were, and the next take came so much easier. (Years later, Jack and I would star together in *Dreamer*—the bowling movie, not a comedy, where Jack's character literally bowls himself to death.)

In high school, I could barely talk to my peers. And acting with them in a theatre class was even worse. I'd grow anxious and feel incredibly self-conscious. With adults, however, and with several of the biggest stars on the planet, I somehow felt buoyant and accepted.

And a new feeling: I felt like I belonged.

On *Divorce American Style*, Dick Van Dyke would tell hilarious stories for hours to Gary Goetzman (child actor, megaproducer, lifelong friend; more on Gary later) and me while we all played Ping-Pong with Debbie Reynolds. Dick Van Dyke was in the Fonda camp, keeping the set loose between takes.

Jason Robards (*All the President's Men, Parenthood*) was also in that movie. A Broadway guy newer to Hollywood, he treated Gary and me like real actors from day one, never once patronized us like the kids we were. In his eyes, we were equals—he just had more acting experience—and it made every scene with him so comfortable. It was like talking to a friend.

JACKIE GLEASON, ON THE OTHER HAND, WAS THE FIRST STAR I knew with his own personal assistant. With a glance, this guy named Arnie would bring Gleason a cigarette or a glass of water on the set of *How to Commit Marriage*. Besides the assistant, Gleason also traveled with a mountain of suits, each suit in *three* sizes to match whatever his weight was on that particular day. "My weight goes up and down," he explained to me one morning.

Gleason was a supernova. Today he would be compared with Tom Hanks for his dramatic and comedic talent and to George Clooney or Jay-Z for his position in popular culture. *The Jackie Gleason Show* and *The Honeymooners* were already considered the television gold standard, and his Oscar-nominated portrayal of Minnesota Fats in *The Hustler* was revered by every actor in the business. In the 1950s, he signed a TV deal that included a *guaranteed* twenty-year commitment. For his *How to Commit Marriage* contract, Gleason purportedly bargained his deal for three weeks of work with the bold statement: "What's the biggest contract an actor's ever gotten for three weeks on a film? I'll take one dollar more."

Now he was doing that film with Bob Hope. And me.

Gleason played my father in the film, and one afternoon, we tried rehearsing a scene but weren't getting very far. Besides Gleason, Hope, and Jane Wyman, the movie was about teenagers and the hippie lifestyle, and so there was a lot of fresh blood on the set— including an actual band (the Comfortable Chair). My romantic interest, JoAnna Cameron (*The Secrets of Isis*) hadn't done much work, either, prior to this film. While the director tried to rein things back together, Gleason put his arm around me and pulled me aside.

"Kid," he said, leaning closer. "You and I are the only ones here who know what we're doing. Let's get this show on the road and get outta here."

"You got it, Mr. Gleason," I managed. "Yes, sir."

It was such an honor. All those days and nights as a kid watching this man on our television, and here now getting his stamp of approval. I was so energized, I could have shot *three* movies that month.

Which was important, as the actual movie we were doing had become a hot mess.

In these days, a runner would drop scripts off at actors' homes at all hours of the night. So when you opened your door in the morning, you would have the *LA Times*, the *Herald Examiner*, *Variety*, the *Hollywood Reporter*, and your script for the day, all in a neat stack waiting for you. The green-sheeted script for the Gleason-Hope film showed up one morning (a color indicating we were already four rewrites in), but it now included a long scene with Hope and Gleason playing a round of golf against a . . . chimpanzee.

There had been no chimp even mentioned in the script I had signed on for. *My God*, I thought. *We're in trouble.* (A decade before anyone had heard of "jumping the shark," we'd now "golfed the chimp.")

But the film pressed on. At the wrap party, Hope gave the cast and crew gifts of every kind of booze you ever heard of in bottles shaped like oversized golf clubs. Gleason gifted watches to everyone, from the fourth lighting guy to Jane Wyman. Mine was an engraved pocket watch ("To Tim, from Jackie") with a little arm you could open like a stand to set beside you when you traveled. (It's resting on my nightstand as we speak.) Class and grace from both legends throughout.

Mostly.

To be fair, not everyone was treated as well. And behavior in 1969 was slightly different than today—still, sometimes the *same*. Class and grace are relative, and these megastars *were* from a different Hollywood.

One day, Hope and Gleason sat at a table before a long line of chorus girls and actresses parading in front of them. I watched from afar as these young women postured back and forth, answering questions. These were young actresses, I soon realized, giving some kind of impromptu audition. This was mostly through the movie, and I couldn't make sense of what they were doing there, since everything, including the chimpanzee, had already been cast. Only days later did I lurch up in bed and finally get it. And discreet questions the next day on set confirmed it.

Hope and Gleason had been casting their lunch "companions." They were merely picking which girl—which hopeful actress—they wanted to spend the early afternoon or evening with. If you wanted a contract with the studios, you played nice, and occurrences like this were still part of that twisted world. It shocked me, honestly, especially with how public it had all happened. But despite earlier promises, I was still far too young, and selfish, to question or protest. That's "just the way things were done" in 1969. The next time there was an impromptu "fashion show" on set, I made sure to steer clear. Again, having been raised by women, I knew this sort of thing wasn't going to be part of my career.

ALSO STEERING CLEAR OF SUCH THINGS WAS MY OTHER INFLUENCE on that film: Leslie Nielsen. He'd worked on just about everything since 1950, and long before *Airplane!* and *Naked Gun*, he'd been a serious actor (part of why he's so great in those films). Leslie's advice to me was simple: "Read the paper." Between takes, he'd just find a quiet corner and read the daily newspaper—no scripts or "getting in character"—and eventually I asked him about it. "Acting is just something we do," he explained. "It's not all we do. See what's going on in the world, Tim. Follow a sports team. Have a life and interests outside"—he waved his free hand at the set—"whatever *this* is." (Perfectly related, this is also a guy who, for years, loved to carry small gag fart noisemakers around in his pants pocket that he could squeeze randomly during awkward silences or mundane conversations to embarrass the hell out of people.)

The lesson: Don't take this, whatever *this* is, so seriously. And as a kid who could fall victim to being a perfectionist, this was much-needed guidance.

———

WHILE NOT A HOUSEHOLD NAME, SADIE SHOULD BE ADDED TO THIS list of mentors in my teenage years. Sadie Embry Dodson Lewis. My Grandma Sadie.

The fiercest, strongest-willed woman I've ever met.

A Virginia girl, born April 10, 1880. Freed men and women still lived at the house while Sadie was a kid. She was vehemently *anti*-racist, a devout liberal, and a vocal supporter of civil rights. When my dad or anyone used foul or bigoted language, she'd always angrily shut it down.

Grandma Sadie was also elegant, a Southern belle in gloves, a simple dark hat, and a big purse folks then called a pocketbook. "Women should never smoke in public," she'd tell me, and ask me to light her a Kool cigarette in the privacy of her own home. She'd take three puffs and then put it out and let it sit in the ashtray for half an hour. Then she'd take it up, light it again, and she'd smoke two or three more puffs before putting it out again. One cigarette lasted fourteen hours. When I was a kid, after she left for work, I'd pop one into my mouth, light it up, and type out stories on her typewriter while drinking shot glasses full of Pepsi, playing Cary Grant from *His Girl Friday*.

She had married my grandfather Louis, who owned a lumber yard. He killed himself when my mom was still a kid, so Grandma Sadie regrouped and became a traveling teacher who taught in Cuba and all around the south of Florida. Meanwhile, her three kids, including my mom, stayed at home with my grandmother's mother, who everyone called "Ma'am." The oldest child, my uncle Byrd, soon ran off with the carnival (people really did this) and then joined the Merchant Marines. But my mom and her sister stayed on, the whole family barely surviving the 1918 flu epidemic before heading out to Los Angeles and a better climate.

In L.A., Grandma Sadie became a notary public and opened up a little storefront office downtown, like a UPS store, with postboxes and a lithograph machine for making multiple copies. If one of her customers, who were like her second family, needed something copied—Sadie would take the carbon paper and retype it herself. Sometimes, we'd go next door and eat at the Southern Soul Café— the sign in the window said "Good Food for Good People"—where Grandma swore it tasted like home.

She would take in the mail for the guys who lived on Skid Row. They were mostly veterans from Korea and World War II, struggling to adjust, long before anyone knew what post-traumatic stress disorder was. They would have their veterans checks delivered to her address—because they often had no place of their own—and she'd hold on to the checks when they were busted for vagrancy or being drunk and disorderly. Once out of jail, they would always pay a dollar or two or whatever coins they could put together for her help. She kept that loose change in her purse.

Whenever we visited as kids, she'd say, "Well, it's time to clean out my pocketbook," and she would reach in there to pull out handfuls of coins, dimes to half dollars, and then divide them evenly between my sister and me. We'd stack it up: *Oh my God, this is amazing.* Knowing we struggled with money in those early years, she was always so generous.

At nineteen, I was living in Van Nuys in my first house, the new house with my mother and my sister. My uncle Byrd, who drank too often, had picked up my grandmother and gotten into a terrible car accident. After weeks in the hospital, she also moved in with us to rehab for months. Between talks with Lucille Ball and Dick Van Dyke, I'd sit and talk to Grandma Sadie. She'd tell me about the old days, and of course, I didn't ask her enough questions.

My mom, sister, and I eventually took turns driving Grandma back and forth to her business, because she wanted to get back to work right away.

A year later, she had congestive heart failure and stayed with us again, trying to recover. But it was different this time. In the hospital with the oxygen tent up, she still wanted a cigarette. "You can't smoke in here," I said with a smile. "You're gonna blow us all up!"

Grandma Sadie winked at me.

She never made it home.

Here was a woman who'd taken care of business. Did her job and reinvented herself, however many times it took, to survive. I could see where Mom had gotten that same spirit. A strength, resourcefulness, and fear of failure I would need to call on time and time again.

—

I was nineteen. With Gleason, Ball, Van Dyke, Nielsen, and Grandma Sadie, one final mentor had appeared to shape my last days of boyhood. Another family member, you could say.

Uncle Sam.

Hollywood Leatherneck

MELSON LOOKED, SOUNDED, AND WAS AS TOUGH AS MIKE TYSON.

We had no idea who Mike Tyson was yet—Iron Mike was only two in 1968—but for the sake of telling a story, it's the best comparison I have.

Melson *wasn't* two years old. He was nineteen and from the South Side of Chicago. There were rumors he'd killed a guy in the Windy City. That he'd already done a tour in Vietnam and was just doing boot camp again for fun. That someone had seen him dribble a bowling ball. That he drank napalm.

Melson. It was his last name, but like Bono or Zendaya—he only needed one name. This guy scared the shit out of me.

He also scared every recruit at the Marine Corps Recruit Depot in San Diego. If we could just get him in front of Ho Chi Minh for five minutes, the People's Army would likely surrender and the war in Vietnam would already be over.

The rest of Melson's squad was mostly, notoriously, made up of inner-city tough guys. These were guys who had been given the choice, usually by a judge, to go to jail or join the Marines, and Melson was their king. The baddest man of all the platoons. Now my squad was facing Melson's during pugil stick exercises—where cadets thwack at each other with large, padded poles as part of training for rifle and bayonet combat.

My platoon was lined up across from Melson's. Forty-plus young men. Face-to-face, each awaiting a mano-a-mano bout. I did some careful counting. I was sixteen recruits back from the start of my line; Melson was eleven back in the other line. *Bingo!* I was clear and my platoon mate Jackson was screwed; he was going to have to face Melson. I could now safely cheer on my platoonmates and bullshit with the guys in line around me.

I had been making jokes and not paying enough attention. Closer to the start of the line now and my turn in the ring, I looked to my left to see Jackson, who was not supposed to be there. Everyone in my platoon was looking out for themselves (very un-Marine of them) and was shifting spots to avoid having to face Melson. Now I'm five guys back and stare across the line at Melson, who is also five guys back in line and already looking at me like I'd recently pugil-sticked his mom.

Near the front now, the drill instructors were watching us like hawks and I was too close and too late to dare attempt to peel off. Better to face Melson, *I somehow convinced myself,* than a drill instructor's foot up my ass.

I weighed 160 pounds at this point (which looks great on film). Melson didn't care about his close-ups, and my best guess is that he weighed 220. His trapezii grew straight up into his chin. I didn't even know what a trapezius muscle was, only that he had no neck. He already stood helmeted, pugil stick in hand, and waiting as if Roman senators were watching.

My drill instructor jammed a football helmet onto my head and snapped the chin guard. He studied me briefly and then took one look at Melson. Then he laughed. "Good luck," he said, and handed me my pugil stick.

"TAKE YOUR STANCE!" barked another drill instructor.

I stepped forward and heard the whistle blow.

I had only one choice: Attack! I mustered up a yell (or yelp) and charged Melson at full throttle. *KABAM!* I hit the Chicago kid as hard as I could. Dick Van Dyke would have been in traction for weeks. Melson, however, just stared at me with narrowed eyes. His head hadn't even moved.

Then he threw down his pugil stick. *Uh-oh . . .*

"Retreat, hell!" I reassured myself with an infamous Marine battle cry. (I'm not going to pretend I didn't think about it.) I braced for impact as Melson dove at me. Or, more so, flew through the air like a Second City Superman.

We crashed backward in a heap onto the ground, 220 pounds filling my whole world with an eruption of dust. His fists began pounding into both sides of my helmet. Melson had gone full South Side, where they don't wear helmets.

I heard loud cheers and louder laughter. Meanwhile, I'm in the most horrifying moment of my life and Melson is bloodying his hands beating my, for the moment, impenetrable helmet. "NO, MELSON!" the drill instructors were shouting with hilarity. "HIT HIM WITH THE STICK!!!" Eventually, the drill instructors got Melson off me and pulled us back to our feet. Then the worst thing I'd heard yet in the Marine Corps:

"GO AGAIN!!"

———

THE NOTION OF BECOMING A US MARINE BEGAN WHILE I WAS driving my childhood buddy Mike Stokey Jr. to Camp Pendleton a couple times. Nicknamed "Up North" for North San Diego County, the camp was about an hour and a half south from my home in Los Angeles. (Mike's dad was a producer and the successful game show host of *Pantomime Quiz* and *Stump the Stars*.) Mike liked game shows fine, but he worshipped the Corps.

I, meanwhile, still had mixed feelings about the war in Vietnam and mixed feelings about what, if anything, I should do. The Summer of Love, 1967, was the previous summer, and I had dropped out of college for a part in a pilot that didn't sell. I wasn't exposed much to active protestors anymore. Everyone I knew over thirty-five or so was *for* the war—"America: Love it or leave it"—because, I suspect, they weren't going to be asked to go fight. Meanwhile, all us kids under twenty-one, who couldn't even yet vote, were the ones being sent over. (The US amendment lowering the voting age to eighteen wasn't passed until 1971.) As an L.A. teenager, I was almost obligated to be *against* the war. But the geopolitics of it all was an enigma I couldn't quite crack; I just knew I wanted our guys home from Southeast Asia.

Also, I had zero interest in personally learning where Dien Bien Phu was.

I'd just made a movie with Henry Fonda and Lucille Ball. Genuinely passionate about my craft and my career, I greedily didn't want to give that up.

Yet I also sincerely felt an obligation to my country, that I needed to do *something*. (Keep in mind: This is a time I'd soon marry a woman because I'd slept with her. I was older-school before old-school was a thing.) I spent a lot of time during those months trying to figure out if I was a proud citizen, an activist, a coward, or just selfish. Probably all four rolled into one.

Earlier, I'd had a temporary six-month hardship deferment (to help my mother with some financial matters), but that had since passed. I'd then had a school deferment, but I had dropped out and the local draft board now had me as 1A: eligible for military service. If drafted, I figured, I'd be dead meat. I was a theatre kid with little experience in fighting, shooting a gun, or in not getting killed. (In 1968 alone, more than sixteen thousand Americans were killed in Vietnam.)

Maybe I could go to Canada. This was a common notion in 1968. Lots of people were going up north as an act of protest and out of fear. But I didn't want to give up my whole life in the States, knowing I couldn't come back. Goodbye, contracts with Warner Bros. Goodbye, Mom. Goodbye, lunches at Hollywood's famous Musso & Frank Grill and the Brown Derby. Even so, I seriously considered it.

Reserve units were available for people to volunteer and join. By joining the reserves, I'd be removed from the draft. The trade-off was the reserves were a six-year enlistment. It worked like this: You signed up for the reserves and immediately began a six-month active-duty period. This included basic training, combat training, military occupational specialty training (a government way of saying "your job is . . ."), and whatever else they wanted to do with you for six months. After that period, you went home to civilian life for all but one weekend a month and two weeks of active duty every summer for additional training. For the next five and a half years.

The Navy Reserves—full. Air Force—full. Army—full. Even the Coast Guard recruiting office told me I'd have to wait years for a spot in its reserves. That left the Marine Corps. And since the Marines were the toughest warriors on earth, they were understandably not very popular with people trying *not* to be tough. But I convinced myself: *If I ever end up in combat, the training in the smaller and "tougher" Marine Corps will serve me well.* I'd be better prepared to handle myself and survive than if I'd just been drafted into the Army and rushed through with the herd.

In a ridiculous coincidence, the day of my real-life draft physical, my character in *Yours, Mine and Ours* was scheduled to have *his* movie draft physical filmed. The studio had to reschedule the shoot, and Uncle Sam gave me my 1A clearance a full week before Tom Bosley checked my vitals for the world to see.

For the penultimate scene of that movie, my character, Mike Beardsley, rushes into the courtroom and presses the adoption judge, saying, "I leave for Camp Pendleton in an hour. . . . I was trying to speed things up." The director had put me in a Marine uniform for the scene. I didn't yet know any of the military etiquette or anything; I only knew that I felt like a real phony wearing that uniform. In costume, I walked down a Hollywood street to get lunch near where we were filming.

Someone yelled out, "Hey, Marine!"

I didn't know what to do. Whether to explain I was still just play-acting or turn and nod politely like a real Marine might. But

I still had no idea what a real Marine even was. The older man who had called out saluted me from across the street and, not sure what else to do, I returned the salute—which I later learned was really bad form for a private.

In the very final scene of the movie, my character Mike is in uniform and waving goodbye as he heads off to Camp Pendleton. FADE TO BLACK: THE END.

But when the director yelled cut, in a strange moment of art imitating life, the real Tim Matthieson was heading straight to basic training.

——

I WAS FIRST ORDERED TO THE MARINE CORPS RECRUIT DEPOT IN San Diego, one hundred acres next to the San Diego airport. The base's main mission was to train all recruits from west of the Mississippi but also—for some unknown reason—a few eastern lands, including Wisconsin, Louisiana, and metropolitan Chicago (thus my new pal Melson). It would be ten weeks of weapons training, rigorous physical exercises on the obstacle course, Marine Corps history, close-order drill, and—shockingly at first, but it quickly made sense for most of the guys I was with—a full litany of personal hygiene. The ultimate goal was to survive and thrive throughout boot camp, where squads face many obstacles requiring not just physical strength but also teamwork. *My* ultimate goal was just to survive to week 2.

It'd sure seemed fun dropping my friend Mike off at Camp Pendleton and meeting his Marine pals. I realized too late that I had never dropped him off at boot camp and had never once met one of his drill instructors.

Guys who couldn't take it would always try to escape. When they did, they always got caught and were brought back to an area in the middle of camp where the rest of us could watch them get their punishment. They would be ordered to dig a hole on one side of the field, then carry that dirt to another hole on the *other* side of the field and fill it—and so on, back and forth, for days. We saw first-hand that going AWOL was not the best idea. Between the ten-mile forced marches, the legendary and grueling obstacle course, the marksmanship training, live-fire drills crawling under barbed wire, and the image of the AWOL guys' constant digging, these ten weeks were among the toughest of my life.

You would think it was the running or marching or close-quarter combat we all feared the most; it wasn't. Everyone hated the needles. We'd gotten *seventeen* shots and vaccinations over eight weeks, sometimes from a nurse with a needle and other times from a medieval pneumatic-gun device that would slice you open if you flinched.

There *were* some flashes of hope.

On Sundays, we had a day of rest from training. We had more free time, got to sleep in a little, and enjoy a nicer breakfast. The only order we had to follow was to go to a religious service. I'd gone along with most of my platoon to some nondenominational Protestant service in the cavernous base movie theater. "IF YOU'RE NOT A GOOD CHRISTIAN, GET OUT OF THIS CHURCH!!!" the minister bellowed at us. "And if you don't love this country, you should GET OUT OF THE MARINES!!!" I don't know what his rank was, but I'm certain he was God's drill instructor.

I went back somewhat dazed and complained to my squad mates, who hadn't come to the service. They just laughed. I was in a squad with a lot of other middle-class, educated reservists from Los Angeles, and a good third of them were Jewish. "Our service was amazing," they bragged. "Bagels, lox, girls from the B'nai B'rith . . ."

"Girls?"

"Oh yeah, many. We danced. And you can smoke all you want." Cigarettes were on drill-instructor command/allowance only. In those days, we all smoked.

"I wish I could go . . ." I groused. What did it matter I wasn't one of the Chosen? "I'll show them my circumcision."

"Just tell them your mom's Jewish," one cadet suggested a better option.

"She isn't."

"No kidding. But *they* don't know that." *Well, maybe it's worth a shot.*

First, I needed the chutzpah to pitch this lie to my drill instructors. I gingerly approached the closed door of the imposing command hut, took a deep breath, and pounded firmly on the door as we'd been instructed to do in an emergency. It was the first time I'd done so—proving how important this was to me for some reason. The squad bay door was jerked open by a scowling drill instructor.

"What??!, shithead?!"

"Sir, the private requests permission to speak, sir?" (All sentences began and ended with "sir." And you never dared use pronouns like "you" or "I.")

"Speak, asshole."

"Sir, the private requests permission to attend the Jewish services, sir!"

His eyes squinted. "*You're* a kike, Matthieson?"

Here comes the chutzpah . . .

"Sir, no sir! The private's mother is Jewish, sir."

"Then you're a kike!"

Every Sunday thereafter became the best hour of my week. The nosh, the schmear, the music, the girls from B'nai B'rith. The rabbis were thoughtful and funny. Collectively, these were the nicest people I'd ever met. I just told the people running the service that my mother was Jewish but that we weren't very religious growing up, thus explaining why I didn't know *anything* about the faith. And my Jewish squad mates, good mensches all, continued to help me sell the lie all my years in the Marines. That little bit of humanity each week saved me.

Boot camp in the Corps proved one of the most profound experiences in my life. Its purpose, or at least the one I took away, was to discover that you can do much more than you think you can. Spending most of my time in recording studios or acting classes, I'd never really done anything physically taxing or even seriously played sports. I smoked two packs a day back then. Hey, it was 1968, everybody I knew smoked two packs a day. I could run a little, but that's about it. And here I was with a group of guys, many from the rural South and raised on sports, hunting, and physical activity. The physical activity was the core of the training, but what you learned about yourself, mentally, how far you could push yourself, is really how you got through all of it. You were learning that there was a reserve and a resource inside you to call on to go further than you ever thought you could.

There was one young man in my squad, Quackenbush, from Louisiana. His father was tired of him lying around the house after graduating from high school. To show his dad how tough he was, he'd joined the Marines. If you looked at Quackenbush, he would have been the one you'd pick to fight Melson. But on our second day in camp, he melted down during a brutal five-mile run. His body looked like it had been chiseled from stone, but here he was, crying in the dirt. I jogged up and—out of fear of the drill instructor or with some reserve of leadership I didn't know I had—I grabbed this kid by his utility shirt and yelled at him: "Get up! Come on, Q! You're tougher than me, stronger than me! If I can do this, so can you!" We made it back before both our butts were kicked.

The Marine Corps has a way of finding the best in you. Later that night, I was made a squad leader. This made me responsible for twelve other Marines *and* their behavior. If they fucked something up, didn't finish a drill, or got out of line, I was going to be held responsible as well. As an actor, I was experienced in doing what I was told to do and being directed. Turns out the Marines really like this quality in a young man. When we graduated from boot camp, I was honored to be promoted to private first class. And I thought the hardest part was over.

Next up was a month with the Infantry Training Regiment (ITR) at Camp Pendleton, where we learned hand-to-hand combat, first aid, basic survival, weapons training (if it had a trigger, we fired it), and the reasons for actually running *toward* enemy guns when caught in the open with no possible cover. At this point, I'd begun to believe we Marine recruits, especially me, were pretty tough stuff. Forged into the fiercest warriors on earth.

Then, early at ITR, in a remote-field chow hall, my unit crossed paths with a dozen guys seated off at a table away from everyone else. They were dressed differently and kept entirely to themselves, and I'd never seen a group eat as much or as fast. They also looked like guys who could eat Melson for breakfast—like stuntmen from a superhero movie, who turned out to be actual superheroes. "Who are those guys?" I asked quietly, somewhat in awe.

"They're SEALs," my tablemates answered and quickly set to their own meals as if the discussion were over.

I'd never heard of Navy SEALs until just then. And I've never forgotten those first guys. I'd officially met the limits of my emerging warrior potential. There were no reserves or resources inside of me to ever get a seat at *that* particular table. But I was okay with that. As Dirty Harry would famously quip in one of my next films, "A man's got to know his limitations."

———

THROUGHOUT ALL OF THIS, I MADE SURE TO KEEP MY LIMITED HOLlywood identity a top secret. Just imagine if Melson knew I once swam in Beaver Cleaver's pool.

My Marine pal Mike Stokey Jr. was always kidding me—*warning* me—about Hollywood Marines. Child stars like my old pal Tony Dow from *Leave It to Beaver* or Johnny Crawford from *The Rifleman* were both serving in the Army at this time. Jimmy Stewart had a stepson in the Marines, and everyone knew it.

The last thing I needed was "Oh, here comes Mr. Hollywood! Oh yeah, Steve McQueen, let's get you down here! Twenty-five knuckle pushups, *Bullitt* boy!! Squad, ten-hut! Lucy's kid is going to show us all how to throw a hand grenade!"

From the second I went into boot camp, I made sure I didn't mention anything about *Leave It to Beaver* or *Jonny Quest* or going on a studio-arranged date with some young actress (yes, these dates were something the studios arranged to get their actors some press). Nope. I was just another dropout from Cal State Northridge. I made sure to fly below the radar, a pattern I kept for the next few years as best I could to make for a smooth enlistment.

One late afternoon during boot camp, our whole platoon was marching back and forth on base directly past the base movie theater. The marquee lit up to entice everyone permanently stationed on base to come experience, in their precious time off, Columbia Pictures brand-new movie *Divorce American Style*, starring Dick Van Dyke and Debbie Reynolds!

What it didn't say, thankfully, was, "And guest-starring your very own squad leader, Private Tim Matthieson, as their teenaged son."

A thousand Marines must have seen that movie over the next week or so. But because my role was minimal, nobody paid much attention to the older kid in the flick. Clearly, actors are the only ones who scrutinize the billing or film credits scrolling up the screen at the start of the movie. I waited all week for the *Semper Fi* hammer to drop, and nothing. No one connected the dots.

I was scot-free.

Then Bob Hope opened his big mouth.

———

THE LAST STEP OF MY TRAINING WAS TO LEARN A SPECIFIC JOB, MY primary military occupational specialty (MOS—not sure why they don't just call it JOB). I was selected to be a 2531, or in lay terms, a field radio operator. The good news was that I wasn't being sent to the infantry. The bad news was that radio operators were always *with* the infantry and the first guys who got shot at. Why? Because to operate our radios, we had to raise what seemed like a 30-foot-tall antenna. The enemy knew the lieutenants were standing right next to the radio operator and the giant antenna, which might have well had "Hey shoot over here" written on it. I was trained on the PRC-25, a.k.a. the Prick 25, the most widely used radio set in the Vietnam War. General Creighton Abrams, who ran the war from 1968 to 1972 on our way out, later called it "the single most important tactical field item in Vietnam." I don't know if that's true or not. I just know I could take the sucker apart and put it back together again with my eyes closed and that it weighed about as much as a third-grader.

After finishing my time at radio school, I had eight more weeks of active duty to serve. I was put on mess duty mopping floors and cleaning pans and hoping our division didn't get activated to go to Vietnam before I switched to reserve duty back home for the next five and half years.

Then, I got the call.

Lucille Ball wanted me to go to New York City to be on *The Ed Sullivan Show* to help promote *Yours, Mine and Ours*. All the other kids were going to be there to do some corny dance number (which you might recognize if you've seen *Licorice Pizza*). The notion of escaping mops for four days sounded pretty good, but . . .

"No way," I said. "They'll never let me." And I didn't want to ask, either. I hadn't yet once pulled out the Hollywood card to help me with anything. All that would do in the long run, I knew, was hurt me. "I won't have leave for another month," I said. I hung up and looked for my mop.

Days later, my sergeant stepped into the kitchen. "Pfc. Matthieson!"

"Aye, aye, Sergeant."

"There's a car coming to pick you up tomorrow."

"Sergeant?"

"You're getting four days of liberty to go to New York and do *The Ed Sullivan Show*."

I sighed deeply.

"You some kind of musician or something?" he asked.

After I'd declined the invitation, Lucille Ball called Bob Hope. Hope had called the Marine Corps headquarters in Washington, D.C., and personally asked the Commandant of the Marine Corps to "deploy" me to serve on *The Ed Sullivan Show*. (Fifty years of USO shows will give you that sort of power. Hope was already a cultural icon for his dedication to America's troops and the legendary USO tours he'd started during World War II. These tours continued until the Gulf War in 1990. There is a reason airports and roads are named after him.)

Now it was an order. The order might as well have been for everyone to give me shit 24-7 for being a Hollywood Marine.

A CAR PICKED ME UP AT THE BASE THE NEXT DAY AND TOOK ME TO the airport, and I got a first-class seat to New York. I only had a single dollar in my pocket, not enough for breakfast when I arrived at the Plaza Hotel.

This was all quite different from being in the Marines. For four and a half months, I had become an expert at doing only what I was told to do. Now, I'm sleeping in a nice room in the Plaza, going out to eat with the cast of *Yours, Mine and Ours*, taking in a Broadway show, and killing time seeing the sights of New York City (for the first time) with Jennifer Leak, Gary Goetzman, and other cast members.

It was during these tours of NYC that Jennifer and I first had any kind of spark. During the shooting of our film, I'd had very few scenes with her; I was focused on doing my job and felt she was out of my league anyway. She was a sophisticated former Miss Toronto, and I was a Valley guy from Burbank. But here, in New York, killing two days before having to be on *Sullivan* for ten minutes, there was plenty of opportunity to talk and flirt.

Fresh off the Marine base, I was quite ready for both.

We all rehearsed at the Ed Sullivan Theater. It was a silly routine involving bunkbeds and pajamas while singing the movie's corny theme song. It was surreal. I could only imagine my fellow Marines scrubbing toilets and digging foxholes back at Camp Pendleton while I pranced around the stage and hit Gary Goetzman with a pillow.

Shepherding us around that weekend was a young production assistant in his early twenties. He proved super helpful and friendly. He'd only been with United Artists, our studio, a few weeks at this point, but you could tell he loved Hollywood as much as I did and he spoke of moving to L.A. soon to start a career in film. His name was Jonathan Demme. (He would later become one of Hollywood's most sought-after directors and win an Oscar for *The Silence of the Lambs*. He would also direct Tom Hanks to an Oscar for *Philadelphia*. Both films were produced by Gary Goetzman. Entertainment is clearly an interesting—and small—world.)

After rehearsals, Demme led us to a press conference with Lucy and all the other kids. There, Lucy was quick to point out that "Tim is just back from the Marine Corps, just like his character in the movie."

"What are your views on Vietnam, Tim?" chirped a reporter.

Oh shit . . . The reporter had shouted out from the back, and the whole room now went silent, waiting for my reply. The year was 1968, and this was a deliberately controversial question. There were definite sides on this subject. I was against the war, but I was also a proud Marine and ready to fight if called on. Trying to explain that balance would have gotten me killed by both Lucille Ball and the Marines. I started some hemming and hawing, clearly going nowhere. I'd never had to speak to the press before. I was trapped and panicked, a total public disaster the likes of which I'd never faced.

"It's a complicated thing," Gary Goetzman interrupted my rambling and leaned toward the mic. "You know . . ." Keep in mind that Gary is fourteen at this point. "Tim's serving his country, which is really inspiring, you know, and there are people with views on both sides of this conflict, of course. But . . . that's not what *this* movie is about."

The press conference moved on.

Fourteen years old. Gary bailed me out like a seasoned pro.

(I've always believed that this very moment is when Demme decided that *this* was the guy he wanted producing his movies.)

It was not the last time Goetzman would come to my aid.

Gary Goetzman

Coca-Cola. Triscuits. Gouda cheese.

We were living the good life. We'd stock up before an afternoon by the pool. Gary and I thought we were quite sophisticated poolside, and it was the gouda cheese that put us over the top. And Lenny Bruce albums; we loved listening to Lenny Bruce.

Both Gary and I were still teenagers. I'd recently bought a house in the Valley. We soaked up the sun, ate gouda, and talked for hours about all the things we were going to do. Awards won, companies started, dreams of the better-than-good life.

We'd met on Divorce American Style playing—what else?— brothers. He was the funny thirteen-year-old with the confidence and wisdom of a forty-year-old. I'd never met a kid like him. Because of our ages, we were still required to have a chaperone on *set. My mom was working, so Gary volunteered his usual chaperone for both of us. She was a nineteen-year-old hottie who drove Gary to and from work every day. There was definite electricity between the chaperone and me. Gary kept telling me she had the hots for me and that I could "make a move on her, if I wanted." I never did make my move . . . or any move, for that matter. I couldn't let Gary know at the time that I was a shy idiot; I didn't have any moves to make.*

A year later, we were brothers again for Yours, Mine and Ours. *With more screen time, we were now hanging out twelve hours a day. In between shooting, we were poolside with our gouda, planning world domination.*

Yes, he sold waterbeds and ran a video-game arcade (Paul Thomas Anderson's Licorice Pizza *is based on Gary's childhood); Gary did many things. Eventually, the kid who'd been thrown out of high school for truancy produced the Talking Heads concert film* Stop Making Sense, *directed by Jonathan Demme, our old production assistant pal from New York. The filming spanned four nights at the Pantages Theater in Los Angeles. Gary invited me to all four shows. The next night after filming, Saturday, he rented out a club for the entire crew, the band, and pals like me to celebrate the wrap of the filming. It was incredible! And with the success of their concert film, Demme and Goetzman continued to collaborate and made little movies like* The Silence of the Lambs *and* Philadelphia, *winning enough awards to impress even Meryl Streep.*

When I was ready to try directing again myself, I told Gary, and he had me directing a Joe Lamont MTV video before you could say "gouda." To finance the production, we met with a guy named Joe Isgro, a powerful record promoter who had worked for folks like Neil Diamond, The Who, Elton John, Diana Ross, Stevie Wonder, and the Jacksons. And he was also a reputed soldier in the Gambino crime family. He apparently carried on for decades "because no one dared testify against him." Gary walked us in there like he was meeting a childhood friend—and he probably was. He put me imme-diately at ease with Joe and always handled himself so well in every situation.

Making Philadelphia, *Goetzman met Tom Hanks and coproduced Hanks's 1996 directorial debut,* That Thing You Do! *The two soon co-founded Playtone, one of the most successful production companies in Hollywood. Their* Band of Brothers *for HBO brought the miniseries to another level, and I tossed my directorial hat in the ring for a coveted shot at their follow-up:* The Pacific.

Gary's response to my request for directorial consideration: "Keep Christmas open!"

He proceeded to stick his neck out for me and cash in some chips to get me on the short list for The Pacific. *HBO was open to the idea, thanks to Gary, but insisted on seeing me handle one of its other shows first before taking on the prestige stuff. To help prove myself, Gary hired me to direct an episode of* Big Love *(a Playtone/ HBO show where another producer told me he'd "loved me in Wings" mistaking me for Tim Daly). But as I prepared to capitalize on Gary's abiding support and prove myself to HBO, Lifetime offered me a se-ries pilot,* Criminal Behavior, *where I could be king and captain. At the time, I had no choice professionally. I had to let* Big Love *and my courtship of HBO slide away.*

"You fucker . . ." Gary said in a phone call that same night, laugh-ing at having gone to bat for me—for nothing. He was disappointed, but he completely understood my decision to take the better offer and opportunity, and being the same friend he had always been since we were kids, he was happy for me.

Whenever I get together with Gary now, he's still mostly surround-ed by the friends he had made and grown up with fifty-some years ago—those he'd met, trusted, cracked up with, planned with, and loved decades ago. Nice to be included in that group.

God gave me a sister.

The great casting director Lynn Stalmaster had given me a brother.

The night of our *Ed Sullivan Show* appearance, the Bee Gees were the big musical guest of the week. No disco yet, they; Barry Gibb and the boys sang "Words." Then George Hamilton sang something and Jerry Stiller & Anne Meara (Ben Stiller's mom and dad) did their shtick. Some kind of Irish band came on next. All the while, we hung backstage in our ridiculous pajamas waiting and waiting to go on. (As John Gielgud once quipped, "I act for free; I get paid to wait.")

Then Lucy came out for a sit-down interview with Sullivan and set up our pajama-clad song-and-dance number for some forty million Americans.

The Ed Sullivan Show was live on Sunday nights. It was a career highlight (thanks, Bob Hope) and a thrill to be on the show I'd grown up watching—despite the silly song and dance. Early the next morning, I put my Marine uniform back on and returned to Camp Pendleton . . . praying that none of the Marines on base were Bee Gees fans.

———

THE *ED SULLIVAN* MISSION HAD EVIDENTLY REMAINED FAIRLY TOP secret.

Ultimately, it was a friend who served in the First Marine Division at Camp Pendleton who truly outed my Hollywood side to the Marines. Dick Liccardi was an active-duty Marine who I knew from civilian radio school. He ran the Marine newspaper at Pendleton and wanted to interview me about being an actor. Before warning me, he'd pitched the idea to his superiors about coming out to talk to me, and his superiors had contacted mine before I had any idea. Dick had thought he was doing me a favor getting me out of a day of training, but my cover was now blown.

The next days were exactly as I had always feared. Filled with a whole lot of "you Hollywood pussy" and "fag" from my superiors. I considered reassuring them that my recent work on the *Hardy Boys* pilot as Joe Hardy had been quite challenging, but I kept my mouth shut.

When the day arrived for my pal Dick to interview me, he never showed up. My Tinseltown cover had been blown for nothing.

I was livid. Then I was devastated.

Overnight, the Marines had shipped out the *entire* Pendleton Division of office workers, transportation departments, and paper pushers—not the guys you wanted on the front lines—over to Vietnam. Dick hadn't shown up to our interview, because he was now overseas at war. And not some cushy job miles from the action, but ducking bullets in the jungle.

Around this time, our combat instructor showed us a headline about reserves being activated. They had already activated every other reserve unit in the US military—from the Coast Guard and Navy to the Army. *"All* you reserve pussies are going!" he said, and laughed at us. "You're getting out of nothing!"

I actually might get called up. I went home that weekend and it was, *Holy shit, what's going to happen if I'm activated?* Despite all my recent training, my bravado, and how much I'd grown and all, I clearly wasn't some Navy SEAL. I was just a Hollywood kid who had grown more antiwar over the months and didn't relish the idea of going overseas.

Thoughts of Canada and a life of mayonnaise on french fries had never been stronger. I didn't know what I'd do up there in the Great White North or what might become of my life, but I had a better idea of my life in Vietnam. Still, I chose not to leave.

Fortunately, for me, the call-up never came. I returned home to my mostly civilian life. For the rest of my enlistment, I'd spend one weekend a month with my L.A. Artillery Reserve Unit, next to Dodger Stadium, and two weeks at Twentynine Palms, California, each summer to train on the base. Thanks to being outed as a

"Hollywood pussy," I was assigned to the unit's press department, and we published the reserve unit's monthly newsletter.

———

VERONICA CARTWRIGHT WAS A YOUNG ACTRESS (*THE BIRDS, DANiel Boone*) who would later become a star with the success of *Invasion of the Body Snatchers* and *Alien.* Veronica and I had once gone on a publicity date arranged by Universal Studios just so we could be photographed together for PR. Now she was married to my friend Richard Gates.

Rick had played my older brother, Frank Hardy, in the pilot *The Hardy Boys: The Mystery of the Chinese Junk.* (Our version of the classic book series was not picked up; it would be ten years later that Parker Stevenson and Shaun Cassidy would become *Teen Beat* megastars in the same roles.)

Gates was now in the same boat I'd been in: A 1A in the draft who didn't know what to do. He was worried about the draft and trying to build his acting career at the same time. I felt sorry for him and made some calls, and luckily he got accepted as a Marine reservist in the last open spot. Where he was just starting boot camp, however, I was a year into being a Marine already on reserve duty. I could use my experience, and my ID, to help my friend get used to his new life.

The first life hack I provided for Rick was telling him about my "Jewish mother." He was no more Jewish than I was, but he started going to the hospitable Jewish services from day one. *Mazel tov!*

The second favor was sneaking his new wife Veronica onto the base.

With my active-reserve status and my Marine Corps ID, I could drive onto the Marine Corps Recruit Depot to attend religious services on Sundays. One Sunday, I picked up Veronica before dawn, and we headed south to San Diego for Shabbat. (Yes, the Marine

Corps had moved Shabbat—the Jewish day of rest and relaxation celebrated on Saturday for thousands of years—to Sunday morning.) At the guard gate, the MPs welcomed me and demanded to know who I was bringing on the base. "This is my sister Veronica; we're going to temple," I replied, and they waved us through. Rick had no idea, a total surprise, and he almost choked on his bagel. The three of us played Veronica off as my sister for the whole morning (convenient when three professional actors are performing a lie together).

After the service—by both accident and abundant good fortune—an older couple was going to show home movies they had taken on a recent trip to Israel. Rick and Veronica grabbed seats in the back. I sat a few rows ahead. The lights dimmed. The film started. The Wailing Wall filled the screen up front. The older couple began their lecture.

And my "sister" Veronica, without being seen by anyone, performed a "mitzvah" on her husband.

Veronica and I left and never dared, despite Rick's ardent pleadings, to attempt a repeat performance. Yahweh had already favored us enough that day. Rick Gates, Marine legend: the only boot-camp recruit ever, I suspect, to receive such a mitzvah from the Mrs. while in basic training.

———

IN 1968–1969, EVERY ACTOR MY AGE WAS BEING ASKED TO PLAY counterculture hippies, so to gain employment, I'd grown my hair out once I was off active duty. But since I was still in the reserves, I had to report one weekend a month for training. Every time I'd go to my reserves unit, I'd have to get up predawn on Saturday morning to properly jam my real hair up into a preposterously short wig I'd gotten from Universal.

Which worked out for about two years; then the shit hit the fan.

My superiors figured it out, and my commanding officer called me into his office. "You gotta lose the wig and cut that damn hair, lance corporal."

"But, sir, I'm the exception that proves the rule," I assured him. Not even clear now what that means, but it froze him pretty good. "I *need* the longer hair for my civilian career."

He wasn't sure what to do.

A particular old, salty gunnery sergeant was less undecided on the matter. He'd been the first to spot the wig, write me up, and rat me out. When our captain didn't punish me as expected, the sarge took matters into his own hands. He full-on tackled me in the hall, ripped the wig off my head, and roughed me up. "You fucking commie!" he shouted from on top of me. "YOU HIPPIE PIECE OF SHIT!!!"

Several senior officers had to pull this guy off me. "Are you nuts?!" they shouted at the gunny. "You can't hit an enlisted man!"

"Not in public," one added, eyeing me askance.

Uh-oh. I got off a quick letter to my US senator, Alan Cranston, pleading my case. How I needed to keep my hair for my work, that it was easier to do the short wig several times a year than a long wig every day, and how I was the financial provider for my family. He now got involved, but because of his intervention, the heat on me at base only intensified.

"We're gonna activate you, Matthieson," another captain told me. "You're going to 'Nam." Then: "We're kicking you out, Matthieson. *And* we're making sure the Army knows you're available again for the draft."

Boot camp, training, almost three-plus years in the reserves was all about to go down the drain. It wouldn't even count. Over a haircut. But hiding my Hollywood roots (pun intended) was clearly no longer a concern to me. *Adam-12* needed a kid with long hair! I was a weekend warrior, only, unless called on. If the reserves legitimately called me up, then fine, I'd cut my hair and do my duty. But for a couple of hours once a month? Ultimately, Senator Cranston helped me cut a deal. The Marines and I parted ways. It wasn't honorable or dishonorable. It was "Convenience of the Government"—Marine-speak for "We're done with you, Actor Boy." With almost four years left in my six-year enlistment. After all this, I now waited again for my draft number to come up.

But America was already bringing home a hundred thousand military members a year.

In two years, the war was over.

I was, and am, proud to have been part of the brotherhood of Marines. There is a bond with your fellow Marines that will never go away. You've gone through something together. Supported each other. I'd trained and worked beside men who had served and died in Vietnam; they are heroes. Even if I was never deployed, I learned to respect and admire everyone who puts on a uniform for our country. The Marines had fostered a deeper love and understanding of country. And a deeper understanding of myself.

I'd grown from some Valley kid into a man, thanks to the Corps. The kid who had spent a lot of time waiting for adults to tell him where to stand and which lines to emphasize had learned how to take control of a room and command. (I don't imagine I ever could have become a director later without this experience.) My biggest takeaway was the exact opposite of the false civilian notion of mindless warriors doing only what they're told and being spat on when they returned from combat. We'd learned instead: The buck stops with me. Semper Fidelis. Always faithful.

My real-life uniform had gone into the closet.

It was time instead to put on a cowboy hat.

Climb in the Saddle, Be Ready for the Ride

(Part One)

MICHAEL LANDON IS GOING TO *KILL* ME.

Pa Ingalls. Little Joe. Angel Jonathan.

(Hence, this was quite the achievement on my part.)

His face red and scrunched in resentment. His eyes look nothing like Little Joe's anymore. I am twenty-four and, as goes with that terrain, have done and said something stupid. "What the hell were you thinking?" Landon snarls. His hands are clenched at his hips to keep from pummeling me. The restraint was appreciated.

"It was taken out of context," I tried, not for the first or last time.

"I'm not sure what we're going to do about this," Michael said. He was producing, writing, and starring in *Bonanza*, the show that inspired me to buy a TV. I'd been on the show for less than a month, as a new series regular, and it suddenly looked like that's where my stint on the Ponderosa would end.

As the young new star of the hit show in its fourteenth season, I'd been asked to do an interview with *TV Guide*—the most important and influential magazine in the TV business. Everyone read *TV Guide* every week. Being twenty-four, I had some hot takes for the chat.

The biggest was that "old-style westerns were over." They'd grown stale. "Outdated." The days of *The Big Valley*, *The Rifleman*, *Death Valley Days*, and *Gunsmoke* were done. As a genre, we'd already wrung out of the western all the western we could. America had grown up and was now looking forward for its ideas, not to our past. "New concepts are coming up to take their place," I foretold. *Pretty impressive, yeah?*

TV Guide also thought so and ran my thoughts.

"You have any idea what these 'silly westerns' mean to the people on this show?"

I didn't. But I was learning right quick.

"There are men and women on this crew who have worked on this show for *fifteen years*," Landon scolded. "They've gotten married, had kids, lost family. Lost Dan Blocker. They've devoted half their fucking career to this 'silly western.'"

"Michael, I never said—"

"You're here for, what, three weeks? But this is all 'old-timer' stuff to you, right? Unoriginal? Old-fashioned? Worse . . . just another job."

"Mr. Landon . . ."

"Get out of my sight, Matheson," he said.

———

THE COWBOY YEARS BEGAN, ODDLY, ON *ADAM-12*, A COP SERIES SET in modern L.A. I was freshly out of the Marines and starring as the criminal of the week: a Texan hippie who—like all "freaky" teens in 1969 network TV—had gotten high on acid, had stolen a horse in L.A., and was riding that horse back to Texas.

"Grand Theft Horse?" was the episode title, with the question mark and everything. Sideburns. Hippie necklace. A little Southern drawl. Some country singin'. Some horse stealin'.

You never know who's watching.

Executives at Universal (which produced *Adam-12* for NBC) also produced *The Virginian*, and it just so happened they were looking for a fresh young face to add to the popular western for its ninth year. Universal liked what they saw on *Adam-12* and offered me the job, including a term contract, which meant—in classic Hollywood style—they paid me monthly whether I was working or not. (They'd make sure to keep the contract actors busy!) This is why you should always try to bring your A game, even to shit assignments. (Like Gary meeting Jonathan Demme in NYC, you never know where a one-day job will lead.)

Film School Boot Camp

Someone Is Always Watching

After working months before on *How to Commit Marriage*, I was walking on the Paramount lot for an audition when a man I'd never met approached me on the lot. "Hey, Tim!" he said, "I'm Ron [Ron Sinclair]! I'm the editor of *How to Commit Marriage*. Great work! Funny stuff! You're a good actor!" Wow. That made my day. But it took me years of working to realize that he probably told other people the same thing about me during the editing process. It never hurts to have someone like that talking positively about you from day to day.

I'll never know how many jobs, both as an actor and as a director, I got because someone who I'd never met had seen the work I did in another show. Here are some of the ones I do know about:

- *Adam-12* led to *The Virginian*.
- *The Quest* came about because of a favor I'd done for Columbia TV when I filled in at the last minute for an actor

who got sick and they needed someone on set in eight hours—plus was damn good in it.

- Martin Davidson cast me without an audition in *Almost Summer*, because he'd seen some episodic show I had done for Universal while he was deep in the South shooting another show, and he really liked the work I'd done.
- Episodes of *Cold Case* and *Without a Trace* that I directed led to my being hired as an executive producer/director on *Cold Case*.
- Directing on *Burn Notice* and *Psych* led to becoming a pilot director with *Covert Affairs*.

You never know how your work will affect someone somewhere down the line and possibly lead to another job or a breakthrough part or possibly change your life forever. Of course, this is a two-way street. I don't know, and never will, how many casting lists I was taken off by casting directors, producers, or directors who didn't like my work in something I'd done months or even years before.

Two pieces of advice here. The first is that you can never tell someone what to think. Just do your best each time, and let the chips fall where they will—you can *and will* drive yourself crazy if you don't let it go. Second, the people watching are taking in everything. When you're cast in a production, they are hiring you for a role, but the role is only part of what you do. You bring the character to the screen, but you are also bringing *your own self* to the job. How you treat the crew, the other actors, the staff. Everyone can come back to help you win a job in the future. Or can help you lose one. Work begets work.

The Virginian hyperboosted my training in all ways.

It started with the wranglers and stunt performers—the real cowboys and cowgals tasked with managing the horses and dogs, doing stunt work, and teaching us actors to look authentic. They immediately got to work on my feeble L.A. ass. Taught me how to drink. . . . Oh, and chew tobacco; they didn't tell me not to swallow the chew, but I learned that quickly.

Stevie Myers was one of the head wranglers I worked with. She could drink, chew, spit, and ride with the roughest guys on set. Her longtime assistant was her girlfriend, and nobody gave a shit. The wranglers didn't care who was fucking who; they just knew she was a real wrangler and that's all that mattered. (Stevie would come up to Oregon years later and work with the horse ridden by the Neidermeyer character on *Animal House*.)

I'd sort of learned to ride a horse as a kid. My mother's boss owned one boarded at a stable on the Los Angeles River, and Mom had cut a deal that if I cleaned the stalls, I could ride his horse for a few hours. So the wranglers got me up to fake-cowboy speed in a hurry.

Whitey Sacks was my main wrangler and fifty years old by the time I met him. He would take me to ride on the Universal back lot, an empty stretch of land in the Hollywood Hills that housed the Shiloh Ranch, the hills of *Spartacus*, the *Psycho* house, and the cowboy towns that were ubiquitous on every studio back lot. His task was to work on my riding and the always-tougher task of getting on and off a horse.

When you're out riding with someone for hours, you really get to know them. These are the kind of people I was getting to know.

WHITEY SACKS WAS ONE OF THE MORE EXPERIENCED AND SALT-OF-the-earth cowboys, and he sure had some stories.

When Whitey was maybe eighteen, he'd been working in the MGM stables, cleaning stalls, feeding animals, and working with livestock on set for over a year, when the head wrangler told him he was being laid off and replaced with another teenager who happened to be the relative of a studio executive. Worse, Whitey had to train the exec's relative on his way out the door. The new kid's first job was simply to take one of the trained dogs, Buster, from the stables to the set for a scene. Begrudgingly, Whitey accepted his fate and agreed to train the other guy.

But, apparently, Whitey had a secret to help his trainee with Buster or any dog the newbie would later work with. He walked the executive's relative back to an empty stall in the rear of the stable. "Simple as pie," Whitey told him. "Just bring the dog back here fifteen minutes before he's needed on the set. Get him to lie down and rub his belly. Then when he's relaxed, you just jerk him off. Tug on his pecker. After that, the dog will do anything you want him to do."

"Really?" the other teen asked.

"Absolutely. We all do it. That dog will do whatever you want the rest of the week."

"Gee, thanks!" the poor guy squeaked. "Thanks so much!"

The next morning, this kid arrives early for work, takes Buster into a back stall, and starts masturbating him. The dog gladly goes along. Suddenly a commotion breaks out in the stables. "Boss, boss!" Whitey yells. "C'mere, quick!!" Whitey had grabbed the head wrangler and led him quickly down to the stables. "Look what this pervert is doing to Buster!!!"

The head wrangler was outraged. "Christ on a cross!" he shouted. "You pud-pulling pervert, git the hell outta here!" When the kid protested that he was only doing what Whitey had told him, Whitey just shrugged innocently. "Whitey," the head wrangler said, making a decision, "that boy wouldn't make a pimple on a cowboy's ball. Get this poor dog over to Stage Twelve for his scene. Looks like you got your job back."

Whitey kept that job for another forty years.

Lingo and Sagacity
Learned from the Wranglers

- [ ] *"They've been around since water"*: any old-timer
- [ ] *"That's too much mustard"*: someone who's bragging
- [ ] *"They're a roper, not a doper"*: comparing cowboys to hippies
- [ ] *"A hitch in their giddy-up"*: someone who's injured
- [ ] *"It's ace-high!"*: something that's top-notch
- [ ] *"That dog won't hunt"*: something that won't work
- [ ] *"Airin' the lungs"*: cussing
- [ ] *"Barn-sour"*: when a horse, or an actor, refuses to cooperate
- [ ] *"They can smell the barn"*: horse or someone who's eager to finish with something
- [ ] *"Want a snort?"*: when offering a drink
- [ ] *"Gettin' all roostered up"*: getting drunk
- [ ] *"Barkin' at a knot"*: doing something useless
- [ ] *"All hat but no cattle"*: a phony
- [ ] *"Don't squat with your spurs on"*: don't be stupid
- [ ] *"Rode hard and put away wet"*: finishing the day tired and ragged
- [ ] *"If the job is too hard, it's cuz you're doin' it wrong"*: figure it out!

The actors on *The Virginian* were, shockingly, cut from the same denim as the wranglers.

One afternoon, Doug McClure, who played Trampas, looked at his work for the next day and said to the director, "You know, I'm gonna be busy tonight. How about we let the kid play this scene?" He was referring to me, and he'd just given me two pages of material to do so that he could party harder with whatever stewardess pals were in town and not come into work the next day. McClure was a pro, and he'd learned all the ropes. When he felt the show was wasting his time or when he had other pressing social matters, he passed the baton to me and spared himself the silly stuff. The writers and producers figured out the rest. Eventually, I'd show up for work and Doug wouldn't be there. There would be some quick rewrites, and off we went. McClure had more free days and I had more screen time. It worked out well for both of us.

McClure was always regaling me with stories of his latest conquest and asking me about how it'd been "fucking" my wife the night before. (I'd recently married; more on this soon.) "How was it, Tim?" Doug would press. "She like talking dirty? Bet you ride that gal hard all night, don'tcha? What'd you two do *last* night?"

"Doug," I'd grumble. "You . . . you can't be saying stuff like that. It's not cool, man."

"I'd be home fucking her right now," he'd advise me, and then wander off again. This wasn't a one-shot discussion; this was just about every day on set.

Meanwhile, Jim Drury, the other star of *The Virginian*, mostly taught me about Jack Daniels. He assured me he'd drink a fifth of it every day. And I believed him. But the man could surely hold his liquor; I never saw him drunk. He was a total pro—but also a complete cutup. He and some of the crew would have water balloon fights, ambushing each other from the catwalks above the sets. One time, our weekly director got hit by a water balloon and instantly fired the two electricians he thought had drenched him. Jim took the heat; it *was* his water balloon fight, and Jim refused to go back to work until the electricians were reinstated. Of course, not all his behavior was appropriate. Jim would also screen pornos—before VHS or internet, doing so required an actual small projector and screen!—during our lunch hours.

The Virginian was a ninety-minute show, filmed on an eight-day schedule, usually with just one camera—a lot of work on such a short schedule. Our only saving grace was that TV westerns always used as much stock footage as possible. At the start of the season, the cast and crew would take several days away from Hollywood and head to a working cattle ranch. There all we did was ride, ride, ride, so that that season's stock shots could be captured. Ride camera left *with* the cattle. Gallop camera right *without* the cattle. Ride toward the sunset. Ride toward the sunset with a carriage. Follow the wagons camera left. Just the wagons only this time. You get the idea. (This is why Marshal Matt Dillon and the rest of us always had the same outfits on.)

It was another great show to learn on. The best part was the guest stars. In the 1990s, everyone who was anyone acting in New York City was in an episode of *Law & Order*. *The Virginian* was like this in Hollywood in the 1960s: Leslie Nielsen, Joseph Cotten, Dennis Weaver, Slim Pickens, Jack Elam, Strother Martin, William Shatner, Bing Russell, and many more, all came to the Shiloh Ranch while I was there. But the two most impactful were the great Joan Crawford and President Richard Nixon, who stopped by the set for a visit.

Dozens of us were gathered around the then president with our "six-shooters," and his protection detail never gave any of us a serious look.

"You know an actor shot Lincoln, right?" I joked with one of the secret service guys.

"Please don't," he said.

But that was nothing compared to the days that Joan worked on *The Virginian*. Joan Crawford was one of the queens of old Hollywood, and the set was designed to treat her that way when she worked. They added extra days so she wouldn't be rushed, cooled the set to fifty degrees so she wouldn't sweat (the crew wore parkas!), stocked Pepsi products everywhere out of respect for her husband, who was CEO of PepsiCo at the time, and we all had specific ways to behave when she was there. No chitchat or messing around—nothing with even the remote possibility of distracting our Mommie Dearest. The one day I worked with Crawford, after rehearsal, with finger jabbed in my direction, at the top of her voice, she shouted to the director, "*Tell this kid not to look at me!*"

At the time, getting scolded by the legendary diva was very embarrassing, but today, the whole "No more wire hangers!" simply makes much more sense.

HAVING SUCCESSFULLY SURVIVED JOAN CRAWFORD, AND AFTER completing the first season, I now looked forward to sleeping in a bit. And late one morning, I was still lying in bed reading the day's issue of *Daily Variety* when one particular article grabbed my attention: It was about my show. NBC was renaming *The Virginian* to something called *The Men from Shiloh*. Hmmm, that didn't sound good.

The article went on to confirm my suspicions: NBC intended to drop *everyone* in the current cast except stars James Drury and Doug McClure, and to fill out the cast of the new show, they were adding Lee Majors and Stewart Granger.

None of those guys was me. I was devastated. I'd just been fired and had to read about it in *Daily Variety*. This was another actor "achievement unlocked," for sure, a Hollywood cliché finally come to life.

So much for sleeping in.

There was no call or word from Universal Studios, the producers, or my agent. I knew enough to know that by the time a story was published in *Variety*, everyone in town already knew about it, so I was, evidently, the last to know. Later that day, Universal finally called my agent—not me and not about the show. They were *also* dropping my term contract. Confirming again that a position in Hollywood wasn't in any way permanent.

No more than, say, a hasty marriage.

Marrying My Sister

STRAPPED TO A GURNEY IN WHAT COULD ONLY BE DESCRIBED AS A glass room, my head enclosed by tiny electrode needles jammed into my scalp. Two of the glass walls are clearly two-way mirrors, and government scientists are measuring and monitoring my every move.

The static voice came over the intercom again. "How are you feeling, Tim?"

"Huh? Fine," I muttered.

"We'll continue then." This same cybernetic voice had been asking questions and telling me what to do all morning. "Tim, could you please multiply three times three times three times three?"

Hours before, the US government had given me marijuana to smoke in a narrow brass pipe. The ole muggles. Mary Jane. Jive. Catnip. It was terrible weed. Earlier, I'd joked, "I could get you better grass at a hundred different parties tonight." They didn't laugh.

So I just kept smoking. By now, bad weed or not, I was getting pretty stoned. But there was real work to be done. *Three times three was nine. Okay . . . and so . . . twenty-seven. Okay . . .* "Twenty-seven!" I called out. "So . . . wow, that's. . . . that's. . . . sixty . . . twenty-one. . . . Eighty-one? Eighty-one."

"Hold on, Tim." The voice in the ceiling never told me if I was right or wrong. It just vanished for a minute or longer before hitting me with another question or more weed to smoke. The EEG needles stabbed into my scalp began to itch. A constant tapping sound emanated from some speaker above me, possibly testing how I reacted to the distraction.

I'd signed up for this crap.

It was 1970, and UCLA was conducting early tests for the government on the effects of marijuana. Down the hall, they were probably having other twentysomethings drop acid, trip the light fantastic, and lick toads. My test paid $50 (about $415 today).

And I needed the money. Badly.

The Virginian had been canceled. My Universal contract canceled. And there were no new projects on the horizon, only fleeting prospects on various back burners. "Hang in there, Tim," my agent said. "Something will hit." I was sending letters to creditors with a $10 check—you read that right—and the promise: "I swear to you I will pay back the rest as soon as possible." I'd become Popeye's Wimpy: "I'll gladly pay you next Tuesday for half a house payment today." It was humbling to beg for another month, week, day. The creditors responded with lawsuits.

The world didn't care I'd been in films with Dick Van Dyke and Jackie Gleason and Lucille Ball. That I was the voice of Jonny Quest. That I'd starred in *The Virginian*. That I was a US Marine. That I wanted to be an actor. That I had a new wife at home. That I was poor again. That I really, *really* needed to pee.

Strapped to this table for hours, I truly needed to use the restroom. ASAP. I had asked earlier and was rebuffed by the tinny voice in the ceiling. To take my mind off it, I tried relaxing, letting the buzz take hold. It *was* crappy weed, but I could work with it. I closed my eyes and let my mind wander before the next math puzzle or word problem. Thoughts and sentiments rolled and collapsed upon each other like campfire smoke or maybe the surf at Abalone Cove. I breathed deeply.

We should get a divorce . . .

The thought was small at first and then grew, becoming a mantra, demanding attention. *We should get a divorce.* It wasn't a question or an option but a fully formed decision. Like a neon billboard in all the other haze of ideas and emotions. Total clarity.

Jennifer Leak and I had not even been married for a year and a half. But she was miserable with the money struggles, and I'd been screwing everything I could for most of our marriage. Beyond our early coupling, she and I truly had little connection or passion for each other. I still confused sex with love, and it would be years before I understood the difference, and it would take even more years to learn you *could* find both.

There really was only one answer.

"Tim," the static voice said, "what five-letter word typed in all-capital letters can be read the same upside down?"

Opening my eyes, I replied, "Divorce."

———

JENNIFER HAD PLAYED COLLEEN NORTH, MY STEPSISTER, IN *YOURS, Mine and Ours*. It would be better for this story if we'd started hooking up on set and if Henry Fonda had caught us in flagrante delicto. But none of that happened. She was clearly beautiful, but she and I were rarely in scenes together and didn't even flirt when killing time between shots. I had numerous scenes with Lucy, and my focus was on the work and not embarrassing myself in front of a Hollywood legend.

My liberty pass from the Marines to do *The Ed Sullivan Show* was the first time Jennifer and I had any time to flirt. And we took it. After New York, I had the Marines to get back to, and Jennifer and I kept in touch only with a couple of letters. Once off active duty and in the reserves, I finally called and asked her out.

I still had almost zero sexual experience at this point. I'd been a literal little guy all through high school—barely five foot six—and had not developed any pickup game during that time to compensate. To compound things, I was still perilously shy. Jennifer, fortunately, had more familiarity with such things and took the wheel, as it were. I spent the night with her after our first date. *This is great,* I thought, and we started full-time courtship right away.

Jennifer was much more mature than I was. She'd been born in Wales and moved with her parents to Canada, where she'd been a Miss Toronto before coming to Hollywood. She had lovely red hair and a melodious voice with a hint of an accent that all would have made her Welsh ancestors quite proud. To nineteen-year-old me, Jennifer Leak was exotic, sophisticated, and further along in her career than I was. I was charmed. I was smitten. I didn't stand a chance.

We got a place together on the beach along the most northern fringes of Malibu. (Malibu folks would have called it Oxnard, but it worked for us!) I had to get up at 4:00 a.m. to go to work at Paramount in Los Angeles every day.

My mom warned, "Don't go crazy and get married or anything."

"Don't worry, Mom. That's the last thing I'll do," I told her.

Three months later, Jennifer and I were married.

WE'D BEEN HAVING SEX FOR MONTHS, LIVING TOGETHER, SO IT only made sense for us to get married, right? This is how hard-wired my conservative 1950s brain was. Everyone else in 1968 was screwing anyone they wanted, no strings attached. But I kept thinking, *If you sleep with a woman, you should marry her.*

My mother wasn't the only one with reservations. Gary Goetzman, all of *sixteen,* grabbed me by my arm in the church hallway bare minutes before the Mendelssohn wedding march started. "Dude, my car is parked right out front and it's gassed up." He was dead serious. "If you want, we can be in Vegas before anyone knows what happened. Portland. Chihuahua, Mexico!" Gary was still a teenager, and yet even he knew this marriage was a terrible idea. But sitting in the pews of the Little Brown Church in Studio City (where, ironically, Ronald Reagan married Nancy) were all my friends and family. Even if Gary was actually making a lot of sense, I couldn't back out. I gulped and married Miss Toronto.

It didn't take long to confirm what my young best friend had already recognized: My new wife and I actually weren't very right for each other.

She was a fancy city girl, interested in fashion and expensive big-city things. Always new furniture, dinners out, costly trips, new clothes: the best. I was a West Coast guy who grew up poor running around beaches and back lots.

To help keep up with my young married life, I collected cards: Amex, Visa, Diners Club, Gilmore Gasoline. I grabbed every card I could. These were great; you could buy stuff before you could afford it and then take care of it when—if—the money finally came in. I could also always walk into my Screen Actors Guild credit union and get another $50 loan, arriving back home with enough to get through another month. One afternoon, there was an envelope from the Screen Actors Guild and a residual check for $2,500 for all the cartoons I'd done years before ($20,000 in today's money; it was like hitting a small lottery!). Freshly loaded with cash, I paid off all the cards and small loans, and we had enough money for another few months of waiting for the next professional opportunity.

Besides the money struggles, I should have taken my behavior as the first sign of a problem: I'd started cheating on my bride every chance I got.

Everyone was sleeping with everyone else, and now that I had some actual experience in the matter, I joined the party. One weekend, Jennifer's friend visited. This young woman and I waited patiently for Jennifer to go upstairs to sleep so we could screw on the couch downstairs.

Yes, I know, horrible. *I was horrible.* A terrible husband. I knew this even then, and it was a nightmare. I felt so guilty but had no idea what to do, how to fix this mess. I was twenty and miserable. I tried to find sparks with Jennifer and couldn't, but finding genuine sexual sparks with others outside my marriage—no problem.

So now I'm driving home with the munchies from this UCLA marijuana test but at least I have the answer. We were barely twenty, with no kids. *We don't have to do this; we can just walk away.* I could stop feeling guilty and miserable all the time, and Jennifer could get on with her life and the world she imagined for herself.

I practically bounded into the house for our big talk. For the first time in months, I knew the answer. I was going to be direct, pragmatic, heart-filled, and honest. "Let's just call it quits," I told her. "We rushed into this too soon. You'll be happier, *I'll* be happier."

Pause . . .

"What are you talking about?" she asked. "Are *you* unhappy?"

Oh no. She somehow had no idea there were issues in our marriage. She was currently sitting on the couch where I'd banged her friend, but I'd still taken her completely by surprise. She was shocked. And furious. I wondered if any of that terrible UCLA pot would help her see the light.

We fumbled along another few weeks. Marriage counseling. Awkward talks. She wanted to get pregnant and pulled some moves in that department, that old chestnut for "fixing things." But I was now fully committed to the divorce idea and got her (unpregnant) an apartment, a therapist, and an attorney.

PART OF WHY JENNIFER AND I DIDN'T GET ALONG WAS THAT SHE and my mother hated each other. We'd go out to a restaurant together, and one or both would end up in angry tears, shouting at each other down the freeway on the way home. I'd strain at being the peacemaker, but mostly I just hunched low and drove. When my mother had lung surgery and needed a place to recuperate, Jennifer would not allow her to stay in our home. "I don't want HER here." *Hated each other.* I gave in, and my mom had to move in with one of her friends. I felt terrible shame about that choice; nothing should come between family, ever.

Now, a few weeks after we had separated and Jennifer had moved out of the house, I got a credit card bill for $3,500 (over $30,000 today). During divorce proceedings, Jennifer had contacted my mother, and the two had gone shopping together to punish me—a guy smoking pot with pins jammed into his head to make ends meet.

Mom was apparently still pissed at my father for leaving us. She decided to join Jennifer in retaliatory outrage against all wayward bastard men—including her own son.

It was nice to see them finally getting along.

DURING A RAY OF CAREER AND FINANCIAL HOPE, I'D GOTTEN THE lead role for a new western called *Lock, Stock and Barrel*. But during casting, in the middle of our divorce proceedings, Jennifer called me: "I just got a call to audition for *Lock, Stock and Barrel*," she said. "It's between me and one other actress!"

And there went my ray of hope. This marriage was never going to end.

The producers called next and told me how sensational it would be if a husband and wife had the starring roles opposite each other; they had already started figuring out ways to spin it for extra publicity.

I could have told them about when Jennifer's friend visited or my credit card bill or the yoga instructor I'd nailed just the day before. I could have told them about the impending divorce. But I kept my mouth shut.

Jennifer deserved the shot. I couldn't mess with her career just because I was destroying her life. All I could do now was hope she didn't actually get the role.

I did test scenes with both Jennifer and Belinda Montgomery (later, the mom of the title character in *Doogie Howser, M.D.*). Belinda, thankfully, got the part.

The cameras had shown everyone what I already knew: Jennifer Leak and I had no chemistry.

———

JENNIFER LEAK WAS THE LAST WOMAN MARRIED TO TIM MATTHIE-son.

During a screening of *How to Commit Marriage* (ironic, I know), the post department accidentally misspelled my last name, deleting one of the *t*'s *and* an *i*. When I first saw it on screen, I was furious. My name was often being misspelled and mispronounced but usually not this badly. And after all attempts to have it changed proved too costly and time-consuming, I decided to embrace it as part of the new me: Tim *Matheson* was born.

———

TWELVE YEARS AFTER OUR DIVORCE, I WAS IN MY DRESSING ROOM while doing the play *True West* off-Broadway, when a woman I didn't know approached and told me, "Jennifer sends her regards; she'd like you to call."

Jennifer Leak had lived in the Big Apple with her husband for years. I called my ex for the first time in over a decade to say hello and to offer her tickets to come see the show. But she flatly refused, something about her husband probably not liking the idea. We did spend some time catching up on the phone.

She had married a very successful architect, lived in a high-rise condo on Park Avenue, spent weekends in the Hamptons, and so forth. It was the life she'd always dreamed of. "Let me tell you a story that only you would appreciate," she said.

I smiled before she told it.

"I wanted a dog," she told me. "But my husband told me no. 'Too much trouble,' he said. But he promised he'd get me a new mink coat if I dropped the dog thing."

"Which one did you get?" I asked.

Jennifer laughed on the phone. "I got both."

I laughed also. Yup, that was my "sister." It was exactly what she'd always wanted, and I could not have been happier for her.

Grateful to Uncle Sam for giving me that government-grade reefer, Jennifer and I said farewell a second, and final, time.

Feel Lucky, Punk?

I was in Italy when Dirty Harry came looking for me.

Ironic, I suppose, given that Harry Callahan, a.k.a. Clint Eastwood, was also the once and future king of spaghetti westerns.

A buddy and I had decided to get super original and backpack around Europe together guided by the 1957 bestseller *Europe on Five Dollars a Day*.

Bonanza, the show I'd recently joined, had just been canceled.

My four-year Universal Studios contract also canceled.

My marriage to Jennifer was *also* now officially, legally, . . . canceled.

I'd returned to being just a freelance actor on his own again. A life I'd lived since I was twelve, running from audition to audition all over Hollywood. Now I'm twenty-five, back on unemployment, and collecting "Nos" again three times a day. Not easy. Europe and its renowned sites, wines, and women sounded like a much better time than sitting at home waiting for the phone *not* to ring.

So it was exciting when my agent tracked me down, through the William Morris office in Rome, to tell me the producers of the *Dirty Harry* sequel wanted to see me right away. The original movie had been a massive hit two years before—the fourth-highest-grossing film of 1971. The follow-up had a bigger budget and a great script from a pair of upcoming wunderkinds (John Milius and Michael Cimino, who would go on to write movies like *Apocalypse Now* and *The Deer Hunter*). Eastwood, it seemed, had managed to escape TV and was becoming an actual movie star. This sequel was likely going to be another king-size hit, and my agent had aggressively worked my name into the final mix for a possible role.

The protests of my traveling pal still ringing in my ears high over the Atlantic, I'd opted out of the rest of our European tour and was on the next flight back to the States. The plane couldn't land soon enough. I was fidgety and talking to myself as I stared out the cabin window. The kind Italian nonna sitting next to me kept asking in careful English if I was "all right?" or "on reefer?"

"That might help, ma'am." I'd turned to her. "Do you have any?"

She stayed quiet the rest of the trip and allowed me to swirl again in my mile-high stardom fantasies. I was clearly stoked and, back in L.A., spent two full days rehearsing my audition scene, getting into character as a vigilante cop even dirtier than Harry. This was an adult villain, not the troubled teen I'd been playing for years. I needed to nail this audition—there was no series role in the works and I hadn't landed a film in almost five years—and I wasn't going to miss this opportunity for lack of preparation.

Arriving at Warner Bros. with such confidence and swagger built over the past few days, the people I passed probably mistook me for Steve McQueen. I wasn't sure if director Ted Post might be there or even Clint. Who would I be auditioning for and with? It didn't matter. I was ready.

Normally, when you enter an audition, there are at least five people already waiting in the room: a producer or two, maybe the director, maybe another actor, and *always* a casting director who is going to read with you.

Today, there was only one person in the room. Some guy who looked like a high school football coach. "I'm directing this picture," Ted Post introduced himself.

"Great," I said.

"How tall are you?" he asked.

Huh? "Six foot two," I reported.

He studied me and then looked down at my head shot: my picture and actor information—*which included my height* proudly displayed in a sixteen-point font.

"Clint's six four," he said.

I nodded. "Okay . . ."

"We shot *Hang 'Em High* together . . . Six two, you say?"

"Yup."

"Okay." He tossed my headshot back down on his desk. "Just wanted to make sure. Thanks for coming in, Tim."

"Wait, don't you want me to audition for Officer Davis?" Davis was the best role of the four rogue cops and what I came back from Europe for—what I'd spent the last two days preparing for.

"Oh, no . . . That part's already cast. David Soul is Davis. Just needed to see that you're really six two. You'll play Officer Sweet." He then shook my hand again—like he had exactly eighty-six seconds before—and shepherded me back out of his office.

That was it. Done. Not another word. Canceled tours of the world's great art museums, the rush home, the scared woman next to me in 23E, the forty-eight hours of intense character preparation. The Steve McQueen star power. This guy just wanted to see, in person, how tall I was.

Just out of high school, I'd had a commercial audition that had gone like this: "You look like you're very tall," the casting director said. I'd finally gotten to maybe six foot one at this point. "Sure," I agreed, "I guess." And then I gave a *great* audition. "You were really, really good," she agreed after. "Perfect. But . . ." *Here it comes . . .* "I think we're going with someone taller."

This was equally ludicrous. *I ran back from Rome for this?!* And, I'd come back from Italy to be Officer Davis, not Phil Sweet. I stamped to the nearest pay phone on the lot and called my agent, baffled. "They just told me they needed to see you right away," he swore. "That's all!"

A contract soon arrived. It took a day or so to get over the disappointment of not getting a chance to show what I could do as Officer Davis, but Officer Phil Sweet was good enough for me.

I was back in the movies.

———

I'D BEEN STUDYING STRASBERG, STANISLAVSKI, SHAKESPEARE. I'D been in major motion pictures with Henry Fonda, Lucille Ball, Bob Hope, and Dick Van Dyke. I'd been a Marine. And so, I believed categorically that I was hot shit. And with a new motion picture contract in hand, this perilous worldview only intensified. It was a far cry from my early days on *Leave It to Beaver* and my impassioned "Gee, Beave! That's some snow cone!"

It was 1972, and method acting was the rage with every coach, teacher, and actor in the world. If you were cast as a teacup, it wasn't enough to understand the motivation of the teacup; you had to actually *be* a teacup.

I was going to play an adult, an adult villain against Clint Eastwood's Dirty Harry in his next blockbuster. Clearly I'd be christened as the next Marlon Brando, so I talked Warner Bros. into sending me up to the San Francisco Police Department for two weeks to do research. I was already familiar with handguns from my Marine Corps days, so I qualified easily on pistols at the SFPD pistol range. I also did ride-alongs and hung out with officers night and day. Really becoming a 415/Fog City police officer, but that wasn't enough— I'm not going to act, I'm going to *be* Officer Phil Sweet. I'll know what he ate for breakfast the day he met Harry, what coed had first broken his heart, how many men he'd killed in Vietnam—all of the backstory to inform the character to *be* the character.

One night, two actual police officers and I drifted slowly through a parking lot directly past a bar riddled with long-haired bikers. As we passed, one of the bikers yelled out, "Fuck you pigs!" I was so happy. The guy thought I was a cop.

"Yeah! Keep driving, pigs, or we'll shit down your neck!"

The officer I was driving with had now stopped the squad car. There was a three-foot fence that surrounded the bar deck and a dozen bikers sprawled on the other side of that fence. I pondered what Stanislavski, creator of method acting, would want me to do.

The two sides—cops and bikers—stared back at each other for an hour or maybe ten seconds. "Should we . . . get out?" I asked.

The San Fran cop looked at his partner. They both laughed and he slowly pulled away.

"Fucking actors," he said.

Film School Boot Camp

Chimps and Scrubs

One of the greatest perks of being an actor, and especially a director, is being admitted into places, homes, jobs, and lives that you would normally never get a chance to encounter. For two weeks, I had total access to the SFPD for *Magnum Force*. I did ridealongs with police officers and qualified at the department's pistol range with other rookies. Later, for a TV movie, when I played an anesthesiologist framed for murder, I spent several days sitting next to an actual anesthesiologist in operating rooms. I observed a knee replacement and a much longer procedure: a spinal fusion.

Most people only get to do a few careers in their lives. To be trusted to experience firsthand how tough, skilled, and emotional people are in how they approach their lives has always profoundly affected me and stayed with me much longer than the roles I played.

I've ridden with wranglers on a cattle ranch: herding, branding, and corralling countless steers for hours. I've spent weeks tailing doctors around hospitals and emergency rooms prior to *The House of God* and seen how stressful life is for a New York bartender before playing one in *The Good Fight*. I have followed the Vietnam War hero Senator Max Cleland of Georgia, who was severely wounded in Vietnam, around the US Capitol to learn his routine and duties as a US senator for background on *The West Wing*. I also spent a week at MSNBC observing all its shows and shadowed Brian Williams (sans helicopter) for days as prep for *Breaking News*, in which I played an anchorman.

As a director, you spend a lot of time scouting many locations, trying to find the perfect setting for a scene. Sometimes you see a dozen locations until you find the right one. I'll never forget the one house we toured looking for an upper-middle-class home for our lead couple to "live" in. An older couple owned the beautiful and sprawling home. It was very cluttered with boxes stacked in many areas, and there were pet or child gates and barriers all over the house. It turned out their grown daughter had recently moved back in with her animals: several dogs and a chimpanzee. Why a chimpanzee? Go figure. Needless to say, we didn't choose that house to shoot in.

On another project, I found myself sitting across from CIA director George Tenet and asking for permission to film scenes inside CIA Headquarters at Langley, Virginia. He was enjoying a cigar and I politely quipped, "Director Tenet, that wouldn't be a Cuban cigar, would it?" He took a long pull and filled the air with smoke before giving me a response I'll never forget: "Mr. Matheson, our policy here at the CIA is to burn *all* illegal contraband." He agreed to let us spend two days filming at Langley for *In the Company of Spies* and even gave us the honor of allowing us to film a scene in front of the hallowed CIA Memorial Wall.

DAVID SOUL, MY COSTAR (ONLY SIX FOOT ONE, FOR THE RECORD) and I had some . . . history. Less than a year before, the very last episode of *Bonanza* ever filmed had centered on my character, Griff King, posing as the husband of a beautiful woman as part of some convoluted plan to bring a gang of Civil War criminals to justice. A stunning actress named Karen Carlson played my wife. Karen had just costarred with Robert Redford in *The Candidate* and was an actor on the rise. She also happened to be married to David Soul.

David was still three years from being on lunchboxes as half of *Starsky & Hutch* and having a #1 hit single "Don't Give Up on Us." This week, while Karen worked on *Bonanza*, he was just a struggling TV actor with a very pretty, much-more-successful wife.

Karen and I got along well, very well, that week on *Bonanza*. There was a definite spark between us, just like in the story. It'll happen. But as I was a "serious" actor, I'd vowed never to become involved with an actress during shooting, as I wanted nothing to distract from the work. Would Brando or Montgomery Clift screw a costar? Okay, probably yes—but this was a rule I had. And *mostly* kept. David didn't know how safe his wife was in my arms.

Nevertheless, he'd clearly gotten wind of how well Karen and I were getting along during production, the perfectly innocent flirtations between us, and one day, David showed up on our set. He visited for a short while with Karen, was pleasant enough to me, and then said goodbye.

An hour later, Karen and I were shooting a scene together, and I could tell she was a little bit flustered. I took her hand. "You okay?" I asked.

"He's watching." She looked straight down at the floor.

"Who?" I laughed, glancing around a soundstage filled with maybe seventy-plus people.

"David." Her chin lifted again to give me a wide, bright, alarmingly fake everything-is-wonderful smile as she pulled her hand away. "In the catwalk."

David hadn't actually gone anywhere. Instead, he'd climbed onto the platforms above the sets where the lighting was rigged. I removed my Stetson cowboy hat casually and then casually looked around the soundstage again, casually taking in the rafters above. There was a whole lot of *casual* going on.

Sure enough, there was someone up top, only half lost to the shadows. David Soul. Perched within the catwalk darkness like Lon Chaney but starring in *The Phantom of the Ponderosa*.

The next scene, naturally, included a kiss. Moonlit stage lighting, a recent scripted gunshot wound to get my shirt half off. The dim wisp of David Soul drifting just above.

"Don't think of me," Karen said. That is, her character, Theodora Duffy, said.

"I can't do that."

"Well, try . . ."

Both of us were wondering when some two-hundred-pound stage light or sandbag would fall on me from the darkness just above. As Karen tenderly brushed back the hair from my forehead, I could hear Soul slowly inhaling and exhaling up there. Or I thought I could.

I leaned into Karen anyway—I was a professional actor and had a job to do! The heat lifted from her lips, a nervous tension twining through her whole body. We stared at each other, a real panic firing between us that only added to our already-healthy spark. (Oddly disturbing that her husband watching was actually making this hotter . . .)

"I care for you," I told her.

"Don't fall in love with me, Griff," she said, but I heard her say "Tim."

The hug came next, then our first real kiss of the show. A clinch that lasted a second or two longer than maybe it should have. The warm sensuality of Karen in my arms had never felt more real—or more fatal. At this point, both of us had clearly resolved to face the wrath of her jealous actor husband.

The door behind Karen burst open! Four Confederate war criminals, guns drawn, stopped the kissing. It was in the script but still startling to me, knowing who it *might* have been. The director yelled, "Cut! Print!"

Stealing a peek above, I glimpsed a six one shadow stepping back into the total darkness again, vanishing for good.

Weeks later, Karen and David separated. And since she and I weren't working together anymore, all my actor rules were off. *That's judicious, right?* Dating began almost immediately. A spark's a spark. It didn't last long, but I'd always presumed David wasn't pleased.

On the first day on the *Magnum Force* set, of course, the ghost of Hollywood past was suddenly present and future: David Soul and I had a scene together. I got the sense he was sizing me up, probably trying to figure out what caliber Mr. Matheson was packing. I hoped Soul's jealousy wouldn't become a problem while he and I worked on this career-important film together.

"Hey, Tim," he said first. We shook hands. "Great to work with you."

Impressive. He'd clearly set his jealousy aside for the sake of the film. Or perhaps his confidence was especially high for another reason.

Soul was cast as Officer John Davis, the leader of our police crew—and the part I'd prepared so hard for. The vigilante cop with the most lines and screen time. The main villain against Dirty Harry. Meanwhile, as I've mentioned, I was Phil Sweet. The first bad cop to die. Off screen thirty minutes before the other guys.

There are no small actors, just small parts.

We shot the picture for two months.

David Soul never mentioned Karen. Not once. He was professional and even friendly throughout the whole filming. As if he had no memory of *Bonanza* or catwalks or who his ex-wife had been banging for a couple of months.

Maybe the jealousy was gone. Maybe David Soul was a Taoist master.

Or maybe he could just never be jealous of Phil Sweet.

Third Cop Through the Door.

———

I DIDN'T KNOW MUCH ABOUT CLINT EASTWOOD. HE'D BEEN ON *Rawhide* for seven seasons, but it was not a distinguished TV show, to my mind. I knew he'd recently done several spaghetti westerns that had made a lot of money. But having never seen them—not "artistic enough" for me at the time—I deduced Clint was just a good-looking guy who probably couldn't act much. A TV guy who'd gotten lucky is all. *There but for the snubs of God go I . . .*

We all came to the set of the indoor pistol range, where our first scene together was being shot. Clint introduced himself to all of us, and then we roughly walked through the scene.

I was, again, remarkably ready. I'd even qualified at the San Francisco Police Department pistol range with the service revolver that was a big part of my first scene. The prop master on the movie, Eddie Iona, gave me a working .357 Magnum to keep at the hotel, and a set of empty dummy rounds so that I could practice speed loading, which I had to do in the film. I'd sit at the end of the bed in my boxers ejecting prop shells, muzzle down, align the loaded speed-loader with the cylinder, push until the click! And again . . . and again . . . trying to get a second faster each time. We were all three years before *Taxi Driver*, but there was definitely some standing-before-the-hotel-mirror-and-talking-to-myself stuff going on that week.

Now I was ready to go for my first scene with Clint. After the walk-through, I approached him to make myself available to rehearse or run lines, if he ever wanted, offering to basically do him a favor.

Up close, he was genuinely a friggin' handsome guy. Also, two inches taller than me.

Tall, handsome Clint smiled and said, "Thanks, but I like to say the lines for the first time on camera. There's something special about that first time."

Now I knew for sure this clown wasn't a real actor. All real actors rehearsed, and rehearsed and rehearsed. That's what the pros always did. Trained actors. Actors like Peter O'Toole, Richard Burton, Paul Newman, Lucille Ball, James Dean, Marcello Mastroianni. Actors like . . . well, me.

Good thing you're six four, is all I was thinking now. Out loud, I said, "Sure, okay," and we parted while they lit the scene. It was his movie, after all, and I thought, *Fuck it, we'll just get through this. I hope he knows his lines.*

We started filming. I was firing my .357 Magnum at the indoor pistol range, and when I finished, Clint, David Soul, Robert Urich, Kip Niven, and I had a short scene where Clint and I exchanged maybe two or three lines.

Damn it.

Eastwood *listened* more intensely than any actor I'd ever worked with. Not just waiting to say his line but actually *hearing* and considering what the other character is saying. (It's the listen that ultimately makes a great scene.) I'm not sure if I've come across an actor since who has possessed this skill more sincerely. I was stunned.

His what-I-thought-was-bullshit about getting it on film the first time and not over-practicing was exactly why he listened so well. Clint was genuinely interested in what my character was going to say, and how. The payoff: He was totally real, relaxed, and in the moment.

This approach helped me be better in the scene, also. We weren't acting! It was a real talk. In one take, Clint changed a word of dialogue when speaking to me, and I adjusted my response using the word he'd changed, and then he played off my change with his next line—all with ease and a smile. This is the take that made the film.

Later I would learn that the celebrated director John Ford (*The Searchers*, *The Grapes of Wrath*, *Stagecoach*), like Eastwood, rarely allowed his actors to over-rehearse. He wanted to capture the spontaneity of the words the first time the actors performed them and, importantly, the first time the actors heard them. And as an actor, I began to ask directors to take my close-up first, particularly if it was for an emotional scene. Some actors need many (many) takes to get their emotions where they want them, but thanks to Clint, I learned that my best stuff was usually the first time.

Eastwood impressed me that day in a way that few actors have. I went back to the hotel realizing what an arrogant tool I'd been and gladly conceding, *This guy is the real deal.* I could see why he was a star. Much like what Henry Fonda once said to me about acting, quoting Spencer Tracy (which shows how these truths are passed down): "Walk in, hit your mark, look the other fella in the eye, and tell him the truth."

That was Spencer Tracy. And Henry Fonda.

And that was Clint Eastwood.

Now I just had to focus on being me. Or being Officer Phil Sweet.

MY DEATH SCENE IN THE FILM CAME WITH ME STANDING IN FRONT of a doorway, delivering a warrant to a bunch of mobsters. I objected to the height-conscious, gym-teacher-looking director Ted Post. "I wouldn't stand in front of the door like that," I argued. "I just trained with the San Fran PD. I am US Marine! This character is supposed to be ex special forces, for God's sake. Phil Sweet would *never* stand in front of the door like that!"

"But . . ." Post explained, "Phil Sweet needs to die."

I stared at him, realizing the conversation had just ended. He walked off to do something else, and I positioned myself, as directed, in front of the door for Phil Sweet's untimely death.

WHILE I MOSTLY KEPT QUIET, EASTWOOD AND POST ARGUED. A LOT.

Clint had recently directed his first film, *Play Misty for Me*, and you could tell he was used to controlling the process of filmmaking. Even though he wasn't directing *Magnum Force*, Clint wouldn't put up with doing many takes. He wanted to avoid having his scenes become stale and overacted. He kept the work of making a movie easy and fun. We never worked long hours, would always go home early, and rarely did unnecessary takes. The more takes you do, the more practiced and perfected it seems to get. Clint taught us there was no perfect way to do a scene.

Today, as a highly respected and two-time Oscar winner for best director, Eastwood is known as "one-take Clint," and I am lucky enough to know why firsthand. For actors, this approach always kept the performances fresh and honest, with a certain rawness. Clint proved a massive presence as an actor and a man. His accomplishments in the world of cinema are unparalleled. He is John Wayne and John Ford all rolled into one.

He'd also helped me—at a very important age, when it was most needed, even though maybe I didn't know it at the time—to pull my own head out of my actor ass. To start trusting my gut and heart as much as all the craft I'd collected in my head. To be open-minded. To give my coworkers every chance to show me something new like Clint just had. To never stop learning.

More importantly—or, so I thought then—I was going to be in a big Hollywood movie. To hell with *Bonanza* and Universal Studios. I watched *Magnum Force* for the first time opening night at the legendary Grauman's Chinese Theatre on Hollywood Boulevard. The one with all the foot and handprints outside. The audience cheered and oohed and awwed like they were watching Jerry West and the Lakers. Eastwood had another hit, and I was back in the game, baby!

Enjoying my Grauman's popcorn, there was no way to know it would be five more years before I made another film. That my career—like poor Officer Sweet—was standing directly in front of a door. That my childhood dreams of being in pictures were both ending and yet just getting started all at the same time.

Climb in the Saddle, Be Ready for the Ride

(Part Two)

"TELL UNIVERSAL TO GO FUCK THEMSELVES," I SAID. MY AGENT WAS on the phone telling me the studio wanted to reinstate the contract they had canceled. At the same pay rate as before. No thanks. Plus, I still felt terribly mistreated and disrespected by Universal. I'd worked hard for them on *The Virginian*: never once held up shooting, came in whenever asked, took over, and quickly learned a new part whenever Doug McClure had a conflict between an invite to the Playboy Mansion and the scenes he had on the call sheet, spent spare weekends doing unpaid publicity junkets when requested instead of taking days off. And I didn't even get a call, a thank you, or a "sorry" when I was fired.

Thanks to them, I'd become a human guinea pig at UCLA, had all my credit cards maxed, and I now slept in the basement apartment I had to build in my own house (renting out the top), to survive. "No way," I said. "Not without a raise!"

"Tim . . ."

"*And* an apology."

"They'll never agree to either," he warned me.

For weeks, he and I would argue. My agent kept telling me the studio kept saying "no." Having gone through months of financial hell since being fired from *The Virginian*, I was not in the mood to do any favors for Universal. I was adamant in my refusal and stood on principle. "I want a meeting with them," I demanded.

"This is a doomed meeting," my agent said. "Doomed."

"I'll take my chances!" Righteous anger is the best anger.

The agent and I went to Universal together. He kept quiet throughout, no surprise, giving me enough rope to hang myself and wanting to prove to me that this was a lost cause. Pete Terranova, the Universal executive, sat there as I meticulously itemized all the extra work I'd done for the show. Work I had done and for which I had been rewarded by being fired without so much as a thank you. He listened patiently while I told him that I, Tim Matheson, wanted an apology. And a raise.

"I agree with everything you've said," Terranova told me. "That was no way to treat anyone."

Had there been water around, I'd have spit it dramatically from my mouth. "Ah . . . thank you," I got out. "I want to—"

"But," he stopped me, "the studio will never give you that raise." I could feel my own agent gloating at me in the terrible silence that now followed. "However . . ." the executive said.

"However?"

"What I *can* do is give you your old contract back—"

"That's not going—"

"*Plus* slip you another check for $200, per week, extra." (This would be an $1,800-a-week raise today; not too shabby.) "Under the table, as it were."

I leaned forward in my chair, clasping my hands like a curious Michael Corleone.

"Also," the Universal executive continued. "I'm sorry we didn't call you to thank you for your hard work." He stood, smiled, and offered his hand. I shook and agreed to the deal, with the promise to keep it quiet. "We don't want other actors coming in here to demand raises, too," he said.

"So, what's the plan?" I asked. "What's this pilot you have in mind?"

The executive patted my shoulder. "Continue west, young man."

Film School Boot Camp

Listen to Your Own Voice

Universal is where I learned one lesson firsthand: *Sometimes you just need to listen to your own gut feelings . . . and not your advisers.* I'd personally renegotiated my deal with the studio, at twenty-one years old. And I got the apology I deserved, too. On my own. My agent couldn't believe I'd gotten both the deal and the apology. (Later, I learned he'd taken credit for getting both for me.)

I've discovered numerous truths about agents, lawyers, financial advisers, *and* managers in my many years doing this. In my experience with each of these various advisers, I've learned the hard way that my gut instincts were usually correct. These folks often provided advice that let them "not be wrong" but perhaps wasn't the soundest advice (like my agent who said Universal would *never* give me that raise). I had one lawyer screw up a rights issue because he said he didn't want to run my bill up too high. A financial consultant once told me that there was "no way" I could afford a wonderful property that came up for sale when James Cagney died; a short time later, there was a huge housing demand and I ended up paying the same amount he'd told me I couldn't afford for much less of a house than Cagney's estate. I've had lazy and deceitful managers who felt they were too important to really handle my career personally but who still took the 10 percent from the jobs that I got. They also got fired.

At the end of the day, these people are only advisers. Bet on yourself, trust your instincts, listen to their counsel, and then make up your own mind.

———

A LONGTIME HOLLYWOOD WRITER NAMED RICHARD ALAN SIM-mons had written, and was producing, a possible series called *Lock, Stock and Barrel* about a young frontier couple who elope and are then pursued by the girl's father and brothers across the American West as they join up with an escaped convict and charlatan preacher. This was the pilot that Universal had lost track of, that they were developing for me to star in, when they dropped my contract. *Oops.*

This was also the pilot where they'd cast Belinda Montgomery instead of my soon-to-be ex-wife Jennifer Leak for the role as my prairie missus.

West we headed, as ordered. Costars included Burgess Meredith (*Rocky*) and Claude Akins (*B. J. and the Bear*, Sheriff Lobo). The pilot almost sold to series. NBC loved it. But not enough. Westerns *were* starting to struggle, so they sent Simmons back to the drawing board to make it more of a western *comedy.* Simmons took the same premise—young newlyweds running around the west together—and did a two-hour pilot film called *Hitched*, which we all hoped would get NBC over that commitment hump.

To help, they recast Belinda Montgomery with Sally Field.

The already-famous-all-over-the-world Sally Field. *Gidget* Sally Field. *The Flying Nun* Sally Field. I was intimidated. But not from her fame. I'd met and worked with people much more famous than she was, but Sally Field wasn't Lucille Ball, thirty-six years my senior—Sally was my *peer.* This peer had more money, more organization, and—what I quickly learned—more natural acting skills.

I'd have a scene with Sally, and she'd have to be crying, and just like that, she'd start crying. I'd heard about actors like this but never yet spent time with one. She was just always in character. The director would say "Action," and snap! Sally was Roselle Bridgeman, my blushing bride. It seemed easy for her.

So, acting-wise . . . she intimidated me. But that was just the start.

We became friendly socially, and I started hanging out with Sally and her boyfriend, Richard Dreyfuss. (Richard hadn't hit big yet, but *Jaws* and *Close Encounters of the Third Kind* and an Oscar for *The Goodbye Girl* were on the horizon.) He was then another young actor who had done a couple of *The Flying Nun* episodes and had a few lines in *The Graduate*. Richard mostly dreamed of playing Hamlet on Broadway; that was his vision for his career. (Even after he became a household name, I used to stay at Richard's apartment in New York when he wasn't using it. Always gracious, he told me to just use the place like it was my own; he kept "our" best-actor Oscar in the bathroom.)

Richard's actor pals were Rob Reiner (Carl Reiner's son and a future megadirector) and Larry Bishop (the Rat Pack's Joey Bishop's son; *Hell Ride* and *Kill Bill*). We'd all just sit around and talk about acting. Richard was all heart and passion, so magnetic. He'd just say, "Yeah, *this* is going to happen." And you believed him. Sally, on the other hand, was all brains. Very focused and always smart about her career, about what types of roles to consider next. Like me, she'd been in this business since she was a kid. And far more than anything I'd developed yet, she had an actual game plan. Thus, where I was writing notes to creditors, she had a mansion in Bel-Air.

Sally was maybe twenty-four, only a year older than me. But she already had a nice house and a kid and nannies. She was so grown-up and classy compared to how I was living.

In only one area could I provide her some insight.

Sally Field was one of those people who couldn't stand posing for publicity pictures. She only wanted to focus on the work. We'd have to sit by some tree and look at each other and then look at the camera. She hated it, borderline refusing, and I'd help her through it.

"We'll go out," I joked. "We'll just goof off for fifteen minutes and let 'em take their pictures. We don't even have to look at the photographer. Ignore them. Let's just hang out for fifteen minutes. The rest is up to *them*."

We got through the publicity shots, but *Hitched* didn't get picked up. The pilot ran as a two-hour movie of the week, but NBC still wasn't seeing a series.

Creator Simmons wasn't asked to try a third time.

Sally became the title character in the TV movie *Sybil* and won an Emmy, and a permanent Hollywood star was soon born.

Meanwhile, I did episodes on shows like *Night Gallery, Ironside,* and *Owen Marshall, Counselor at Law.*

On *Owen Marshall,* there was a scene that required some real emotion, some real acting. I was playing a college kid who was responsible for the death of one of his fraternity brothers. We'd blocked the scene so that I would be crouched over the dead boy's body, confronted with the reality that his death was my fault. But when the director called action, I just couldn't do it. *Camelot* couldn't help me this time. I couldn't find the character or any genuine emotions. (Sally Field, I knew, would have pulled it off in one take.) So, I faked like I was blubbering, like I would have at age twelve, and the result was humiliating. We got through the scene, but I knew I'd been awful. I drove home, furious at myself. I remember the drive as a true turning point. I was so embarrassed and ashamed, I knew I needed to learn how to do it right or quit acting.

Film School Boot Camp

Acting Classes for Everyone!

Acting classes come in all sizes, shapes, and worth. Throughout my career, I've jumped from one class to another seeking a positive environment in which to open up in front of a class. A class where there was also a language with which to discuss the acting work without getting into personal issues or petty jealousies.

I'll never forget sitting in on one of the great Stella Adler's classes late in her career in Los Angeles. I was shocked after a scene between a young woman and a young man. Stella berated the woman and told her that she'd have no future as an actor and should just quit. "Get off this stage!" is what she said, I believe, after her tirade was over. I didn't want to be a part of a class, or a teacher, that treated people like that. Your acting teachers should be there to help you grow, not to humiliate you.

In the best classes, you will learn a technique and a language with which you can speak about the play, the scene work, or the exercises that you and the other actors do. When you're in the right place, this will give you a way to talk about people's work without making it about personal feelings. Instead, you can focus on your thoughts about what was just presented on stage. It should never be about a critique of the actors, but it should always be a healthy discussion about the work, the purpose of the scene, and what the audience feels they got from watching it. After all, the audience is why the actors are performing in the first place. As a director, I have never put much stock into what type of technique or training an actor has or doesn't have. It's my job to find a way to speak to them, to support their work, to help them do better work, or to make certain adjustments to help the scene work better dramatically. And with certain actors, sometimes it's not necessary to say anything at all.

Now that Universal was paying me every week again whether I worked or not, I decided to take the opportunity to get my "master's degree" in acting, signing up for everything from acting classes to voice, dance and movement, and fencing lessons. I'd either get better at acting or quit for good.

During this time, Universal "loaned" me to Warner Bros, to work on another cowboy show.

It was time to piss off Michael Landon.

PRE SMARTPHONES OR EVEN ANSWERING MACHINES, I HAD AN answering service. This was a nameless, faceless service you paid each month to collect your missed phone calls and messages. Then, whenever you got a chance, you'd find the nearest pay phone, drop in a dime, and call your service to see if anyone knew you existed. At every break in every acting class I ever took, there was always a mad rush to the pay phone by hopeful actors. In one of my Stanislavski acting classes, I got to the phone first.

The message: Agent Fred Specktor had called from my agency, William Morris. NBC had offered me a new regular role on *Bonanza*, the second-longest-running western series in TV history and the very same show that I'd bought my first TV to watch.

But I was studying and preparing myself for new roles that would expand my range as an actor; part of me felt like I'd already been a cowboy . . . more than once. I called in to seek Fred's counsel and asked, "Should I take the part?"

Specktor replied, seemingly without stopping to even take a breath, "Are you kidding? You're lucky to get the offer. Be happy I called." And then hung up.

Dan Blocker, who'd played Hoss and was one of the show's most recognizable and beloved stars, had gone in for a routine gallbladder operation and not survived, a tragic shock to all. NBC wanted me to somehow replace that huge loss as a fresh face for Season 14, playing a young convict who was being paroled to the Ponderosa. They were also trying to draw a younger audience to the show, since it had been slipping in the ratings for years.

All of this was a great deal for Universal, who took the higher money I was getting paid from *Bonanza* and Warner Bros. each week but still kept me on my new contract pay rate (the extra $200 a week notwithstanding!). In the end, Universal made a handsome overall profit on my contract deal.

But it had also worked out well for me too, giving me the financial security and time to continue studying acting more deeply.

Now I could I delve further into not only Stanislavski's acting techniques but also approaches taught by Lee Strasberg and Michael Chekhov; I could also go deeper into Shakespeare and practical aesthetics. I was finally learning my craft. And I'd bring my newfound skills to the Ponderosa set and try them out. I made a somewhat foolish choice to stay in character all day long, on and off camera, to the confusion, consternation, and annoyance of the *Bonanza* cast and crew.

Very much the method actor now, I suggested everyone on set call me Griff King, my character's name. Almost immediately, Lorne Greene, who had been doing the show for almost fifteen years, basically told me, *Get the fuck out of here.* A few crew members in makeup and catering honored my request.

One day, I rehearsed a scene with the director and cast and used the rehearsal to search for the real emotion of the scene for my character (these blocking rehearsals are used only hurriedly to find positions for the actors and the camera, not for acting!). This effort on my part added a good thirty minutes to our work that day, but I thought it was worth it. After the rehearsal, I asked the director what *he* thought of the scene and the new blocking we had chosen. He grimaced. "Well," he said. "The audience is asleep by now . . . But the blocking was . . . okay."

I assured him I'd speed the pace up when the cameras were rolling.

"Please," he implored, "just kick it in the ass and save the acting for the camera."

MICHAEL LANDON, LITTLE JOE, WAS NOW RUNNING THE ENTIRE show. He'd written twenty episodes, directed, and, of course, acted in each episode, too. He did all this seemingly effortlessly and was beloved by all. (Landon appeared on the cover of *TV Guide* twenty-two times, second only to Lucille Ball.) The cast and the crew had become all very much like his family, and he was clearly the show's father figure.

"Dad" apparently needed a little help to keep moseying along now and again. One day on location, a prop man was filling a large red Solo cup in the prop truck for Michael. "What's that?" I asked innocently *and* pryingly.

"Almaden white wine on the rocks."

This was a notoriously cheap jug wine. Now, I noticed Michael holding this cup, usually after lunch. When the chance arose, I got up the nerve to ask, "Michael, what's with the Almaden? Why not a great French or California wine? Come on, you're rich as hell."

Landon just laughed. "Well, I dunno . . . I just like it, I guess."

This was Landon in a nutshell. Honest, unaffected, and clear-cut.

And he never once looked or acted tipsy. Ever. I was duly impressed. Hell, the two guys from *The Virginian* would have been impressed. On *Bonanza*, after wrap each day, the prop guys would set up an open bar for anyone on the cast or crew who needed a drink—which was just about everyone! This work-hard/play-hard attitude was just the way things were done back then.

Not that I could handle it myself.

One week, Charles Dierkop, a magnificent character actor who had been in *Butch Cassidy and the Sundance Kid* and had just filmed *The Sting*, was a guest star. I'd worked with him, it seemed, a hundred times before, including on *The Virginian*. At lunchtime, I'd invited him back to my place for lunch just down the street from the lot. After eating, he pulled out what initially appeared to be an enormous tampon.

"I got this great joint here, Timmy. What do you say?"

"Well . . . I gotta work," I argued, marveling at the size of this roll. "We're due back in an hour."

"We're not doing *anything* this afternoon," he countered. "Look at the schedule. All the shots are other people . . ." He was making a lot of sense as he lit up. I took a couple of hits and then a couple more. By the time we got back to the Ponderosa, I was utterly bakederosa.

Months before, I'd gotten high while playing Poins in *Henry IV, Part 2* at the Shakespeare Festival in San Diego. During intermission, I'd been offered a toke, and it was 1974—who was I to say no? By Act 3, I was tripping flat onto my face backstage, missing cues, and coming in from the wrong side of the stage; I didn't know the difference between Wales and La Jolla. While lots of actors I knew, *and know*, can perform high almost habitually—all names redacted—I clearly could not, and I swore I'd never ever do it again. I lied.

When Charles and I got back to set, some production assistant gave us the news we were not expecting; "Hey, Tim. We're gonna pull up a scene from tomorrow and shoot it today."

I now had to deliver, *while wasted*, a scene with Lorne Greene in front of the director, five other actors, and a crew of a hundred. Lorne, however, was my full focus. He was almost sixty. He, I assumed, *never* got high. Had never gotten high. He refused to call me Griff King. He undoubtedly hated me and my newfound actor purism. He knew I was high. He wanted to fire me. He had that *TV Guide* article pinned up in his trailer to remind himself daily how much he hated me. These were now the thoughts racing through my paranoid, joint-wasted noggin.

For the scene, there were a bunch of characters all standing in a row as Lorne Greene walked down from man to man. I'm at the end of the line and sweating like it's 140 degrees in the shade. Lorne finally stops in front of me and looks me in the eye. Weed-fueled paranoia raging, I convince myself that he knows I'm high and somehow knows about what I did to his car.

The car!! He knows . . . During my first week of shooting on location in Northern California, he'd parked in front of my room at the motel where we were all staying. It was a huge brand-new Mercedes sedan, and I'd just learned Mercedes had innovated a swivel and pliable connector between the hood ornament and the car. I saw Lorne's car and was curious about how the swivel worked. I pushed the hood ornament slightly to the side, and—*snap!*—it came off right in my hand. *My first week, and I just broke Pa Cartwright's expensive car!* Thankfully, no one was in sight, and I quickly, carefully, balanced the hood ornament back onto its pedestal and got the hell out of there.

But now, as Lorne stares into my eyes, I can only imagine he's back in that big beautiful black Mercedes watching his hood ornament teeter and plunge to the ground when he starts the car. He *knows* it was me. He knows! How does he know?! Maybe he *does* have a reason to hate me?

Focusing with everything I had, I looked Mr. Greene in the eyes and gave my lines. Or I think I did. I must have, because the scene ended and everyone moved on to other matters. My joint pal Charles? I found him later with his boots propped up and sound asleep behind one of barns.

I'm never, ever doing this again, I promised myself. *I'm such an idiot.* To risk a great job for what? *If I have to lie, steal, cheat, or kill, as God is my witness, I'll never be stoned while acting again.* If I hoped to stay on *Bonanza* another few years, I needed to always bring my A game.

Alas, my days on *Bonanza* were already over.

This week's episode happened to be centered on my character of Griff King. Late one afternoon, as we finished the last camera setup of the final scene, Michael Landon arrived on the set with a news crew from the local NBC affiliate, KNBC. Something very strange was up, but nobody—especially me—was quite sure what.

"NBC has just notified me," Michael began, "that as of today, we're being canceled. This is the very last scene of *Bonanza* that will ever be filmed."

Everyone was shocked. There were still eight more episodes left to be filmed to finish the season. "No," Michael confirmed, "we're done." He was extremely emotional since he and this crew had spent almost every day of the last fourteen years together, an extended family, and Michael was very close to all of them.

Landon asked the news crew to roll film for *NBC News* that evening. He spoke now directly into the camera and announced to the viewers that *Bonanza* had been canceled after fourteen years; he thanked the cast and crew and all the viewers and said that this was not only the end of *Bonanza* but also the end of Little Joe.

Suddenly, the red-cup-Almaden prop man stepped into frame next to the news cameras and raised a shotgun. As Michael smiled and waved goodbye into the camera, the shotgun fired *boom*, and Michael was literally blown back fifteen feet through an open door behind him. (Actually, he'd been *yanked* back by a preset jerk line that had been hooked up to his body and pulled by a stunt crew when the shotgun was fired.)

And *that* was Michael Landon. The whole thing staged to help lighten the horrible news. A perfect ending for the show. All of us laughed, and many cried, for the longest time. We were all so stunned that the show was over, and we'd been given no warning. But because of Michael, the ending was fitting: classy, touching, and funny. And all about family.

It was no surprise that Michael had a hit show on NBC one year later. It was about a girl named Laura Ingalls and her family. Nor was it surprising that almost the entire *Bonanza* crew was on that show with him again and remained there for the next ten years. I, however, was not invited to Walnut Grove.

About that interview I gave . . .

It was several years before he finally forgave me. *Mostly* forgave me.

As a freelance actor in Hollywood in your twenties, every day you wake up is filled with hope. *Today is going to be the day! Today I'll get that big job!! Stay hopeful.* Your time after coffee and a shower is filled with working on scenes for acting class, preparing auditions, encouraging your agent to work harder for you, balancing the checkbook, and occasionally falling in love with some of the most beautiful women in the world. It is also probable that you were already out of the business and nobody told you.

1975 was a bit of a low point for me. I'd had to break up with my girlfriend when I discovered that she was trying to screw every one of my pals . . . *and* my agent. (Still the time of free love, I suppose, and I had slept with a few of her girlfriends. I guess I had it coming—turnabout is fair play.) Maybe I was looking for a Band-Aid to cover the fact that I just wasn't doing very well professionally. *Bonanza* was over, and I wasn't finding any work.

But I still had hope.

My agents had gotten me an audition to read with another young actor for a new series. The other guy already had the lead role. I'd never heard of him. You've never heard of him. (In fact, no one has heard from him since.) This doesn't stop him from spending the next two hours telling me precisely how to read all *my* lines in our audition (*Actors "lovvvvveeeee" this.*) and snapping back at me anytime I try and engage in some creative dialogue. This is his first TV show. I've already been in two dozen. I'm utterly miserable, and I try thinking of other career paths but can't come up with anything. I hate the industry. I hate myself. I leave the audition as fast as possible, doing my best to conceal my contempt for all of Southern California and every idiot in it.

An hour later, I am still fuming but have to get ready for what is known as a *meet and greet* with the head of casting at Columbia Television. Meet and greets are exactly what they sound like: You take a shower, hit a few extra sprays of Right Guard, slap on some cologne (hippies didn't use aftershave, and Hollywood wasn't yet casting *actual* hippies), brush your teeth, and try to make a good impression on someone who may or may not someday be in a position to change your life. There's nothing to read. Nothing to prepare. Just be yourself and be charming. It's a thirty-minute drive for a meeting that will last fifteen minutes, tops.

I open the door, and sitting in the waiting room is Kurt Russell. *The* Kurt Russell. Twenty-four and sprawled on the couch like a young Olympian god. My shit day just got even shittier. *God damn it, why is Disney star Kurt Russell in my meet and greet?* His look mirrors my own—but somehow, I don't think he's asking himself, *Why is Tim Matheson in my meet and greet?* He sizes me up. "What the hell is this?" he asks with that gruff trademark Kurt Russell laugh.

"Beats me," I mutter, and collapse on the coach next to him. The speaker on the secretary's desk buzzes, and we hear the head of casting: "Send them in."

Both of us? At the same time? How much humiliation am I supposed to endure in one day? Kurt and I look at each other, shrug, and head into the paneled office of Renee Valente, head of casting for Columbia TV.

Renee tells us how she loves all our work as actors and how David Gerber (producer of NBC hits *Police Story* and *Police Woman*) wanted to cash in some chips and make a western series. He wants the two of us to star together as brothers in *The Quest*, a two-hour western pilot he's doing. Renee then hands us a big, fat script for this two-hour movie. No audition, no read-through, no waiting it out while ten guys all read for the same part. This was an offer! An offer to star in a new show, something that had never happened to me. I was so stunned that I hardly knew what to do, so I quickly looked to my side and mirrored Kurt's behavior. . . .

"Sounds nice," Kurt says with the same energy he would have mustered if someone told him his dry cleaning was ready. He couldn't care less. "Love to read it."

I feigned the same casual attitude, but inside I was doing cartwheels.

I thanked Renee, made some jokes, and left with Kurt. Despite how the day had started—with plans to do literally *anything* else for a living—things suddenly seemed to be looking up.

Hollywood.

Now, THERE ARE JOBS THAT, IN AND OF THEMSELVES, DON'T REALLY amount to much. Then there are the jobs that don't amount to much but can set things in motion and will amount to a whole lot and ultimately change your life. *The Quest* was one of those jobs.

The show was a TV version similar to John Ford's classic film *The Searchers*, the story of two young men on a mission to rescue their sister captured as a child by Native Americans. Kurt played the younger brother who had also been captured and fostered by the Cheyenne people and was recently recaptured by the Cavalry. I was the older brother, raised back East and trained as a doctor. (My mom was so proud she finally had a doctor in the family; little did we know at the time that I was going be playing doctors for the next fifty years.)

The year we spent making the pilot and the fifteen episodes that we ultimately shot during our only season on NBC was another master's degree for my acting studies. Working every day and playing the lead in a series taught me a lot of lessons quickly. There wasn't Jim Drury or Lorne Greene around to do all the heavy lifting. It was me and Kurt, and that was it.

And thank God for Kurt.

His limitless stories—mostly from his days playing Minor League Baseball more so than acting—were always discerning and hilarious. He had one about a woman with "major league yabbies," and the phrase cracked me up for days—so much so that I improv'd my own version years later when auditioning for *Animal House*. But far beyond the great stories and expressions, Kurt just knew the business.

His dad, Bing (who I'd acted with on *The Virginian*), was also an actor and a former Minor League Baseball player. Kurt had grown up in a Hollywood house and understood how things worked before he'd stepped in front of the camera at nine years old. By seventeen, he was starring in several Disney live-action pictures. And then he quit acting to become, like his dad, a professional baseball player. By all accounts, Kurt was a pretty good second baseman and hitter. While playing AA Ball for the El Paso Sun Kings, Kurt was turning a double play when another player collided with him. Kurt tore his rotator cuff, and in the sports medicine view of the 1970s, the injury meant his baseball career was over. He returned to acting.

Kurt brought team spirit and an athlete's healthy attitude to the craft of acting. The Russell Approach taught me as much as, if not more than, my Shakespeare, Stanislavski, and Strasberg techniques combined. Although he was three years younger than me and playing my little brother, Kurt knew so much more than I did. He became the mentor and, in many ways, an older brother to me.

"You work too hard," he told me one day. "You give it your all in rehearsal and in every run-through. You know, you're gonna get exhausted, get sick, or burn out, because we got fifteen episodes. Just slow down some. Take it easy in these rehearsals. Save it for the camera."

He was always relaxed, cool. Nothing frazzled him. Kurt—the Dao master from Thousand Oaks.

If something shitty happened, he'd laugh and say, "Okay . . ." And if something spectacular happened, he'd laugh and say, "Okay . . ." This was from a combo of growing up a jock (in baseball, you're lucky if you bat .285, less than one in three) and a working actor's kid.

Pro sports and pro entertainment are full-contact sports. You're out in front of a crowd all the time and you gotta get a hit when you need to get a hit. There's a lot of pressure, and one way athletes deal with that is just giving each other shit all the time, constantly busting each other's balls. Being brutal with each other in a joking way so that the real pressures seemed less important. Once, when I visited the Miami Marlins clubhouse before a game, the manager introduced me to a young lefty pitcher they'd just brought up. "Way to go," I told the young man. "Congratulations. Welcome to the Bigs!"

The manager laughed. "If you're a lefty and you've got a pulse, you're in the big leagues." This kid was barely twenty, but the manager needed to keep him in his place, not letting the hurler take himself too seriously when he headed out to the mound later that week in front of 30,000 people.

That's the attitude Kurt brought to the set each day: It's no big deal; *I'm* no big deal. Let's get on with the game.

Film School Boot Camp

The Dao of Kurt

Working with Kurt Russell on *The Quest* was a master class in teamwork and partnership. What Lucy taught me about comedy, Kurt taught me about team. (He was a professional baseball player, after all.) We'd make notes about our questions regarding the scripts together so we were always on the same page. Then we'd meet with the producers or writers to implement changes or adjustments if necessary—together whenever we could—but always looking out for each other.

His was the kind of wisdom I never heard in any acting book or class I ever attended. I've used his advice and our experiences as a personal tent pole of my career in all areas. Here are some of the things I lean on the most, and maybe you will too: Kurt once described his approach to breaking down a script: "There are only two or three scenes in each script that I can really do something with," he said. "In the other scenes, I don't try to do too much. Just be there and deliver the mail." One director we had on an episode had been an actor himself. He kept doing take after take on my coverage—each time changing the performance a tiny bit and adjusting my readings again and again. More takes and adjustments than I'd ever done on our show. When he tried to do this on Kurt's coverage, I could tell that Kurt didn't like it. After about three takes, Kurt just looked at the director and said, "That's as good as I can do it," and let him know he wasn't putting up with this actor's-studio BS any longer. (As a director, I never give more than a couple of adjustments, and all the actors I've worked with have Kurt to thank.) Kurt also taught me to give back to the crew, to be gracious in success and failure. We bought *The Quest* belt buckles for everyone and threw a holiday party for the crew even after the show was canceled. We even had Santa ride in on a Wild West-style stagecoach! Kurt taught me to share the stage and screen. It isn't a competition between you and the other performers. It's a system of cooperation and support. A family.

Kurt was always very generous and gregarious with people who recognized him from all the Disney stuff he'd done. We couldn't go anywhere, especially around younger fans. He wasn't a Beatle, but you could have fooled me, considering how people would go nuts when he walked in. Kurt would just smile, be courteous, and move on with his life. He didn't glamorize the industry or fame, and his approach was really insightful for me. Kurt always just did the job and treated it *like* a job.

In its final push before the premiere, *The Quest* had the two of us do publicity shots together, in costume on the horses and all. After all, this was a show about *two* brothers searching for their abducted sister. That week, the Sunday *LA Times* published its TV magazine with a picture of only one brother, Kurt, alone on the cover. I understood; he was a bigger star. But it still stung. When I arrived at work on Monday, I could hear someone yelling loudly. Turned out it was Kurt, laying into the press department and the press agent who had foolishly come on the set that morning—thinking they were going to get an attaboy from Kurt for the layout in the paper. "What the fuck?" Kurt railed. "You can't do that to us ever again. That's not okay. It's me *and* Tim or no one." He was totally coming from *This is a teammate of mine, and we're on a fucking team.* "Don't let this *ever* happen again!" Kurt thundered away, and I was left in awe.

There are not a lot of people in this town or business—in *most* businesses, I suppose—who would take a stand like that. I began to see casts as more of a team than ever before. To stop thinking about myself so much.

To that point, I learned some lessons the hard way: Always be respectful and treat all crew members with dignity and kindness. I'd spent a lot of time on sets but I hadn't yet picked up this part of Kurt's lessons. I'd always been too focused on what *I* was doing—or trying to do.

When we started *The Quest*, being inexperienced, I put great pressure on myself to make *every* scene perfect and real. One day, I got all worked up about a silly costume issue and got into a shouting match with the set costumer. We'd shot a scene where Kurt and I had "checked into a hotel room the night before," but no one had laid out our clothes or belongings in the room like they would have been in real life. It was a small detail, but I was in my relentless searching-for-the-truth mode and blamed the costumers, who blamed the prop team. The costumer, I insisted, had screwed up, and we traded harsh words *loudly*. I knew enough to feel bad about it that night and went to apologize first thing the next morning, only to find out that he'd been fired for being "out of line" with me, one of the stars of the show.

I was horrified. I tried to get him hired back, but it was too late. I'd gotten this poor guy fired because I had been a self-indulgent actor and a complete jerk. Not only had I treated him badly, but I'd also done it publicly in front of the whole crew. And that behavior, rightly, didn't go over well with many in the crew.

The revenge came quickly and simply and was priceless.

The costume supervisor, a bearded, Harley Davidson–riding, cross-dressing giant got even with me by putting lice in my character's hat. My head started itching later the same day, and I scratched and scratched. It took three days of special tarlike shampoo and nightly grooming to get rid of them.

The lesson I learned: Never peck *down* the ladder; it's always too easy and a cheap shot. And never publicly upbraid anyone, ever. If you have a problem, take the person aside, have a quiet conversation about the issue, and always allow them to save face. My biggest overall lesson: Stop being a jerk and so self-involved. Actors' jobs are no more important than anyone else's on the crew. We're all part of the same team, and all should be treated with kindness and respect.

(Years later, I ran into the fired costumer while directing an episode of *St. Elsewhere* and fell all over myself apologizing. He was good-natured about it and maintained that getting fired had freed him to work on other, better shows.)

As good quests are meant to, I came out of my *Quest* with a whole new perspective on my career and on myself. I felt more mature and had a better sense of how to do this job and a better sense of trusting myself.

Kurt had just about everything to do with that.

I will always love and admire him so much.

When I first started directing, I was at the Warner Bros. lot setting up a scene when all of a sudden I hear this voice behind me. "Wowwww! . . . Are you . . . are you Tim Matheson?" This was all delivered in this high little weaselly voice I did not recognize, and I turned slowly, expecting the worst. It was Kurt. (Not the last time he's snuck up on a set I was working on and surprised me with a quick joke.) "Boy, I never wanna do that," Kurt said of my new directing path. This coming from a guy who could do it in his sleep.

Every time we run into each other, I'm taken back to when Kurt and I used to stand around the back lot at Warner Bros. It would be Friday night, we'd be working late, and we'd say to each other, "I can't believe we're getting paid for this."

The Quest was aired on Wednesdays at 9:00 p.m. to target an older audience.

Two channels over was *Charlie's Angels.*

People could now decide between watching two young cowboys running around . . . or Jaclyn Smith, Kate Jackson, and Farrah Fawcett running around.

The Quest was canceled just before the season ended.

Michael Landon might not like it, but I'd been right in that *TV Guide* article. The classic TV western was over. (It would be another forty-plus years before Kevin Costner trotted onto Yellowstone Ranch.)

After four-plus years in a Stetson, it was time to hang up my spurs.

Theatre Nerd

(or How to Make $100 per Week)

WHEN DIRTY HARRY AND *MAGNUM FORCE* DIDN'T PROVE THE career lift I'd hoped for, I humbly returned to episodic TV to find steady work acting in episodes of many of the early 1970s classics: *Hawaii Five-O*, *The Magician* (with Bill Bixby), *Police Story*, *Rhoda*, *Medical Center*, *Kung Fu*. And while I enjoyed learning from actors like David Carradine (who spent time between our scenes picking plants in the desert he could ingest later and teaching me to find sacred datura for the best hallucinogenic), I knew there was still work to do. The shame of my *Owen Marshall* cry-fail hadn't waned. The lack of feature film roles still frustrated. And I wanted the better roles, not just the bit parts.

Theatre, I'd decided, in light of actor autobiographies and the talk in all my acting classes, was obviously a path to learning more about, and getting better at, the craft. I knew theatre paid like shit and, so, had avoided for it years. But it was time, no matter how small the check, to return to my first public success as an actor: the stage.

——

THE THREE SCARIEST MOMENTS OF MY LIFE.

In the first, I'm eighteen and standing in the doorless side of a Piper airplane traveling 110 miles per hour some 7,500 feet up in the air, skydiving in the Mojave Desert. I'm in my first, and only, semester of college, and I'm doing this for fun.

"Okay, Cappy! Shut down the engines!"

Not what you expect to hear, ever, on an airplane. Then, "Okay, Matthieson!" The instructor pulls me forward. This was back in the day where there was no expert latched to your back as a safety net for new jumpers. I was instead, at least, connected to a static jump line so that the chute would pull automatically once I was ten feet away from the sputtering aircraft. The strategy now was for me to climb out of the gaping wound of this plane and hang on to the narrow strut that held the wing up. When this "instructor"—a term I previously believed would involve teaching me something, beyond what I had learned falling off a swing set when I was three—yells "GO!" I'm supposed to let go of the only thing that is keeping me attached to the airplane and launch myself toward the ground. Dangling from the strut, I'm thinking, *Who thought this was a good idea? What the fuck am I doing here? I paid for this? I'm gonna die.*

The second time, a grown man I've never met is screaming at me and shaving my head aggressively on the first day in the Marine Corps. (But you already know that story.)

The third, I'm twenty-six at the San Diego Shakespeare Festival. The opening-night audience is there, the play has begun, and I'm getting ready to enter through the lobby doors. The play is *Romeo and Juliet*, and I'm playing Romeo, who doesn't come on until about seven minutes into the show. *"Is the day so young? Ay me, sad hours seem long."*

While waiting for my cue to enter, late arrivals are being held outside the theater, and they're not happy. The ushers are explaining to them that because of our entrance, the fair Romeo (me) coming down the aisle through the crowd to the foot of the stage, these late arrivers now have to wait before being allowed to enter. I turn to see the commotion and am suddenly face-to-face with my own mother. *My mother! She* was one of the late ones.

But I didn't let that distract me. I still had enough to think about. This is my first professional theatre production. I am about to deliver five-thousand-plus words in iambic pentameter Elizabethan English to a live audience while also presenting a real-life character via feelings and tone and movements and reactions. Halfway across the theater door threshold, I'm thinking, *Who thought this was a good idea? What the fuck am I doing here? I'm barely getting paid for this. I miss skydiving. I miss Melson.*

It was, I realized too late, exactly the same feeling I'd had skydiving the first time or mostly every day during boot camp. Terror. Neither crawling beneath live rounds for the Marines nor appearing on *The Ed Sullivan Show* nor working a scene alone with Lucille Ball was as terrifying as the stage and a live audience.

But parachuting proved great; my chute opened, and the whole experience was exhilarating. I did five more jumps. The Marines taught me more about myself in ten weeks than I'd learned in the previous eighteen years. And *Romeo and Juliet* proved no different. I did forty more performances. Once I learned to appreciate the fear, it actually energized each performance, even though, admittedly, I was great on some nights and not so much on others. On those mediocre nights, it was merely hard work.

I've always enjoyed live theatre as an audience member, and as an actor, I respect those who can do it. But it never fit me personally. I was a film kid, a TV guy. I wasn't one of those actors who stands in the wings, and goes, "Oh, this is so great!" For me, it always felt like my primary career went to the back burner while I was doing theatre. (The Shakespeare Festival, for instance, was five months long. *Animal House* was shot in five *weeks*. The math didn't add up.)

Plus in film, you do the tough scenes two, three, ten times, and then it's there. It's done, forever captured on camera. In postproduction, they pick (hopefully) the best take, and that's what everyone sees. Not so in the theatre. There, live on stage, you have do those same tough scenes *every single performance*. Stanislavski said, "If you can hit an average of 70 percent of truthful performances, you're doing great." Imagine if airline pilots took that same outlook. To Stanislavski, 100 percent every night wasn't possible, but you futilely still try anyway.

The stage, for me, served mainly as a chance to grow as an actor and to work on my craft. It was good to do something over and over again in front of an audience, to find out what works and what doesn't. I *was* getting better. And there *were* times I genuinely loved being on stage: working at the wonderful Williamstown Theatre Festival in Massachusetts, doing a play with Dick Cavett, playing Petruchio in *The Taming of the Shrew*, and toying with a one-man show as Ronald Reagan. But for many reasons, I mostly kept live theatre at a ripcord's length.

It started out well. I acted in my first play, something about Sacagawea, when I was eight. I'd had a couple of good lines, and I remember getting my first laugh ever on a stage from an audience. I won't pretend I didn't like the attention and immediate feedback. And I wanted more. Almost twenty years later, I'd learn that some people never grow out of that desire.

I'd been doing a production of one-act plays by George Bernard Shaw.

The lead actor I performed with in one of the short plays was a selfish, pompous man . . . and a good actor. He was playing Napoléon, and we spent a lot of rehearsal time trying to get the humor to work better. The play *was* funny as written but was still landing flat in dress rehearsals. Then on opening night, a wonderful accident: I knocked and knocked and then kicked open the set door to make my entrance as usual, and this actor happened to be standing in front of the door. He'd been off his mark. The force of the door knocked him aside and now behind the door. I strode onto the stage looking for, but not finding, my Napoléon.

The audience howled.

Every line I gave after this entrance was met with growing laughter, and when the scene ended, the audience applauded us both— not the play, mind you, just the scene. It had worked that well.

This went on for the rest of the week. Kick. Laughs. Applause. Success. We'd found what the play was supposed to be—more slapstick and broader humor. But our star had had enough. They weren't *his* laughs. The next night, I kicked the door open and he was standing ten feet away. Literal crickets were heard chirping from the street outside. There were no laughs that night, and the whole one-act play died right in front of that night's audience. The Napoléon actor hadn't liked a younger actor getting the big laughs and decided that a play about Napoléon, that is, a play *about him*, would be more interesting. It wasn't. And he'd harmed the entire show, including the other one-acts, making the whole night less enjoyable. Having never run into it in television, I'd finally learned about being upstaged at the theatre. And it pissed me off. Three nights later, I "missed my cue," waited a few beats longer, kicked the door open, and hit him square with the door again. Kick. Laughs. Applause. Success—*for all of us!*—the rest of the evening. And the rest of the run.

Film School Boot Camp

Upstage Isn't Just a Place

I've experienced lots of actors who either consciously or unconsciously don't like it when other actors shine. So, they do things to upstage or pull the focus to themselves instead of their scene partners. One such time, in rehearsal on an episodic TV show, I found some business for my character to do in a scene. It was a funny physical bit. We got ready to shoot the scene. On the first take, the other actor took the business that I'd made up in rehearsal and did it himself on *his* line right before the line I was going to do the business on. Now, it had become his business. And he got away with it.

On another show, there was an actor obsessed about keeping the scene always about them. I had a very lengthy and touching speech in the middle of a scene, and we rehearsed it, blocked it, and got ready to shoot. The director called action, and as I began my dialogue, this actor started to cross the room. In rehearsal, the actor had originally made the move on their own line, which was the proper way to do it. (There's a law in the theatre and in film: You never cross or move on another actor's line; you move only on your own lines. Onstage, moving while another actor is speaking draws the audience's attention from the actor speaking and onto the actor moving. On film, it forces a cutaway from the actor speaking. Otherwise, the audience will be confused when you cut to the character at the bar who has now magically moved to the table.) When I objected to this movement on the speech, the actor claimed to have done it that way in rehearsal. I asked the camera operator if that was true, and he tactfully shook his head no. However, the director was green and didn't know how to protect the scene from upstaging tricks like this. In the final cut, the editor had to cut away from my emotional speech to the actor crossing on my line, and kept the scene about them, which had been the person's objective all along. The other actor and I had a constructive heart-to-heart shortly afterward.

My advice is to be aware of what is going on around you and to learn, in your own way, how to protect yourself when someone is playing diva or showboating to steal a moment or scene. Hopefully, you'll have a good director who will stop these things from happening and keep the scene playing as written. But most importantly—a scene with others is *never* about *you* or *your character*. It's about the scene. Help keep it that way. Only you can prevent scene stealing.

Five years later, I'm at the Mark Taper Forum in Los Angeles doing a play called *Division Street*. I was playing the lead: Chris, a retired radical hippie trying to find a normal life surrounded by every possible misfit you can imagine. Rehearsals had started the same day our playwright, Steve Tesich, won an Oscar for *Breaking Away*, the classic bike-riding film about the Little 500 at Indiana University. His new play was also a solid script, and I was still getting enough Sacagawea-level laughs for the play to keep my attention.

I had one of those aisle entrances again. These entrances are great because they give you a moment in the crowd and everyone turns to you. However, in most places, *everyone* turning to you isn't some famous person you revere. This is what happened at the Mark Taper Forum on opening night.

Oh shit! There's Neil Simon! I also see Richard Dreyfuss, Richard Benjamin (*Westworld*, *The Sunshine Boys*), Paula Prentiss (*The Stepford Wives*, *Where the Boys Are*), and star after star in the audience. I've never been so distracted and taken out of the moment in my whole life. But it's live theatre; you refocus, and the show must go on.

The reviews the next day were split. I'd auditioned twenty times for this role and, in the middle of serious improv training and work, was nailing these auditions. While the part didn't fit me perfectly, I found a way to both find the humor and make this character work. And the casting people kept saying, "You're so good in this part, but you're not right for it . . . but you're so funny." Finally, they just couldn't find anybody else better, or available, and cast me.

The *LA Times* had reservations about my performance and agreed that I was miscast. But Lawrence Christon of the *Los Angeles Herald Examiner* loved me and thought the play was great. In either case, the show proved successful enough in L.A. that the decision had been made to take it to Broadway. The big time. Gordon Davidson, a Tony winner, was running and producing our show. He called us all to his office to discuss the big move to New York and the Great

White Way. To do so, he was bringing actors in one at a time while the rest of us sat excitedly and waited. I cannot overstate how big a deal this is for an actor. It's Broadway—even if you don't like the theatre, it's Broadway!

Over time, I'm the last guy left.

"Tim," Gordon says once we were finally alone, "I know this has been a tough run. We're . . . we're gonna. . . . we're gonna get somebody else to play Chris on Broadway."

There were no words. There had been no hint that this was coming.

"You know, it's the way things go sometimes," he offered.

Another guy who thought I was miscast, the hit show's producer.

Mostly, I couldn't understand why he'd made me sit outside his office for two hours before the Broadway coup de grâce. This might have been done a hundred different ways.

They replaced me with John Lithgow—clearly going a different route with the male lead. That version of the play flopped on Broadway (not that I was paying attention), and a brief 1987 revival was blasted again for the "miscasting of the main role."

You know, it's the way things go sometimes.

———

DANIEL STERN WAS TRYING TO MURDER ME. (THIS IS THE BUG-EYED banger of checkout girls from *City Slickers* and the *Home Alone* bandit *not* named Joe Pesci.) I'd come back to theatre again, off-Broadway, to work on my acting chops and instead was taking nightly shots *to* the chops. This guy couldn't keep his hands off me.

The play was *True West* by Sam Shepard (the magnificent playwright and actor who won more Obies, the off-Broadway Tonys, than any other writer or director). It's about a sibling rivalry between two estranged brothers who have reconnected. I played the intellectual, struggling screenwriter, and Daniel played Lee, the ne'er-do-well older brother. The brothers would quarrel and fight.

And big brother Lee (Daniel) would beat me up. Each night. In front of a live audience. *Hilarious.* This was supposed to be acting, and it was acting in rehearsals, but on stage . . . Daniel really started beating me up. Losing control. Real slaps, full punches to the chest, my neck caught in the crook of his arm as I fought for air. One of the lines on the play was "Brothers . . . they kill each other in the heat mostly," and it was getting heated for real on stage.

The first time it happened, I tried talking to him: "Got a little crazy out there tonight, pal. Stage fighting, remember?"

Gangly Daniel slapped my back. "I got carried away, sorry. You know how it is."

He wasn't on drugs or anything; he just couldn't turn off his natural look-at-me-everyone rowdiness. Each performance, it got more violent. We had soft, safe props to throw, but some nights, I was getting hit with real glass, toasters, and furniture.

"Danny," I said as I grabbed his arm after the curtain shut, "you're getting way too rough out there, man. It's not cool." I'd pulled up my shirt to show him actual bruising from an earlier performance.

He looked at me like I was the asshole. "We're supposed to fight, right?"

"We're supposed to *act* like we're fighting, yeah. You really need—"

"Won't happen again," Daniel said and walked off.

Oh, but it did happen again. I said something to the director and producers, and nothing changed. As soon as we were in front of an audience again, this guy went full UFC on me—the "Most Dangerous Man on Off-Broadway." There were deep nail scratches on my arms, a gash in one knee, and welts across my neck and shoulders.

Eventually, I decided I was going to fight back.

One night, I put stage fighting aside and didn't pull my punches as I had been taught years ago on *Bonanza*. Nothing was for show. If this jerk wanted to tangle on stage for an audience of two hundred, let's go. The only issue is that my character was supposed to lose these fights. So anything I dished out, he came back three times harder. I'd push him off me, and he'd lunge back like it was a back-alley brawl. The audience would openly gasp. Furniture would break. Two grown men were actually fighting on stage, and Sam Shepard would probably get another Obie award.

In the final scene of the play, my character strangles his brother with a telephone cord. This scene had been staged very carefully so that neither Daniel or I got hurt. This night, I might have allowed myself to get carried away just a tad. Sorry, not sorry.

We were only eight weeks into the twelve-week run of the play. I called the producers and protested, "You guys get this guy in control, or I'm walking."

"Tim, you're so right. We'll talk to him."

Nothing changed. If anything, the nightly beatings increased.

"I'm out," I finally decided. "I won't be in tomorrow."

That same night, I got a call from my agent telling me they were firing Stern. *But*, he added, Daniel was finishing out the week and if I didn't show up to work, I could expect to hear from the show's lawyers.

For three more shows, I took beatings from a disgruntled, already-fired Daniel Stern.

—

I'D READ SOMEWHERE THAT SIR ANTHONY HOPKINS (*THE ELE-phant Man*, *The Silence of the Lambs*, *The Remains of the Day*, King Lear, Macbeth, Odin, etc.) was always off book on day one of rehearsals when he did a play. "How can I be walking around as a character with a script?" he'd asked. This acting legend had set such a high standard for himself, and I did my best to follow his lead.

In 1982, I'd been invited to St. Edward's University, a private college in Austin, Texas, that hired one or two professional actors annually to join their theatre students in a big professional production. There were to be six to eight weeks of preparation for *The Taming of the Shrew* for the students. I was to come in for one week's rehearsal, then perform a four-week run as Petruchio, the male lead.

A couple years before, Broderick Crawford—a wonderful older tough-guy actor who liked to drink, who I loved on *Highway Patrol* when I was a kid—had gotten the gig, and one of the college kids was tasked, every night, with keeping a water pitcher on the prop table for him. However, the student was also tasked with making sure that the water in the pitcher contained a certain percentage (100 percent) of vodka. (On *Highway Patrol*, they had apparently done afternoon filming mostly with his character Detective Dan Mathews leaning against the car hood or a wall, because alcohol and standing up don't always mix.) I wanted to set a better example, an Anthony Hopkins example.

Cast as Petruchio, there were a considerable amount of lines and, leading up to my trip south, I'd learn twenty to thirty of them every day. The next day, I'd review them and then add twenty more. This went on for weeks until all six hundred lines and 4,633 words were locked in. When I showed up the first day, I was ready for blocking and character direction. "I'm ready to go!" I assured them. Many of the college kids had also been practicing for weeks and were ready to shame the pro a bit. But I truly *was* ready to go, and we hit it off. They knew instantly I'd come to have fun and really give myself over to their experience.

Every time I did Shakespeare, there was something new to pick up.

During my repertoire run in San Diego's Shakespeare Festival, I'd played Poins, a small part in *Henry IV, Part 2* as a pal of Falstaff and Prince Hal. No small parts, only small actors, I'd come exclusively to learn. Falstaff was played by Victor Buono, who had been nominated for an Oscar for his role in *Whatever Happened to Baby Jane?* I'd stand in the wings and watch him every night for weeks and learned so much. Victor, as Falstaff, turned his soliloquies into stand-up comedy routines and played them differently as improv every night. Now more than ever, I'd learned the value of seeking out an old pro to learn something new.

Coming off *Henry IV* and Romeo, I'd auditioned for *The Runaway Barge*, a pilot/TV-movie shot on the Mississippi in the ides of winter. The movie included a young Nick Nolte months before he filmed *Rich Man, Poor Man*. Doing my best Victor Buono impression, I landed the part. Theatre *was* genuinely helping.

Yet I didn't spend all my summers doing Shakespeare . . .

Endless Summer

"Where's Anna?" the gruff voice on the phone asked.

"I have no clue," I replied. She was next to me and half-dressed at most.

"Tim," Rocky asked again. "I need to see Anna."

Rocky Pamplin was a professional bodyguard. He outweighed me by fifty pounds, all muscle. He'd played running back for the University of Oregon and been drafted by the New Orleans Saints. (He'd also recently been a centerfold in *Playgirl*.)

He'd been tasked with collecting Anna, and right at this moment, I really liked Anna. "Haven't seen her," I lied again. I was convinced that a lie, as weak as it was, was the best chance I had of keeping my face intact.

"Okay," he said and hung up as I moved on with my afternoon.

Fifteen seconds later—*bang, bang bang!*—a heavy fist was slamming on my hotel room door. "Open up!" It was Rocky.

No way to get out the fifteenth-floor window, I looked to Anna wide-eyed, but she was already up and fully clothed again with a shrug. I plodded to the door and opened it. Rocky shook his head at me. Now it was my turn to shrug.

"Let's go, Anna . . ." he said. My crash course in Rock Star 101 had just hit a new level.

SHE PATTED MY CHEST AS SHE PASSED AND SMILED. "MAYBE I'LL SEE you later," she said. All I heard was—*"And we'll have fun, fun, fun till Rocky takes the groupie away . . ."*

MIKE LOVE, A COFOUNDER OF THE BEACH BOYS AND FRONT MAN, had written most of the soundtrack for *Almost Summer*, a so-so movie I'd just finished for Universal Pictures. A light drama about seniors in high school foretelling a run of films like *Fast Times at Ridgemont High* and *The Breakfast Club*. To help promote the film, it was agreed that Lee Purcell (star of the movie with Bruno Kirby) and I would travel with the Beach Boys to promote both the film and Mike's new songs.

Brian Wilson—reclusive virtuoso and leader behind the Beach Boys success—had cowritten some of the songs with Mike and recently come out of retirement to join the band on this tour. The musical savant behind the classic album *Endless Summer* was now going to help promote *Almost Summer*. Perfect!

Bodyguard Rocky belonged to Brian. Not to protect Brian from other people but the other way around. Wilson's social cues were so famously off-kilter—he'd pluck a cigarette right out of a stranger's mouth and start smoking it or put a local news reporter in a headlock—that Rocky had been hired as an extrajudicial warden to save Brian from himself whenever possible.

For several weeks, we traveled throughout the southwest together—Texas, Arkansas, Arizona—on private planes. Each morning, Lee and I would do the local radio and television stations to push the movie and that night's concert. And each evening, we'd run out onto the stage with, "Hey! Hey! How you doing, Dallas?!" or wherever we were, and show a quick clip from the film before introducing the band. It was my first introduction to the rock-and-roll lifestyle.

Drugs were everywhere: pills of every color, coke, booze. Young women. Every cliché you'd imagine. It was a Costco for vice. It was 1978, but the Beach Boys were still living like it was 1968.

There were thousands in the seats each night and the audience was always 70 percent female, the mothers who'd grown up listening to the Beach Boys and, now, their teenaged daughters. It was the first time I saw the true power of a rock star—far from the stage reaction I would get doing Shakespeare. And this is the Beach Boys, mind you. This wasn't Zeppelin or Mötley Crüe. These guys played poppy classic hits from a decade before and the audience still trembled and gaped like it was a religious revival or a summer pagan fertility ritual. The boys in the band had their pick of the ladies. And pick they did.

I'd seen some things in Hollywood and had enough experiences myself—checked off the threesome box and whatnot—but these guys were at a whole other level. Sex and drugs seemed the goal of the day; the music was just the means.

My new friend Anna, after being sprung free from my room, spent the next several days with Brian Wilson. She'd spent the *previous* several days with Dennis Wilson. Not totally bad for my ego, but they don't call them groupies for nothing.

There were always a lot of groupies around: locals but also favorites who the Boys flew in. The partying went on until 4:00 a.m., and I'd grab enough sleep to hit the radio stations the next—uh, *the same*—morning.

Dennis Wilson, in particular, was crazed. Shockingly, the Beach Boy who had been friends with Charles Manson was a wild man. His appetite for *everything* was insatiable. He'd screw a snake if he could get it to lie still long enough. He was taking on two or three girls a day in between the drinking and the cocaine. Then Dennis would give a killer performance for two-plus hours and start again until the early hours of the next day. (Coincidence: Dennis later married Karen Lamm, an actor in *Almost Summer*.)

I'd been with these guys for only two weeks, and I already needed to get to rehab. My body felt bloated and my vision was blurry. I was running on fumes while the experts were just getting revved up. The only thing that saved me from corporeal collapse was Mike Love, who was deeply into transcendental meditation. I was toying with meditation at the time myself, and he and I would meditate together every day. Getting those few moments in the day of restoration is the only way I survived.

After promoting the film on stage, Lee and I would stand in the wings and watch the show. Most nights, the band members would toss us a tambourine to bang on and get us out on stage beside the backup singers to help out with "California Girls" or "Sloop John B." Eventually, Lee and I headed back to L.A. and the Beach Boys continued their tour. Days later, following another concert in Arizona, Dennis was arrested for sharing drugs and alcohol with an underage girl in his hotel room.

Meanwhile, I completely detoxed and slept for days. I'd been on the road for less than a month, and it exhausted me. These guys—the three Wilson brothers, Mike Love, and Al Jardine—had somehow been doing it since 1958.

———

IN *ALMOST SUMMER*, I LOVED THE PART I PLAYED BUT FELT A BIT typecast. The handsome jock surfer guy. I yearned to play more outrageous, wilder, and funnier parts and knew it was time to reinvent myself—it was time for my seven-year switch. My career would end in a whimper if I didn't do something new. Improving my comedic skills and working on improv seemed a natural extension of the work I'd been doing on stage.

I joined a new improv troupe in L.A. called the Groundlings.

The Groundlings had started in a basement but were now renting a permanent work space. Future *Saturday Night Live* cast members Laraine Newman and Phil Hartman were around. Pee-wee

Herman (Paul Reubens) was in the class just behind me. This crew was unmistakably different from my formal and rigid Strasberg/Stanislavski training. In improv, rule number one is just say yes. Yes to your partners' choices, yes to the situation, and don't try to be funny—trust what is there and go with the group. For a year, I was gaining confidence about doing this new type of acting.

While working with the Groundlings, my agent sent me a script, telling me it was the funniest he'd ever read. I read it that night, and not only was it the funniest script I'd ever read too, it was also written unlike anything I'd ever seen. It was outrageous, bold, and innovative. It was also filled with profanity and observations on racism and sexism, and crossed about every line of cinema propriety I'd had to adhere to for years, all with a knowing wink and intelligence. Its attitude was a full-frontal assault against the boring, straight-laced attitudes of society, in the spirit of the movie *M*A*S*H*, which I worshipped.

I knew I *had* to be in this movie—that if I got this part, it would change my life. I called my agent back the very next morning.

"Did you see a part for yourself?" he asked hopefully.

"Eric 'Otter' Stratton," I replied. "Rush chairman of Delta House. Damn glad to meet you."

Double Secret Probation

Sigma Alpha Epsilon's credo is dubbed "The True Gentleman," 125 words about good will, self-control, honor, and the feelings of others. Every fraternity brother has to learn it before being initiated, so the seven SAEs who were currently beating the crap out of me all knew it.

The night had had a more promising start.

The cast of *Animal House*—minus John Belushi, who was back in New York doing *Saturday Night Live*—was partying at the Sigma Nu house at the University of Oregon, Eugene. The Sigma Nu house was the one we'd rented for the *interior* shots of Delta House (the exterior shots were of an abandoned halfway house next door). The cast had joined the film crew *and* Sigma Nus to paint the inside of their house for the film. The brothers of Sigma Nu were good guys. Their motto was "Love, Honor, Truth," and they didn't disappoint; we were welcomed with open arms from the first handshake, paintbrush, and beer.

While at the Sigma Nu party celebrating the day's painting, Bruce McGill (Daniel "D-Day" Simpson) and I had hit it off with a couple of the female college students in attendance. They asked if we'd like to join them to check out another fraternity party.

Why not? Let's go awhile and have some fun. We'll go be "college kids." Stanislavski would be so proud.

"Great!" I agreed, threw my arm around one of the co-eds, and waved over James Widdoes (Hoover), Peter Riegert (Boon), Karen

Allen (Katy), Tom Hulce (Pinto), and even James Daughton (Marmalard). It was the only time during the entire production we let an Omega hang out with the Deltas.

The young women took us straight to this enormous colonial mansion: the Sigma Alpha Epsilon house. "It's the hottest best fraternity house!" our lovely Oregon tour guides assured us.

I'd embraced my Otter role and shepherded us all through the gauntlet of drunk young men armed with red Solo cups and cigarettes into the house. We clearly didn't belong. Everyone in our group, except the actual co-eds and Tom Hulce, was in their *very* late twenties. We were also dressed like actors from New York and L.A. These college students, twenty-one at best, were mostly from rural Oregon and dressed, with all respect, as if Lyndon Johnson were still running things. James Daughton, the women, and I had worked our way upstairs to where the main party was. Only later did I learn that not everyone had made it inside; half our squad had been blocked at the front door.

The top floor had an enormous billboard of New York City covering the giant ballroom's wall, the whole city skyline. I'd been in Hollywood all my life, and this was still one of the most impressive homes I'd ever been in. This floor served as the SAE's own disco, and the *Saturday Night Fever* soundtrack was pounding like a backwoods Studio 54. The young women who brought us upstairs got us some drinks, and we were talking again. Seemed the night was off to a fine start and a predictable (wink wink) end. Once again, I was wrong.

A few minutes later, James Daughton was pulling at my arm. "We gotta go . . ." he said. I'd just met him a few days earlier, but I'd seen that same fear in some eyes during basic training.

"What's the problem?"

"I just I ran into a guy . . . Said he's president of the frat or something. They want us out. They're really pissed."

"Why? What's the issue?" I wasn't worried. Yet.

"He said the party's for SAE members only, and we should *not* be here." James's eyes darted wildly around behind me.

"Let me talk to him," I said. I was Otter, a rush chairman, after all. *How hard could this be?* "I'd be 'damn glad to meet him.'"

Several SAEs were already approaching. "Hey, guys . . ." I said, and held out my hand to shake. I noticed instantly that while I'd recently gotten a bad haircut to look 1962-ish, these guys had that same haircut. It was 1977. "I'm Tim and this—"

"You need to get out of here," the shortest of the three guys began. All three were clearly drunk. "You don't belong here."

"Yeah, that's what my friend was telling me," I agreed. "We didn't mean to crash, man. These girls invited us and—"

"They don't invite. *We* invite. And you're not welcome here. So get the fuck out."

I held up both my hands high now. Forget this. "Okay, okay . . ." I deescalated. "I get it. You're absolutely right. No disrespect meant. Just a misunderstanding. We're sorry, and we'll get going. We'll collect the rest of our crew and—"

"You'll get the fuck out now."

Right. (Of all social frats in the US today, SAE is the only one founded in the antebellum South; I'm just gonna leave that here for now.) I collected James and the co-eds, and we were all swiftly ushered back down the steps. I tried to keep calm as we descended the stairs, reassuring the SAE "escorts" that we were sorry to have offended and would leave ASAP.

I got James and our hostesses out and into the yard, and then I turned to look for everybody else in our group. By this time, three frat guys around us had become fifteen. *Thus the point of fraternities, I guess.* There was blood in the water, and the sharks were doing more than circling. Stepping out onto the huge front veranda, I could see a situation had developed. In the yard outside, Bruce McGill and my other cast-mates were about thirty yards away, separated from me by what seemed like 400 drunk guys in light blue button-downs all talking shit.

"You Hollywood faggots trying to fuck our girls?" one of the guys outside demanded, and his beer-fisted pals laughed.

Jamie Widdoes (Delta House president) couldn't let it go. "That doesn't even make sense," he mocked. Then—in a decision I'll let him address himself—Jamie slapped the red Solo cup of beer out of the hand of a clear descendant of Sasquatch who was taunting him. It flew, seemingly in slow motion, over the frat guys and smashed off the SAE porch wall nearest me and onto half a dozen SAEs in an explosion of Schlitz. Then everything went off.

Beer-spattered SAEs now turned on me in strangely choreographed unison. *I'm a dead man . . .* I recognized. Four of what could only be linebackers had targeted me, and I found myself forced to retreat back into a veranda corner. Fists rained down on me from all sides. I ducked, did my best rope-a-dope, where their fists now only landed on the top on my head. What choice did I have? Hey, I'm an actor! *And* it was four on one.

Then as if sent by divine intervention, a "true gentleman." Probably the only sober SAE in the house, or maybe the only one who actually grasped the credo, stepped in front of me to take on the wrath of these other guys himself. This enormous kid, bigger than the rest by half a foot and fifty pounds, stepped directly between his brothers and me. "Take it easy guys!" he shouted, holding out his arms and physically pushing his own frat brothers away. "Calm down! Just let 'em get out of here." I was back in the corner still, crouched behind this lad. Drunk brothers continued taking cheap shots, and this SAE was still standing tall. This true gentleman looked back at me, "You need to get out of here, man."

"Got it," I said, deflecting another blow.

He kept his arms up for my defense, while I ducked down and tried to get out of there. Reaching the front steps, I got shoved from behind to the ground on the lawn. Bruce McGill had managed to shove his way back from the street to help me and was lifting me up. Karen was outside, ignored by the SAE guys, and just screaming at the top of her lungs, *"Leave them alone!!"* Which only riled them up more.

The rest of our gang had worked safely to the outside of the melee by now. But what seemed like a circle of death had tightened around Bruce and me for some reason. I could see that Bruce had already taken a good shot to one eye. "We know who you pussies are!" they shouted. "Get out, pussies!" *Pussies* seemed to be the only word they now knew. It was fifty-plus of them and two of us, pussies maybe, but discretion was clearly the better part of valor, as the circle tightened.

"Whatever we do," I said to Bruce. "Don't run. That'll just set things off worse." *Wait, was that advice for drunk frat guys or bears?* The punches started again from all sides, and we were both knocked back to the ground. With mouthfuls of dirt, Bruce and I locked eyes and said at the same time: "Run!"

We both sprang up and bolted off like our lives depended on it. I hadn't run like this even in the Marines. A couple of SAEs chased us for blocks, but at this point, Bruce and I were cackling in joy as we ran. We'd wanted a real college experience, and we had gotten one. Everyone made it out, but there *were* Delta casualties: Jamie had two chipped teeth. Bruce had a black eye. Peter and I had bumps and scratches. No one got laid. And filming was set to begin in less than thirty-six hours.

WE WENT RIGHT TO OUR DRILL SERGEANT, CLIFF COLEMAN.

Cliff was the film's first assistant director and an old salt who'd been in the business for years as an AD on movies like *The Wild Bunch*, *Shampoo*, and *The Longest Yard*. There were no troubles we could bring him that he hadn't already dealt with tenfold working with Sam Peckinpah, Warren Beatty, and Burt Reynolds.

Six of us now stood in his tiny motel room, bloodied and battered. There was a ring of emptied beer cans and bottles lined carefully around his four walls; every time he drank one, he'd place it beside the last. We hadn't even begun shooting, and he'd already started the second lap around the room.

"You fucking idiots," he grumbled. "I told you to stay away from townies and college kids."

"What do we do?" Jamie asked, running his thumb along his newly chipped teeth. We were all terrified about what would happen when John Landis, the film's director, found out what we had done.

"You shut your stupid mouth," Cliff told us, getting up. "Landis doesn't ever hear about this shit. You got it? He's got enough on his plate right now without worrying about you morons. I'll take care of it."

And he did. Cliff found a local dentist, and Jamie had his teeth capped the very next morning. Cliff also quietly arranged to have our makeup artist cover up McGill's black eye *before* McGill went in officially for his D-Day makeup.

It was a few days before word somehow got out. Landis was furious. Belushi, true to form, had to be physically restrained from going to the SAE house and seeking reprisal.

I don't think I've been to a real frat party since.

———

I LOVED THE *NATIONAL LAMPOON* AND HAD BEEN READING IT AND laughing at its provocative covers for years. From "True Facts" and "Foto Funnies" to articles by the likes of Doug Kenney, P. J. O'Rourke, and future mega-creator John Hughes and art by Rick Meyerowitz. So when my agent sent me *Animal House*, I knew I had to be in it. Also, it was the best script I'd ever read. (Until I read Aaron Sorkin's *West Wing* twenty years later, this remained true.)

But Landis and the producers (*Lampoon* publisher Matty Simmons and Ivan Reitman) wouldn't even let me audition. They'd seen my TV stuff and told my agent, "No thanks. He's a cowboy or a surfer. He's not for us." Their minds were already locked on what kind of actor I was. And roguish preppie wasn't it.

By this point, I knew enough folks around town and asked a favor from one of the Universal executives (Thom Mount, a future president of Universal and a studio producer I'd just finished *Almost Summer* for). "Just get me in there," I pleaded. "And if I fall on my face, then I can walk away from it. But just give me a shot."

"How about Greg Marmalard?" They offered the snotty Omega Theta Pi president. "You'd be a perfect—"

"No fucking way," I replied. "I'd rather not be in the movie." I was done playing that guy, the squeaky-clean boy next door. And I sure as hell wasn't going to be the guy with the "Is-it-supposed-to-be-this-soft?" dick. I wanted to be the guy with the bigger cucumber.

I begged and cajoled my Universal connection even more and, thanks to a favor to a favor for a favor (which is how a lot gets done, or did get done, in entertainment), eventually, they caved. The producers and director of *Animal House* agreed to let me come in, with my long hair and everything, and give it a shot.

Peter Riegert and I auditioned together, and the audition was one of those that just took off. I tweaked some old Kurt Russell, talked about "major league yabbies," pretended to trim nose hairs while we talked, and whistled "Peter and the Wolf." Peter and I were improvising as if we'd worked together for years, and Landis, Reitman, and the casting team were just in tears. I had a second audition a week later with the same dynamism and result in the room.

"Wait outside just a minute!" Landis grinned with an energy uniquely John Landis. From the hallway, on the other side of the door, I could hear all this commotion going on and gales of laughter. Eventually, the door opened again and Landis came bounding out. "You're fantastic," he held his hands wide like an excited child. "You're going to get this part! You're gonna be Otter!"

I was speechless. Never did a producer or director tell the actor the truth in this situation. They were worried it would weaken their salary negotiation position. Landis didn't care; he was just happy to have found his Otter.

"But," he said, "don't tell a soul that I said that. Don't tell a soul! Swear now, we never spoke! Swear!!"

"I swear, John," I said. I shook his hand. "Thank you so much!"

Outside, I ran to the first pay phone I could find and found a dime to call my agent, John Gaines. "I got the fucking part!" I yelled.

He'd started congratulations when I stopped him with, "But don't tell a soul!"

I'd gotten the dream part. An opportunity to rebrand and jump-start my whole career. Then I could—

Wait. Another hurdle first. *Always* one final hurdle.

This time, that hurdle was Chevy Chase.

—

To get the movie green-lit, *National Lampoon* and Ivan Reitman needed a star—and the studio wanted Chevy Chase. As Otter! But that wasn't John Landis's vision for this movie. He already had a star in Belushi, and Landis didn't want this film to turn into some sort of improv-comedy silly fest. He wanted to surround Belushi with *actor* actors—not comedians.

The story goes that Matty Simmons, Ivan Reitman, and John Landis all took Chevy Chase out for lunch. Matty and Ivan, hoping to convince Chevy to do the movie . . . John, less so. Ivan knew Chevy from the successful Lampoon off-Broadway show, and he and Matty were telling Chevy how much they'd love him for Otter. "This will be great for your career," Landis suddenly piped in. "You do this wild college frat film, and you'll be one of about eight guys, so you won't have to work that hard. And if it bombs, so what? Because it's an ensemble!" Matty reportedly kicked Landis under the table several times to get him to shut up. "Or, you're, what . . ."

Landis continued. "You're gonna do this movie with Goldie Hawn, and it's just you and her, and you're the star, or *she's* the star, of this romantic comedy? And sure, great as a first movie for you *if* it's a hit. But what if it fails? Yikes! You totally wanna be in our gang comedy!"

A little reverse psychology. Chevy's ego won out, and he chose *Foul Play* and the chance to be the sole male star. And I'm sure the real payday didn't hurt. Landis was now free to officially cast me as his Otter.

The part was mine, but there was no money, barely one-fourth of my usual rate. Yet this job wasn't about the money. It was a long-term strategic move, a career reset. There are different kinds of currency.

What *had* been promised at the start of contract talks was second billing. I'd wanted my name right behind John Belushi's when those credits rolled and on the posters and so on. Most moviegoers pay zero attention to such things, but the Hollywood powers that be, who decide what an actor's next job will be, do. In my effort to rebrand myself in the industry as a comedic actor, it mattered. The deal is closed, I'm ready to sign it, and Universal legal drops one last little problem on me.

"John Vernon wants second billing."

Dean Wormer? John Vernon was famous for . . . nothing really. Being the bad guy in Eastwood's *The Outlaw Josey Wales*, I guess. Other than that, he was just a TV guy like me; only he'd been doing it longer. Sounded like we were both trying to rebrand ourselves on this film.

They were pulling all this at the very last minute. Amending the "final draft" of a contract I'd been waiting to sign.

"I'll drop out," I threatened, and meant it. "I'm not doing this part unless I get second billing. It's *that* important to me." After months of begging even for an audition, I was now making demands. I believed so strongly that it mattered.

And for three days, I heard nothing. My agent promised to get back to me after he spoke with the studio. Silence, silence. Ear-piercing silence.

If you watch the film, you'll know what happened.

———

THE UNIVERSITY OF OREGON WAS THE ONLY CAMPUS THAT WOULD let us shoot our film. The producers had made a list of perfect schools, and twelve colleges in six states read the script and said: "Nope, nope." "This is scandalous, outrageous." "No, no, no." "You're nuts." In Eugene, however, brand-new university president William Boyd proved to be Faber College's savior. Years before, as an administrator at the University of California, he'd gotten the script of a film that wanted to shoot on campus and he'd said no because he thought the "script was no good." That movie was *The Graduate*, the number one box office movie of 1967 that earned seven Oscar nominations. It was not a mistake he'd make again ten years later. (So much so that Boyd's actual office, horse and all, was used as Dean Wormer's office.)

In classic Hollywood style, Landis had the Deltas all arrive at the University of Oregon a week early. It was under the pretense of rehearsals, but he just wanted us hanging out and becoming brothers. We spent all day and night together. Landis took us all to a local barber shop and asked for some 1960s-style cuts, and all us Deltas got our hair chopped side by side.

We also all stayed, as did most of the crew, at the Rodeway Inn in nearby Springfield. A two-story brick building that looked more like a row of dentist offices than your standard small-town motel.

From the first night, Bruce McGill's room was party central. Every evening, there must have been thirty-plus people in that motel room at all hours. McGill's character had few lines and, more to the point, was only in Belushi scenes. And because Belushi was only in town half the week (the other half with *SNL*), Bruce had little to do most nights other than play host. There was plenty of beer, booze, pot, and coke (it was 1977, after all). This is where the writers discovered that Bruce could play the *William Tell* Overture on his Adam's apple. It was 1977, and half the people there knew how to play some guitar and people would be singing until 3:00 a.m. It got a little rowdy.

Belushi, for the record, was clean on set during *Animal House*. If he did anything, it was away from the rest of us, and he never gave any signs he was up to anything. Landis had warned Belushi to keep on his best behavior and made sure it was a drug-free set.

I hadn't come to Eugene to party but to give my career a needed revamp. Call me square, but I wasn't going to risk wrecking that with too many late-nighters. My only significant contribution to the party scene was the piano in McGill's room. I'd noticed earlier that the hotel had an upright piano parked to the side of the lobby in the building across from where we were all staying.

"Let's just grab it," I told him. "It's what any good Delta would do."

Five minutes later, we'd somehow forced the piano between a couple doorways and were dashing it across the parking lot like a battering ram to the cheers of those waiting at McGill's doorway. Bruce dropped down and instantly fired up some Bruce Springsteen he knew. The new centerpiece of the party and home to liquor bottles, pizza boxes, and local gals' bottoms for the next five weeks.

Bruce McGill

John Landis did some wonderfully unique things to make sure the Deltas bonded as Deltas. He had everyone fly into Eugene at the same time for a Deltas' cast dinner. He knew there could be some tension between Belushi's fame, the East Coasters' dedication to the art of acting (McGill, Hulce, Allen, and Riegert), and the West Coasters' Hollywood point of view (Stephen Furst and me). And before the meal was over, we had all naturally slid into our character roles so much so that the banter sounded like it has been written for the movie. That night was one of the most important of my life. Not because of Animal House, but because of Bruce McGill.

When dinner was over, McGill shouts out, "Okay . . . So who wants to do tequila shots with me?" It was a test, Bruce being Bruce. This was, to be clear, the first movie where his name would actually appear in the credits (he'd go on to play another 160-plus roles), but he still needed to read the room. I was the only one who took the bait. And we've been together ever since. (Perhaps this tequila bonding saved my face at the SAE house.)

A best friend, the best man at my second wedding, a confidant, the pal who would help me bury a body if called on, and—as often goes with such pals—the guy who almost got us both killed multiple times. One of my fondest honors is McGill asking me to introduce him when he was inducted to the Texas Film Hall of Fame. To mark the occasion, I held up the mic as he plunked the William Tell Overture on his throat, just as he'd done in 1977.

I'm not sure how you know Bruce beyond Delta House—Rizzoli & Isles, MacGyver, The Insider, My Cousin Vinny, Reacher—but you do. And like Gary Goetzman before, you never know from where the real friends are going to show up. The genuine soul mates. For me, Daniel "D-Day" Simpson was one of the few.

Bang, bang, bang! A decade-plus after Animal House, someone was hammering fists angrily on a door somewhere. I awoke groggily and looked around. For half a second, I believed I was still on the Beach Boys tour and bodyguard Rocky was heatedly looking for me! Hotel room. Dallas? Yes, Dallas, I'd roused enough to recall that. So . . . not Rocky. And Bruce McGill, of all people, was asleep and snoring softly in the other bed a few feet away.

That's right! He and I were headed to Scotland to play golf. (A fun sentence to write!) We were single at the time and both productive actors, so a week of golf in Scotland was part of why you fought so hard to stay in this crazy career. I'd recently convinced him it was okay to drop out of a Broadway show he'd grown tired of after two years. I had stacks of reward points to use and promised to cash them in for us. His only job had been to arrange the tee times at the most amazing courses: St Andrews, Muirfield, Carnoustie, Turnberry. Our flight to Edinburgh was out of Dallas, so we'd decided to meet there, play a round, and spend the night first to warm up for the higher Caledonian grasses. By midnight, we were in a local Dallas bar chatting up the local women. The boys from Delta were out!

Wait . . . I sat up fully for the first time and scanned the rest of the room.

A local Dallasite stood in the doorway of the room's bathroom, mostly naked and hastily buttoning up her blouse. Her eyes were wide. Her pants were still only half on. "It's my boyfriend . . ." she whispered.

"Your . . . what?"

"I have to talk to him," she told me.

"No shit," I gaped. "How did . . . ?"

Yes, she'd come back to the room with Bruce and me. Yes, she'd maybe spent time on both sides of the room during the evening. Yes, Bruce and I were in deep shit.

The fist thumping continued further down the hall this time. Her name shouted from the man—loud enough finally to wake my old pal.

Bruce wiped the sleep away from one side of his face, looking at me. And then the girl. Then he laughed and rolled over, away from the commotion.

The young woman cracked the hotel door and slipped outside into the hall. I'd jumped up behind her to barricade the room with door chains and my naked hip. Peering through the fish-eye peephole, my ear pressed against the hard, cold hotel door, I could see his hulking form, her hands against his Dallas chest, but couldn't really hear their muffled conversation.

Suddenly, alarmingly loudly . . .

"I can't believe you slept with Tim Matheson!"

The sentence roared through the walls. People in Fort Worth probably heard this guy. I lunged for my suitcase and some clothes. Bruce was already snoring again.

The young woman somehow got her boyfriend out of the hotel, but the next few hours in Dallas were fraught. I was thankful to have a tee time some 4,000-plus miles away.

Of course, we didn't actually have tee times. This Bruce finally confessed halfway across the Atlantic. Some guy Bruce had asked to set up everything had flaked out, and Bruce hadn't called ahead either. These are some of the most prestigious and exclusive courses and clubs on the planet. You can't just walk on. There was nothing to be done from thirty-five thousand feet over the Atlantic. Bruce was apologetic, both about having fucked up and about neglecting to mention it to me until about 34,999 feet too late. "Road trip?" I winked. Bruce smiled back. "It'll be okay," I reassured him, "We can do anything we want, we're college students."

When we got to the Royal & Ancient Golf Club of St Andrews—a place people make tee-time reservations years in advance—we just walked up to one of the course marshals and explained our situation. The starter put us out as a pair predawn, ahead of the first official group at 6:00 a.m. We teed off ten minutes before the sun crested St Andrews Bay.

The whole trip went like this. From rounds of golf to finding last-minute places to sleep, to getting fortuitous last-second rides to the airport on the way out. Everything always worked out perfectly. Total chaos, yet utterly blessed.

I always knew things were going to be okay with this guy.

Still do.

Animal House writers Chris Miller and Doug Kenney were always the smartest guys on set. Doug, in particular, was the sharpest, funniest man I think I've ever met. He'd founded the *National Lampoon* and been the heart and soul of that magazine, but even that success, I think, left him tortured. By the time he got to Eugene, you could see he was riding a delicate balance. Fame and Doug did not go hand in hand, and he was about to experience an unimaginable success. (More on Doug later; for now, we'll leave him in Eugene playing Delta Dwayne "Stork" Storkman, overseeing mounds of coke at the parties and effortlessly tossing out punched-up dialogue when called on.)

Atop the whole operation, of course, was John Landis. The perfect guy in the right place at the right time. You'd never have guessed he was making his first big feature film. He was an amazing director, his energy ideal for this group and the tight schedule. In our first read through he would exclaim, "Terrible! You were all absolutely terrible! Okay . . ." He'd stop. "*One* of you was good—but I'm not gonna say who!" He kept this same energy up when we were shooting. Without cutting he'd shout, "Do it again, funnier!" We'd laugh, team up, and do it again.

He also reined in the film in two critical ways.

"They *have* to like you. The audience has to like you," Landis counseled. "So, you can't do mean things! To the Omegas and the college, sure. But never, *never* to each other."

There was a line in the script, we're on our way to the Emily Dickinson College, and Flounder does one of his "Oh boy is this great! I hope we get dates and that mine has big tits." And Otter turns and says, "At least as big as yours."

We tried one take, and Landis goes, "No, no, no, no. It's not nice! You can't be mean to Flounder." He was always protecting our characters from being unkind. He even added the quick shot of the Emily Dickinson dates walking back home together from the Dexter Lake Club to show they got home okay. The Deltas were goofs but not cruel.

Riegert and I filmed a scene (which was partially deleted from the final film) where I'm talking on the phone with a coed who is breaking our date, saying, "Oh really? Oh, come on now, she'd want you to go. Oh listen . . . sure, all right." Otter hangs up and Boon jokes, "Let me guess, washing her hair?" And I reply, "No, dead mother."

Again, spot-on *Lampoon*, but Landis was always aiming for a broader audience. And so, he always knew what to cut (like Otter on the phone not being sympathetic). One of my favorite scenes from the original script that Landis, wisely, cut was a moment from our road trip when the Deltas pick up a scruffy hitchhiker holding a sign reading "NY or Bust." This guy sardines himself into our car with his guitar case. "What's your name, kid?" Boon asks. "Zimmerman, Bob Zimmerman [a.k.a. Bob Dylan]. Going to New York to see Woody Guthrie," he mumbles in distinctive Dylanese. Otter looks to Boon and comments, "Articulate son of a bitch, huh?" "Wanna hear a song?" Zimmerman asks. "Knock yourself out," Otter says. Strum, strum: "Hey, hey Woody Guthrie, I wrote you this song . . ." The car slams on the brakes, and we toss Dylan and his guitar out. This exact joke was accomplished better and quicker when Bluto smashes Stephen Bishop's guitar on the staircase. That was all Landis.

Film School Boot Camp

Directing is About More than Knowing Where to Put the Camera

People are always asking me what it was like to work with Belushi in *Animal House*. It was great, but one lesson from that film that I have carried with me throughout my career was taught not by Belushi but by John Landis. Landis made some of the greatest comedies of all time—*Coming to America*, *Trading Places*, *Animal House*—and threw in the *Thriller* music video to boot. I've always believed that one of his secrets was his ability to meet the cast where they were and to find ways to bond them as a cast rather than a collection of actors.

In Eugene, Oregon, Landis used haircuts—of all things—to bond the Deltas. There was only one barber in the shop, an older local fellow from Chicago, and one by one, we'd step into the chair. Belushi absolutely refused to get his hair cut, telling Landis that he had to do *SNL* and needed it like it was. As each of us settled into the chair, we would all vote on what type of haircut each of us would get. Meanwhile, Belushi was waiting for us across the street, in a pub, to see our results. Doug Kenney as Stork: nerdy cut!! Bad, nerdy cut!! Me as Otter: Cary Grant or John F. Kennedy. Then it was Bruce McGill's turn as D-Day. Landis wanted Bruce to have a buzz cut like Lee Marvin's in *The Dirty Dozen*. McGill told Landis that he had a cut in mind he'd like to try first. And, he said, "If you don't like it, then we'll do the Lee Marvin and cut it all off." Landis agreed. Bruce sat in the chair and told the barber he wanted a flattop with fins on the side. Also called ducktails. "You mean a Chicago Boxcar," the barber said. "I used to do ten of these a day on the South Side!" "Yeah!" we all chanted. In about ten minutes, the Chicago barber had transformed McGill into D-Day. And after one look, Landis screamed, "That's it! That's fantastic! We'll keep it!! C'mon with me!" He grabbed Bruce and took his barber cape off as we all moved across the street toward the pub. Once inside, Landis held up the cape in front of Bruce, so that Belushi couldn't see D-Day's haircut. Landis crowed loudly, "John, you are going to be so jealous when you see D-Day's haircut! You're gonna be so sorry you didn't get yours cut!" Belushi smiled and said, "Show me!" Landis pulled the cape aside, revealing D-Day and his cut. "Chicago boxcar!" Belushi screamed along with Landis and McGill. That was what convinced Belushi to get his hair trimmed too and bonded us not as a cast but as the fraternity brothers of Delta House.

The other deft brilliance of John Landis was in keeping us all playing it straight. A couple of fourth-wall breaks to the audience, sure. But the real comedy came from treating *Animal House* as if it were a "serious" film. (The exact same reason he hired Elmer Bernstein, composer of *The Ten Commandments*, *To Kill a Mockingbird*, and *The Great Escape* to do the comedy film's score.)

Landis had fought to get actors like Cesare Danova (Mayor Carmine DePasto), John Vernon (Dean Wormer), and Verna Bloom (Mrs. Wormer)—very formidable actors who had mostly done serious work. And when Vernon kept trying to be funny, Landis would do his now-trademarked "No, no, no, no" to get him back to a villain worthy of Clint Eastwood. We'd be doing the double secret probation scene, and Vernon would offer up some ideas he thought were funny. "I'll do this and then I'll do this," and Landis would just smile and wave off the suggestion as if speaking to all of us: "Just say the lines, guys. It's perfect the way it is."

Vernon or me *trying* to be funny—it's okay.

Vernon or me playing it like we're actual people—you may have a hit comedy.

Bruce McGill and I would drive out to the airport on many Sundays to pick up Belushi, who flew back and forth between Eugene and New York, where he was doing *SNL*. John's wife, Judy, wanted him to get to their house and be resting as soon as possible; there were a lot of drugs around *SNL* back then. John would be in New York Thursday to Sunday and in Eugene the rest. You could feel him just totally relax as soon as he was home with Judy. He'd have to be the Samurai Deli Server, the Killer Bee, or even Bluto, but when he was home with Judy, he was at peace.

Saturday Night Live was the biggest thing on television, and Belushi its most recognizable star. When he walked across the Oregon campus, it was like John Lennon was passing by. The college kids and locals shadowed him and parted for him like pilot fish. I was the most experienced actor in Delta but wasn't the biggest comedian in the world, like John. Whenever we worked together, John and I would build this wonderful support system. He watched me and helped me learn how to be funny and hit my timing; when I got it right, he'd always encourage me with a "That's good." For my part of the relationship, John would look to me on set and make sure he was keeping it grounded to his character and not making it an *SNL* sketch.

The more days the Deltas worked together, the more we bonded. In the scene where Delta House is being shut down and Pinto asks, "What are we going to do?" I suggested that I share with Peter Riegert the line about a road trip. I said, "Look, Otter and Boon are so tight, why don't we look at each other and say 'Road trip!' at the same time?" Landis agreed and we tried it. Little things like that bonded us in real life as our characters came to the forefront.

Stephen Furst (Flounder) took some more getting used to.

Frankly, I hated him when he first showed up.

He was so . . . earnestly innocent. He was all "golly gee" about everything in real life, not only as the bumbling freshman character. After about three days of this, I'd had enough of him: "Please shut the fuck up." The guy was only twenty-three and still managed to bring a wife and kids to Eugene to be there all five weeks with him. I grew very tired of his always being Flounder. And he told these stupid stories, which were *hopefully* made up, about how he accidentally froze his wet dog Fluffy, when he stuck him in the freezer to try and dry him or something. I literally said to him, "I don't like you. I will never like you. Just go away." He simply gave me that dumbass smile that made Flounder famous and walked away.

After a week or two, however, I kind of fell in love with the guy. Stephen just had this way about him, and you eventually capitulated. Landis had brought us together early for a reason.

Landis kept it a very light set, and because of him, we all felt comfortable playing around with each other, always part of his master plan. For instance, we shot the parade scene in the town of Cottage Grove, next to Eugene. It was the same town where Buster Keaton had shot his amazing silent film *The General*, and Landis screened that movie for all of us before our crew filmed there. These were the kind of little things he'd arrange to keep the production familial and fun. A simple box of popcorn and a classic movie next to your new buddies.

This is how we'd somehow successfully shot the movie in five weeks. That, and we had little time for anything else.

Well, we had time for women.

———

LADIES AND GENTLEMEN, I'LL BE BRIEF. THE ISSUE HERE IS NOT whether we broke a few rules or took a few liberties with our female colleagues; we did.

Local women were what got me through that fall, but I also fell in love *again* with a wonderful young actress. Sunny Johnson (who would soon be Jennifer Beals's ice-skater pal in *Flashdance)* had recently been in *Almost Summer* with me as the "prettiest girl in high school." She had a couple good scenes with lead Bruno Kirby and she was just twenty-four and staggeringly adorable. In rehearsals for *Almost Summer*, the director had characters improv together even if they didn't have actual scenes in the film together. After all, we were playing high school kids; it was like chatting in the hallways even if you didn't have class together. Sunny and I created a storyline of flirting classmates who had never gotten together. Very method. I got to know adorable Sunny really well but not intimately.

Then she was cast for a small scene in *Animal House*—a two-line scene of Otter taking another student to the motel where he later gets ambushed by the Omegas. (We shot it, but it didn't make the final cut. She's still listed in the credits as "Otter's Coed.")

So Sunny and I were reunited, and it was great fun being around her again. Everything was somewhat in place, quite frankly, for the opportunity to add a chapter or two to the *Kama Sutra. However . . .* Whitey Sacks, the dog-masturbating wrangler, once advised me in his low, gruff wisdom, "Tim, you don't ever ride the workin' stock." Crude, but it had put on-set fraternization into perspective for me for years. It's unwise to screw around where you're working. Adorable Sunny was safe from my advances as long as she worked on *Animal House.*

We finished the day shooting, a Saturday, the last day of our working week. Sunny came to me distraught. "Tim," she said, "they're making me fly home tonight. I'm done working on *Animal House.*"

How literally, I now wondered, *should I take Whitey Sacks's when-at-work policies?*

"I won't get back to L.A. until two a.m.," she said. "They already canceled my hotel room." She held one sad little adorable suitcase.

"This is bullshit," I said, first trying with the production manager to get her room back. "Not in the budget. Sorry," he said definitively. Innocently, I offered a solution. "Sunny, listen, I've got two beds in my room. No strings. Crash there and fly out tomorrow."

"You sure?"

"Absolutely, and I promise not to hit on you. We'll grab a quick dinner and then you can get some sleep. No big deal." And I meant it, too. My grandmother Sadie would have been proud.

Sunny agreed and came back with me to my room with her stuff. I pointed out her bed, which had never been touched, and then grabbed a beer from my little refrigerator and picked up my script for Monday's scenes. I told her just to settle in, and we'd head out for a bite to eat in a little bit.

"I'm going to take a quick shower before dinner," she announced, and headed straight to the bathroom.

Ten minutes later, the bathroom door opens, and mist bursts out like the start of a rock concert or a *Flashdance* routine. Sunny's got this towel wrapped around her from her chest down to just barely covering the curves of her twenty-four-year-old hips. Steam-slicked legs and shoulders, her skin fairly shimmered. She coyly tugged at the top of the towel. In slow motion it collected again at her feet, as her playful laugh sent actual shivers down my spine and her eyes connected with mine. Romantic and so very sweet. We never made it to dinner. *Sorry, Grandma.*

There was a deep connection between us. I fell and fell hard for Sunny. We gathered again as soon as I got back to L.A. We spent as much time together as we could, but all too soon, I was snagged out of town to shoot *The Apple Dumpling Gang Rides Again* with Tim Conway and Don Knotts. Sunny and I just couldn't get the timing right, and she eventually started seeing another actor named Archie Hahn, a fellow Groundling. So it just never happened for us. Our "high school" and "college" romance came to a swift end.

The timing was clearly not on our side. As a poet once said, "For all sad words of tongue and pen, the saddest are these: *It might have been.*"

Except, of course, for the night she'd been kicked out of Faber.

VERNA BLOOM PLAYED MRS. DEAN WORMER.

In 1977, she had been in *High Plains Drifter* and was a regular TV series player and a serious and successful Broadway actress. She also lived in New York with her husband. She was also turning forty in a few months.

"She'd like to rehearse the seduction scene with you," John Landis told me.

I knew where this was going. Verna had already dropped enough hints herself. We did not yet have the term *cougar* (I was barely clinging to my twenties myself), but I was old enough to understand that nearly 40-year-old women still had a pulse. "We ran through everything two days ago," I detailed. "And blocked it this morning."

"No, rehearse. Like . . . you know . . . *rehearse*. She's staying—"

"What are you doing?" I asked, dazed. "Passing notes in math class?"

"She's three thousand miles from home. Out here alone for five weeks . . ."

"John—"

"Jesus, Tim! She's turning forty!"

"John, stop. No. Way." I stood my ground. Verna was a lovely woman, but I wasn't going to "rehearse" just to make her feel better about an impending birthday.

Hers or mine.

Film School Boot Camp

Don't Sweat the Small Stuff

Bud Ekins was a legend in the movie business. A total pro and an old-school stuntman. He'd done the motorcycle jump for Steve McQueen over the barbed-wire fence in The Great Escape. He was a pal of McQueen's and would ride along with him, Lee Marvin, and Keenan Wynn on their weekly motorcycle journeys. Bud came up to drive the Deathmobile for the parade sequence in Animal House, and I convinced him to allow me to do a ride-along inside when he was doing the stunt. The first thing I noticed was that Bud was down low in the car, with all the Deathmobile rig blocking his view. He had a tennis-ball-sized opening to see where he was going. I asked Bud how he could see where he was going, and as cool as a cucumber, he said, "Hell, I can't see a damn thing. But I just drive into the stands until we stop!" He was so cool. His pulse was probably about 60 BPM. He checked over the way the car was running, how all of the main things were working, picked up the radio, and signaled that he was ready. Meanwhile, I braced myself, strapped in as I recall, and then came "Action!" over the radio. Bud had the car in neutral, revved the engine, and dropped it into gear. The wheels burned rubber, the car shook and launched ahead very, very quickly. Speed built and built as Bud sat stoically at the wheel and adjusted the wheel slightly, correcting his angle into the bleachers. *Boom!!* We smashed into the bleachers with a huge bang and grinding sound, and the car came to a halt, metal smashing down onto the top of the vehicle.

The look of relaxation and concentration on Bud's face said it all. "Know what you're doing, execute it per the plan. Don't sweat the small stuff." Those are the lessons I'll never forget. They apply to acting, directing, mowing the lawn, and everything in life.

———

ANIMAL HOUSE TOOK IN $140-PLUS MILLION ($650 MILLION BY today's math) on a budget of under just $3 million. That's just ticket sales; never mind the posters, T-shirts, DVDs, and TV series spinoffs. An absolutely massive success. It was the number two movie of 1978—couldn't quite catch *Grease*—and remains in the five highest-grossing comedies ever. Twenty years later, the Library of Congress would select *Animal House* for its National Film Registry as a rare work of cinema deemed "culturally, historically, or aesthetically significant."

A bunch of guys and gals in togas.

AROUND 1992, SOME TEN YEARS AFTER JOHN BELUSHI HAD PASSED, I was in Tampa Bay and crossed paths with DeWayne Jessie, who played the "Shout" singer Otis Day. He was now playing with local bands all across the county as Otis Day and the Knights. Preset, I approached to say hello. "DeWayne, great to see you again."

He smiled that huge smile that made him famous. "Otis," he corrected me. "The name is Otis Day." He'd legally changed his name years before. ("Say it right now, baby.") It was my first hint that school reunions are best left to memory and the imagination.

Sunny Johnson died tragically at thirty from a sudden brain hemorrhage. Belushi was gone. Doug Kenney, gone. Stephen Furst, gone. All passed away far too early. The past would have to remain where I'd first left it.

As further proof of the passage of time, I'd visited Universal Studios to do some research on *Animal House* for a possible project about the making of the film. I'd wanted the production notes and all the backstage stuff: prop notes, wardrobe, budgetary notes. But they'd all been tossed as a "fire hazard" when General Electric had briefly owned the studio. *Who cares what the Library of Congress thinks?* Meanwhile, there had also been a fire on Universal's back lot, and the studio had lost many negatives, including outtakes from our time at Faber College.

These bits and pieces are now never to be seen—unless you were in Eugene in the fall of 1977.

I'm damn glad I was.

—

You came for some Belushi stories. I know. He's who I'm asked about more than anyone else I've ever worked with, and I've worked with almost everyone.

Chris Farley's first question on *Black Sheep*: "What was it like working with Belushi?" Ryan Reynolds's first question on *Van Wilder*: "What was it like working with Belushi?" Alexandra Breckenridge's first question on *Virgin River*: "What was it like working with Belushi?"

The LAPD cop who arrested me for my DUI, tugging my handcuffs and shoving me into the back of *his* car: "What was it like working with Belushi?" Honest to God.

And so I would try and tell them. Now I'll try and tell you.

John Belushi

"Nothing Is Over Until We Decide It Is"

THE GUY OWED ME $100. THE *SNL* MEGASTAR.

John had a habit of borrowing money from people. "Hey, man . . . Can I get a hundred dollars? You got a couple fifties? You got any cash?" He and the Beatles were also famous for this; they just never carried cash. And you'd never hear about it again. Nobody would ever dare ask him for the money back or what he spent it on.

When I gave him the hundred bucks, I confirmed that he was going to pay me back—I'd worked for and was protective of every dime I had. "Yeah, yeah!" he said, grinning.

Days went by. Then, a week. At rehearsals, I started: "John, where's my hundred bucks?"

"Yeah, yeah, yeah!" he'd say, and pat my back and off he'd go.

Later that same day: "John . . . a hundred bucks?"

"Yeah, yeah, yeah!"

Finally, days later, I cut to the chase: "Belushi, you owe me a hundred dollars!"

"All right, all right!" He laughed and quickly got the money from somebody else to get square with me. "Here, Tim, here's your money." He eyed me curiously but with a genuine smile. I'd officially earned some respect from the Chicago kid. He'd always treated me as a closer friend *after* I demanded my money back.

I'T's DIFFICULT TO CONVEY THE IMPACT *SATURDAY NIGHT LIVE* HAD fifty years ago, when it first aired. For my generation, it was, "Holy shit! These people look like us and talk like us and are on television making fun of the things we make fun of." (The fact that almost the entire cast and several writers had come from the Lampoon Broadway show should not go unmentioned.) This wasn't *The Jackie Gleason Show* or Ed Sullivan's modern-day take on vaudeville. This wasn't for our parents; this was our friends on TV. We didn't have TiVo, and the VCR was still a new technology that almost no one could afford. With no internet to check out the best skits later, we actually gathered around TVs at 11:30 p.m. to watch the show live. Bars treated it like the World Cup. We would plan where we would go out based on if that bar would put the show on and if the crowds would be quiet enough for us all to enjoy the comedy together.

Belushi and Chevy Chase (now off filming with Goldie Hawn) were the two breakout stars, and John walked onto the *Animal House* set as one of the biggest celebrities in America. Rumors of the wild parties after *SNL* aired each Saturday were already trickling out on entertainment and gossip pages.

We expected a colossal coked-up prima donna to arrive from New York to lead the Deltas. The exact opposite is what we got.

John couldn't have been more wonderful. Everybody was in awe of the guy, and yet he proved so normal. Approachable. Genuinely friendly. All the id and raw energy was for characters in a scene and onstage. John—away from an audience—was quiet, thoughtful, and gentle.

For decades, there's been a conflict between East Coast and West Coast actors: Supposedly, the East Coast actors are more serious and better trained and are in it for the theatre and "the art," while the folks in L.A. are looked at as pretty people who make a lot of money on TV and don't really know their craft. This attitude had come onto the *Animal House* set (thus Landis's first-night dinner scheme), where most of the actors *were* from the East Coast.

But Belushi wasn't buying any of that crap. Firmly grounded in his Windy City upbringing, he treated every actor, no matter where the person was from, exactly the same. As close to a rock star as you could get during his meteoric rise, he couldn't have been more gracious or generous—with his time, attention, respect, or joyfulness.

Not easy to do on the schedule he'd signed up for.

Belushi was only on set for three days a week—Monday, Tuesday, and Wednesday—and then they'd put him on a red-eye Wednesday night to fly him back to New York for *Saturday Night Live*. Hours after the show, and the famed postshow party, they'd pour him back into a plane Sunday morning to get back to us Sunday night in time for some rest before *Animal House* scenes the next morning. It was a whirlwind. Somehow, he and wife Judy still made time for normalcy.

With Thanksgiving coming, Landis asked the cast and crew if we wanted to take the day off on Thursday, in the middle of our shooting week, or push through the week and take Saturday off and celebrate Thanksgiving then. The vote was to work the straight five days and move Thanksgiving to the weekend. *SNL* was off that week, and Judy and John offered to host our belated Thanksgiving dinner. All the Deltas were there; writers Doug Kenney and Chris Miller; producer Ivan Reitman; and several Omegas, too, including Mark Metcalf (Neidermeyer), Kevin Bacon (Chip), and James Daughton (Marmalard). Belushi had invited everyone, deliberately ignoring the unwritten—though mostly enforced—Deltas-don't-hang-with-Omegas rule.

He and Judy traveled with an expensive metal case outfitted with great speakers and the latest technology: cassette tapes. (When *Animal House* ended, I bought John and Judy's same setup for when I was stuck in hotel rooms and set trailers.) While we listened to the blues over turkey and stuffing and wine, I heard all about John's recent trip to the Eugene Hotel lounge for a Blues Night, where John had been fascinated by a young local blues singer and harmonica player named Curtis Salgado and had gotten an idea for a new character. (Also in Salgado's group was a young musician who had had a small part in

Animal House as a member of Otis Day and the Knights. He was a local Eugene student who would go on to become one of the most important blues guitarists in the world: Robert Cray.) By the time we were fighting over Judy's amazing pumpkin pie, I saw the first hints of Belushi as Jake Blues, as he sang along joyfully with the records and did some tryptophan-infused dance moves.

Belushi, an improvisation wizard, was always trying something new. Still a Groundling myself, I'd often stand by the camera and just watch him do his thing. The scene as he moves down the cafeteria food line stuffing his face, and pockets, with food was performed in one take and totally improvised. Landis just told the cameraman to stay with him, and John (sans the planted edible golf ball) did all the rest himself. I was now learning as much from peer Belushi as I had from legends like Jackie Gleason and Lucille Ball.

But this time, I was catching a legend at the *start* of his career.

A long career, we all assumed.

In 1978, John had a number one album (*Briefcase Full of Blues*, as the Blues Brothers, with Dan Aykroyd) and a number one movie with *Animal House* and was still king of *Saturday Night Live*.

He never had a prayer.

WHENEVER JOHN AND JUDY WERE IN L.A., I WAS A (MOSTLY) CLEAN friend who proved great to be around for John. Safe. In return, whenever I was in New York, Belushi insisted I spend time with both him and Judy, and I was more than happy to oblige. John couldn't have been more gracious and generous, so fun, so smart.

But walking on the edge all the time.

He and Aykroyd had done a small tour in support of the album, and I'd visited, taking in the concert before heading backstage to say hello. John now had two enormous bodyguards whose primary job was to keep people from giving him drugs. The misassumption was that John *was* Bluto. Every fan, actor, director, and hopeful woman figured the way to his affection or attention was through drugs: booze, cocaine, ludes, speed, pot, and, eventually, heroin.

These two goons stopped me from passing until Belushi noticed me and waved me over. John looked exhausted, distracted. Even with the bodyguards, he was clearly caught in the swirl.

By the time we worked together again in 1979 on Spielberg's *1941*, it was impossible to not see that the fame and lifestyle had taken their toll. He wasn't the same John. He looked exhausted, distracted. He could still shine, mostly, when Spielberg yelled action, but the focus was gone. And the warmth. To me, it felt like he was just going through the motions. It broke my heart.

But there was nothing, I thought then, I could do to save my friend.

The notion of pulling him aside to scream, "You're one of the *most talented actors* I've ever met! . . . *Don't ruin this!* Get *off* the drugs!" just wasn't realistic. He was a grown man. A megastar. We were friendly but not friends enough for me to free him from this. John was in his own orbit now.

Less than three years later, on March 5, 1982, John Belushi shot a "speedball," a mixture of coke and heroin, at the Chateau Marmont in L.A. and overdosed. He was thirty-three and gone forever. I was filled with sadness but not surprised.

I CLING ONLY TO THE MEMORIES OF THE JOHN I MET IN EUGENE, Oregon. The one before the fame and addictions got too big to battle anymore.

He'd come to my room to invite me out and noticed my slant board, my bike, and some free weights against one wall.

"What the hell is that?" he asked.

"A slant board," I explained. "You do sit-ups with it."

"Why?" he asked.

"John," I defended, "I gotta do a couple scenes with my shirt off. I need to look good."

"You're kiddin' me."

I assured him I wasn't, and Belushi just laughed. "I love it. That's so fucking Hollywood," he said. "Let's get outta here, man."

He and I went to find the other Deltas.

The Clown Princes

As with Belushi, I've been blessed to have had many of our finest and funniest cross my path over the years—from Bob Hope to David Spade, Margaret Cho to Howie Mandel. And too many of them—some of the greats—we have lost far too soon.

Sam Kinison—Sam hit the comedy scene like a hydrogen bomb and was, especially when not screaming "louder than Hell" in his signature delivery, one of the funniest people I ever met. We worked together on a show called *Charlie Hoover* for Fox in 1991. I played a mild-mannered accountant, and Kinison was the id voice in my head who would appear miniature style à la Jiminy Cricket to give me grab-the-world-by-its-balls advice. Okay, so maybe not quite like Jiminy Cricket. It was suggested, briefly, that we do the show with Sam as a full-size id, but ultimately his work was largely done in front of a green screen so he could he miniaturized on my desk or shoulder. The show lasted six episodes before Fox had seen enough. (Sam was born to stand before a live audience, not a green screen.)

Despite his reputation as a major fan of creative pharmacy, Kinison was a straight arrow through our pilot production. After Fox ordered up the series, I'd even congratulated him on getting off drugs. (This was right around the time I broke away completely myself.) Sam laughed that world-famous laugh. "I'm not straight," he said. "You ever have one of these?" He pulled out a plastic sandwich bag from his customary long coat—the bag chock-full with enormous red pills. I was dumbfounded. Kinison just giggled and put the bag away. "Maybe for later," he proposed. Just months after our show ended, Sam was killed in a head-on collision when a drunk teenager's pickup crossed the lines.

JOHN CANDY—JOHN BEFRIENDED ME WHEN I WAS PART OF STEven Spielberg's enormous *1941* cast. In that vast whirl of other actors, it was Candy who made me feel most welcome. He was fresh off Second City and *SCTV*, but his career was just taking off. Though basking in my recent *Animal House* success, I was still new to comedy and John always treated me like I'd been in Second City with him for years. He became a surrogate for Belushi when I realized Belushi had changed.

Candy and I landed on a routine, poking fun at me called "Tim Matheson's School for Actors." Its premise was an actor running a scam whereby he could teach people to act through the mail . . . also available in Spanish. Candy's aim, which cracked me up, was to poke fun at my Strasberg and Stanislavski days. John did multiple voices and characters—many which wouldn't fly today on any movie set or, if they were spelled out, in this memoir. But in 1979, he could get the cast laughing whenever he wanted.

John passed away from a heart attack at only forty-three and close to his top weight of 350 pounds. Like many comedians, I think, he'd fallen into the Oliver Hardy trap of connecting his size and shape to the comedy. He smoked a pack a day, and according to those close to him, binge eating had become his response to any professional setback—which, for working actors, happens often.

With movies like *Stripes*; *Planes, Trains and Automobiles*; *Home Alone*; *National Lampoon's Vacation*; *Splash*; *Spaceballs*; *Uncle Buck*; *JFK*, and so many others all still to come, it's hard to imagine setbacks. But that's how this business works. Anything short of topping the box office as a bona fide hit can feel like a failure if you let it. (This is one of the things I've learned over the years. Home runs are awesome, but you have to love them the same as you do the strike-outs. Many of the tortured artists I've worked with couldn't internalize this, and for some of them, the challenge of putting things in perspective took them from us all too soon.)

I could not have met John Candy at a better time. He was still filled with joy and appreciation for his burgeoning career and would prove to be one of our most brilliant comedic actors.

CHRIS FARLEY—CHRIS WAS SO GENEROUS AND KIND TO ME because he revered *Animal House*. Devotedly worshipped, actually. Belushi was the messiah, and I apparently one of the apostles. My directing career had kept me away from the silver screen for five years, and it had been another ten (oof!) since I had been in a *Fletch*-sized hit. So, the studio insisted I had to audition for *Black Sheep*, Farley's new film to follow *Tommy Boy*.

Auditions are job interviews, nerve-racking no matter how many times you do them. As I went in for mine to play Farley's brother in the movie, Chris showed up, unannounced. He burst in just to say "I love you" with unrestrained joy. "I think you're so great!" I didn't even have the part yet, but he still made me feel so relaxed and at home. Just the two of us talking like real people showed the producers, I think, that Chris and I *could* be brothers—like in the film.

On set, he smoked more cigarettes and drank more cups of coffee than anyone I've ever seen. John Candy was a moderate smoker and consumer compared to Farley. Chris would drink an iced coffee before almost every take. Not every scene, but every *take* of every scene. So, if the director needed a close-up, Chris would pound down *another* iced coffee. Twenty to thirty cups every day. Between coffees, he acted or smoked cigarettes. He had a compulsive personality, and smoking and coffee had replaced, for *Black Sheep*, his well-known drug addictions.

Chris was constantly the class clown. We had one scene with 150 background actors for a political rally and, between takes, he'd entertain them. He was the star of the movie and could have been napping in his trailer or clearing his headspace quietly somewhere. Instead, he was doing a slow striptease for 200 people while the production crew set up for the next shot. Chris couldn't help himself; he truly loved entertaining and making people laugh.

He and I did a bunch of photographs one day for the film to show our "history as college football players," and just hanging out with him alone for that afternoon was so special. He'd made me part of the film's team, made us brothers. You couldn't help but love this guy.

Months later, I saw him at the premiere of his next film, *Beverly Hills Ninja*, and he wasn't sober this time. Off the wagon again. This was dangerous, I knew, because I'd seen how addicted he was to caffeine and nicotine. And I'd seen his hero, John Belushi, meet his own end.

Chris died a year later. He was thirty-three. The similarities with John were heartbreaking. It was devastating, and it felt like losing Belushi all over again.

DOUG KENNEY—"WHERE'S DOUG?" ASKED KATHRYN WALKER on the phone. She had genuine fear in her voice. "We can't find Doug."

"Doug" was Douglas Kenney—cofounder of the *National Lampoon* and virtuoso cowriter of both *Animal House* and *Caddyshack*. The classic golf comedy had been out less than a month and was on its way to making north of sixty million, ten times what it cost to make. It'd already hit the number fourteen movie of 1980. A hit. But Doug was shattered by its "failure."

Animal House, in his thinking, had made more than *twice* that and been the number two movie of 1978—a success that shouldn't have happened and shouldn't need be duplicated. And yet Doug had tragically reset his bar for success to that level.

I knew all this because I'd just seen him in Hawaii. It was the late summer of 1980 and I was vacationing in Maui with my "next fiancée." This was still the phase where *every* girl I slept with, I fell in love with. *Marriage was obviously the next step, yes?*

Who comes strolling into town but Doug Kenney with Chevy Chase and a young producer named Alan Greisman, who was producing Chevy's next movie, *Modern Problems*. (Four years later, Chevy and Greisman would handpick me to play Alan Stanwyk in *Fletch*.) These three men—Greisman had also started dating my old pal, Sally Field—were also staying over in Maui. My then girlfriend and I joined their group.

Throughout, I noticed that Chevy could never let Doug get the last laugh. The *Lampoon* writer would say something profoundly hilarious, a turn of phrase so Lampoonily nuanced that you'd be thinking about the line for years after. We'd all laugh, and then Chevy would make a fart sound or imitate an ape. It was like watching two brothers seeing who could get the most attention.

Between Chevy's fart jokes, Doug kept lamenting the "failure" of *Caddyshack*. With his girlfriend, Kathryn Walker, working back on the mainland (and just starting filming *Neighbors* with Belushi and Aykroyd), there was no real support system for him in Hawaii. All he had was his cocaine and tossed-off assurances that his new film was in fact *another* huge hit, *another* future classic. Doug wasn't buying it.

And now he was missing.

I was back in L.A., and Chevy and Alan had also flown back. Kathryn had come out to Hawaii to stay with Doug for a few days but was stateside again for work. Doug had been left completely alone in Hawaii, supposedly working on his next screenplay.

Kathryn flew back out to Hawaii as quickly as she could when she hadn't heard from him. She'd found only an empty cottage. "Do you have any idea where he might be?" she now asked breathlessly. "Did he say . . . *anything?*"

I played back in my head and scrutinized every conversation we'd had that week: every place he'd mentioned, his suggestions for where my girlfriend and I might snorkel or eat next. Anything. I gave Kathryn all I knew but had no real lead for her. Neither, she said, had Chevy or Greisman.

"Thanks, Tim . . ." Her voice trailed off in disappointment, and she hung up to make the next hopeful phone call.

Two days later, they found Doug's body at the foot of a thirty-five-foot cliff called the Hanapepe Valley Lookout. The Kauai police officially ruled his death accidental. At best, this conclusion was half believed by those who knew him. "Doug," Harold Ramis quipped at Kenney's memorial, "probably tripped and fell while he was looking for a place to jump."

In Doug's abandoned hotel room were notes for projects he'd been planning and an outline for a new movie. He'd written "I love you" in soap on the bathroom mirror. On one notecard, he'd written, "These last few days are among the happiest I've ever ignored." He was thirty-three.

UNEXPECTEDLY, THE TIME TO PROPERLY PROCESS DOUG'S SUDDEN death came on *The Merv Griffin Show.*

I'd done the legendary talk show half a dozen times before (once with Kurt Russell, both of us, bizarrely, dressed as our characters from *The Quest*) and always had a good time with Merv. He'd often invite me out afterward for dinner, where we'd be joined by Merv regulars like Don Rickles, Tommy Lasorda, and Sammy Davis Jr. It was always a blast, a taste of old-school Hollywood stuff, so I was excited when the call came inviting me onto the show again. I had absolutely nothing to promote at the time, but I'd think of *something* to talk about.

Then they told me it wasn't going to be Merv but guest host Chevy Chase.

Okay, I thought, *even better. Something new.* Chevy and I had had pretty good rapport in Hawaii and could have some fun, ape faces and fart jokes notwithstanding. When the show started, I ran out and jumped up into Chevy's arms. Silly, but trying to keep things light and fill the time for the audience with some Chevy-like energy. It got a big laugh, and we were off to a good start. Then we sat to talk.

Chevy says, "You know . . . our dear friend Doug Kenney died just two weeks ago, . . ." and he goes into a long eulogy about Doug. Throughout, his voice was low and slow. This is serious Chevy. And this, I only now realized, was not going to be one of those fun interviews. Chevy went on to detail "poor Doug Kenney, my best friend," and how he thought the writer's death was a conspiracy of some kind, that Doug had been targeted by local thugs, or something. I had no idea where to go with any of this.

Thankfully, my old pal from the Groundlings, Laraine Newman, who was on *Saturday Night Live*, joined us, and I presumed, *I'm now safe*. I could vanish back into the chair and blissfully listen to Laraine stories. But Chevy did the exact same thing to her.

For two hours, he went on about the tragic loss of Doug with all these half-formed conspiratorial questions of "what really happened." The audience had lost interest and, worse, the thread of Chevy's discussion almost immediately.

Finally, I began to process what was really happening. Chevy was truly devastated. I knew they were pals but now, belatedly, understood his very real love for Doug. He wasn't rambling; he was grieving. I could now see the hurt and loss in his every word. That Chevy had asked me on the show to discuss and process Doug's death was humbling—though perhaps in front of a live audience and on Merv Griffin's stage wasn't the place.

I didn't realize it until many years later, and what I wish I could go back and do—what I should have done then—was ignore the lights and cameras, ignore the audience, ignore trying to be funny. I should have stood up, walked over to Chevy, and given him a hug.

Get Me Tim Matheson!

POST *ANIMAL HOUSE*, THERE CAME WHAT I REFER TO AS THE "Otter Bump." The movie was a smash hit, and everyone, it seemed, was finally interested in me. As an actor. And as someone to lay.

Women, many, wanted to date me, assuming I was exactly like the character in the movie. And I did my best impression. But I was not as smooth, or rakish, in real life as Eric Stratton. Still, my dance card was filled for years, thanks to Otter.

Meanwhile, mostly every movie company in Hollywood invited me out for lunch to figure out how *they* could work with me. Was I the next Chevy Chase or a young Robert Redford or Warren Beatty type? If they were really lucky, I could dance like John Travolta. I was invited to many lunches and meetings, generic talk of projects and ideas on how we might work together. Nothing came of it for months. They were all just feeling me out, figuring out what—if anything—they had. Was Otter a fluke?

I took *The Apple Dumpling Gang Rides Again* immediately after *Animal House.* I'd learned the hard way that a good job was more likely to mean that you *wouldn't* work for five years, so I'd taken the quick offer. Plus, I needed the money, and Disney paid me five times what the Lampoon had. In fact, I'd missed the *Animal House* premiere in New York to work on this Tim Conway and Don Knotts film.

It wasn't the greatest project for the résumé, but it paid some bills. And a much bigger fish—the biggest in Hollywood—was about to tug at my hook.

I was driving back to L.A. from the *Dumpling Gang* filming location in Utah and stopped in Las Vegas. I had gone out to dinner, had played some craps, and was just getting up the next day when the phone rang. "I have Steven Spielberg for you," said the voice on the other end.

Um, okay . . . This was after *Jaws* and *Close Encounters of the Third Kind.* The summer blockbuster had just been invented by Spielberg, and I, as they say, took the call. Steven's now-famous voice came on the line. "I want you to be in my movie," he said. "I'm making this film called *1941*, this wild World War Two comedy. I loved you in *Animal House*, and I want you, and Belushi, in the movie."

Like Landis, Spielberg apparently couldn't care less about playing games with actor-salary negotiations. (Or, so I thought . . .)

"Jesus," I got out. "That's . . . Steven . . . I'm just very flattered."

"I've got two parts you can play," he told me. "We'll send over the script, and take your pick."

I got the script as promised and chose Captain Loomis Birkhead. Back in L.A., Steven couldn't have been more gracious. I went over to his workshop—a converted hangar at the Hollywood Burbank Airport, where he showed me the film storyboards and all the artwork. I was being courted by the wunderkind—the new king of Hollywood. I was going to work with this guy!

Then the offer came in. "Whatever your quote was on your last movie," they told me. "That's what you're going to get on *this* movie." In my last movie, I'd played third fiddle to Conway and Knotts. In *Animal House*, I'd taken a discount salary for the opportunity. What did either of these things have to do with Captain Loomis Birkhead and *1941*? But there was no negotiation; it was take it or leave it. Now I understood why Spielberg apparently couldn't care less about playing games with actor-salary negotiations.

I was a bit shocked. I'd convinced myself that Steven and I were pals. We'd literally "looked at his etchings" together. We'd hung out.

He'd let me pick my own part! My first instinct was to say no. It was a shitty deal. To heck with *Jaws* and *Close Encounters*. But the studio wasn't a bunch of dummies. They knew most actors would have *paid* to be in a Spielberg movie.

"The credits will be alphabetical," Spielberg's folks now added. "Your name is going to go between Christopher Lee and Toshiro Mifune." Dracula and the star of *The Seven Samurai*, among the other hundred films these two legends had already made.

"When does shooting start?" I asked.

When I took the part, I realized they could cut my character easily and the film would be fine. It's a two-hour comedy, and my storyline could be the first thing to go. Fortunately for me, Steven wanted the full movie as planned. (Already bulky at two hours, his later director's cut was half an hour *longer*.)

Spielberg, a perfectionist, did every major stunt two or three times, including crashing a plane onto a back-lot reproduction of Hollywood Boulevard. I've still got a couple of T-shirts from the production that Spielberg handed out which read "I will not make this movie if it costs a penny more than $14 million." He spent $35 million, so, technically, he'd kept his word.

I loved working with Steven. He couldn't have been kinder or more supportive. If I had an idea for a shot, he'd say, "Let's try it." Watching the master work firsthand and up close no doubt reawakened my own early desires to be a director. It was impossible not to get excited about making film around this guy.

But Steven wasn't the only one who had me excited.

—

I'M IN LOVE WITH NANCY ALLEN . . .

This was the realization. Or, at least, *falling* in love. (In these younger years—I was "just" thirty-two—I was still hazy on the difference.) In any case, this epiphany would now clearly change the course of my whole life. I just needed to tell her.

There were a lot of guys who had a crush on Nancy Allen in 1979. She'd just starred in *Carrie*, the popular horror film by Brian De Palma, as the plucky blonde who orchestrates the gag with the bucket of pig's blood for prom night. But my crush, I'd decided, was more than a crush. She was my destiny.

And now we were filming Spielberg's *1941* together. And almost every scene I had was with Nancy.

On our first day, we were shooting at Indian Dunes, a mostly barren field about forty-five minutes north of Los Angeles. Not really shooting; more like *waiting* to shoot. It was a night shoot, which gave us a call time of 7 p.m. Steven was filming a John Belushi scene that night, and Nancy and I were merely on standby if there was any time, at the end of the night, to shoot a scene with us before we wrapped around 6 a.m. It was clearly going to be one of those ten-hour sitting-around nights. *I act for free; I get paid to wait . . .*

That being the case, I'd invited Nancy to hang out in my trailer while we waited. All above board, truly. Nancy and I ran in the same circle of friends and had had one brief romantic liaison, years before, when I dutifully played the role of rebound when she was "on a break" from her New York boyfriend. I'm a gentleman on set. There's plenty of time for any socializing to be done *after* the film is over. Sure, she wanted to spend more time with me, but mostly it was because I had a better trailer and they had stuck her in a crappy dressing room for the night. *Carrie* did fine and all, but this was before *Blow Out* or *Dressed to Kill*, and Nancy hadn't yet graduated to the fancier digs.

So we hung out. And talked. And maybe worked on some lines. And talked more. And might have napped a little. And some flirtatious touching, but again, both of us being rather reputable with things. I was dating someone at the time. Living with, actually. And Nancy had just broken up, again, with the New York guy . . .

And now I'm also looking at her in the dingy light of this trailer and I realize, I love talking to this woman. Spending my time with her. I love—

Bang, bang! "Tim!!" Someone is now pounding on the outside of the trailer. Nancy and I sprang up awkwardly from whatever dangerous tableau we'd just been in. "Steven's ready for you!"

I parted the door only just enough to spot the eager production assistant. "Isn't he filming Belushi now?" I asked.

The PA grimaced. "John fell. They're taking him to the hospital."

"John?" I opened the door wider. John had apparently slipped and done a real-world face-plant off one of the wings. (This is the shot Spielberg used in the film; film genius, he.) I turned back slowly into the trailer. "Guess we're on," I said, and Nancy shrugged and smiled impishly.

I was now doubly smitten. But I needed to do things right.

My plan was to drive home and tell the live-in girlfriend it was over. We'd been on-again, off-again for more than a year. After she'd gone back to an ex for a couple of months, we were now giving it another go, but the bloom was definitely off our rose. But I got back from Indian Dunes at 7:30 a.m. to find my girlfriend getting ready for work. I didn't want to hit her with a heavy breakup speech then, so I waited until the next day. While she was at work, I had the whole day to get more pumped up about Nancy. This wonderful woman. So smart and funny and beautiful. I couldn't wait to get back to the set in Indian Dunes to tell her how I felt.

I whisked back north to my Nancy. That night, if you looked up *romantic* in the dictionary, there would have been a picture of me pulling onto the set of *1941*.

Before finding her, however, I ran into Spielberg.

He was chatting with another director. Brian De Palma.

Uh-oh.

I took in the trim dark beard and receding hairline. The hawk eyes. The East Coast posture. De Palma was Nancy's on-again, off-again boyfriend.

"Hey, Tim!" Steven called out, waving me over with that boyish grin of his. He introduced me to De Palma.

"Oh, boy!" Steven said beaming. Or something similar. "You just missed it."

"What's that?" I asked.

"Brian just proposed to Nancy. Right here! On set! Can you believe it?"

I couldn't. I really couldn't.

De Palma had traveled twenty-eight hundred miles west with hat in hand and had thrown his best Philadelphian Hail Mary. His instincts must have warned him to get down on one knee and right quick. I wanted to tell him about the girl back in Los Angeles I was breaking up with so that I could be with Nancy. Or tell him how Nancy also made *me* feel.

But I didn't. I just said, "Ohh . . . That's . . . that's great, Brian. Congratulations." And walked away.

I never told Nancy any of this. Or anyone else.

Until just now.

———

THE MOVIES HAVE A SICK SENSE OF HUMOR.

A few days later, I saved Brian De Palma's fiancée's life.

Nancy and I are forty feet in the air inside a fighter plane positioned on a doohickey that would make the plane rock and roll like we were being shot out of the sky. Nancy is in the cockpit, the plane convulses as special-effect flashbulbs burst throughout the rear cabin to mimic bullets hitting our plane. For more effect, there are pieces of plane seat cushions and feathers flying through the air and—*poof!*—the spark of the flashbulbs catches them *all* on fire.

This isn't in the script or some added effect; it's real-life *fire*.

In seconds, the entire cockpit fills with smoke, and tiny balls of fire arch and drift everywhere. Instantly, there's no air to breathe—a terrifying realization at the first inhale. There's an exit door three feet away from me in the rear of the plane, but Nancy is screaming. I look at the door again, my way out, then back toward shrieking Nancy and have no choice. Into the smoke I charge. Blindly grab her by the back of her costume to yank her from the seat and pull her back to the escape door. I rip the door open and push Nancy out, diving out behind her like some boot-camp drill. The only people more shocked than Nancy and me are the crew members on the scaffolding just outside the plane. They're wondering why we aren't in the plane anymore. No one has yet yelled "Cut!"

Outside the plane, we're both hacking and gasping for air. Nancy is shaking and terrified. The ember of a burning feather still rests on her left shoulder. I'm in shock, having never been in such a dangerous filming situation. (And I'd been on three shows where we wore six-shooters and shot at each other every week.) Two special-effects guys—who had also been inside the plane working the fans—are already on their way to the infirmary.

But Spielberg had been so focused on the monitor, he hadn't realized he was looking at effects that were so real, they *were* actually real!

"It's not safe, Steven," I told him. "We could have been hurt badly in there."

"Well, it didn't look like much of anything happened," he replied.

"Look at Nancy!" I argued. "We couldn't breathe. There's two guys in first aid right now. I honestly thought *we* were both heading to the hospital or worse."

Steven nodded and then sent us off to the first aid office for an exam of our own. There, we learned that the two special-effects men were slightly burned by the ignited feathers and that one suffered from smoke inhalation.

When we returned, Steven and his first assistant director had already gone out to scout back-lot locations for other shots while the plane was being reset for another attempt at the scene. *Forget this!*

Nancy and I went to lunch, and I ordered both of us drinks to help calm us down. She was still terribly shaken. So was I. Meanwhile, production was going along as if nothing significant had happened. The woman who I had, days before, planned to profess my love to, was now shivering in pained silence. What was I supposed to do? I did something I'd never done before (and haven't done since)— I walked off the set. I whisked Nancy back to my place, which was only ten minutes away from the studio, and let production know we weren't coming back until someone called to apologize.

Steven himself called back, asked how we were doing, and said he was sorry things had gotten out of control. He promised he'd make sure we'd be safe in the scene, and told us the crew had already adjusted the effects. Back we went, but when Nancy tried to climb up the scaffolding to the plane again, she broke down sobbing and couldn't do it. A double was inserted for Nancy, and I climbed into the plane to redo the shot. This time without flashbulbs and feathers on fire. The scene went off without a hitch. Spielberg got his shot.

———

THE BEST WAY FOR ME TO PUT THE SOON-TO-BE MRS. BRIAN DE Palma out of mind was to focus on learning from the other masters on this film—not just the one named Spielberg. I'd follow Toshiro Mifune around and watch him work. There was also Slim Pickens (*Dr. Strangelove*, *Blazing Saddles*), Warren Oates (*The Wild Bunch*, *Bring Me the Head of Alfredo Garcia*, *Stripes*), and Robert Stack (*The Untouchables*, *The Tarnished Angels*) to trail after and talk with. I could list names all day; the cast was enormous. Heck, my *Animal House* director, John Landis, even had a part. Spielberg wanted a massive comedy, and he'd built one.

Ultimately, that may be why the film wasn't so successful.

In *Animal House*, everybody had their own unique style of comedy. Belushi's was physical with not much dialogue—he and McGill were almost playing a silent movie like Chaplin and Harold Lloyd. I was the smart-aleck and suave Cary Grant type. Peter Riegert did a Groucho Marx kind of thing. Pinto and Flounder were like Laurel and Hardy. Neidermeyer, Dean Wormer. Everybody got their own distinct voice, and the script and Landis demanded it.

In *1941*, however, everybody had a similar voice: big, broad stuff. Just very frenzied and frantic and amplified. Fortunately, I could play my part pretty straight, but, otherwise, I'd be standing on set looking at guys like Dan Aykroyd, John Candy, and Ned Beatty all standing together—amazing talents with *very* different cadences to give—and the film had all three playing the same notes. I remember that one night on set, Aykroyd described it as, "We're all these Ferraris in Steven's garage, but we're being used like bumper cars."

———

THE *ANIMAL HOUSE* LIFT WAS STILL GETTING ME MEETINGS AND offers, and I'd just finished a film for Steven Spielberg. At an all-time peak, for sure. But, just like with *Magnum Force* years before, there was little way to know that my career was about to stall out. For years.

Bad choices, bad timing, bad luck.

And my love life wasn't going much better.

TIM MATHESON

Damn Glad to Meet You

MY SEVEN DECADES IN THE HOLLYWOOD TRENCHES

Why is my head so big? *(Photo courtesy of the author)*

My first "agency"—Screen Children's Guild—was a scam. These are three of the pictures they made me pay them to take. I got twelve 8x10s for $25 and I *had* to hire them to take them. It didn't get me shit, but they are my first professionally taken headshots. *(Photo courtesy of the author)*

Aunt Estelle, me and my sister. San Bernardino was the only "normal" place I had as a child and where I first discovered a love of acting. *(Photo courtesy of the author)*

Newly moved to Timalot. I posed for a picture with my new best friend. I named the dog "Ichi" short for my favorite action hero: Zatoichi. *(Photo courtesy of the author)*

I found my Elizabeth on set in Bluebell, Alabama. We were married in an intimate family affair in the L.A. Arts District. *(Photo courtesy of Jennifer Lourie Photography)*

The Marine Corps shaves your head and takes your picture in the span of about ten minutes. That's why everyone has the same facial expression of confusion with a slight hint of terror. *(Photo courtesy of the author)*

When shooting in Montemarte, a 5 a.m. call time is the perfect time to read the paper . . . before all the other art lovers arrive. *(Photo courtesy of the author)*

Brothers in films and in life: Bruce McGill, Gary Goetzman and me. *(Photo courtesy of the author)*

This was Jennifer Leak and me at a party designed to share stories from the set with television stations from around the nation for Universal's TV shows. *(Photo courtesy of the author)*

Thanksgiving SUNDAY 1977 at the Belushis'. This is one of my most precious memories of making *Animal House*. As a cast, we all decided to work on Thanksgiving Day and postpone the holiday to Sunday. John and Judy did it right with turkey, stuffing, and I can still taste the cranberry jam. *(Photo courtesy of the author)*

I snapped this picture of Doug Kenney in Hawaii a few weeks before he died. Doug was always the smartest person in the room and the best comedy writer I ever knew. Chevy Chase would be in this picture—but he was sailing the boat. *(Photo courtesy of the author)*

Family trip after finishing *Fletch*. Sue had just passed the bar and it was time to celebrate. They wanted me to come back early for a reshoot, but I wasn't leaving my girls. It had been the three of us against the world for twenty years—it was time to celebrate where we had come as a family. *(Photo courtesy of the author)*

I like to work closely with all of my cast. For *Hell Swarm*, I needed to make sure these bees knew to treat me like the Queen . . . ah, um . . . director. *(Photo courtesy of the author)*

Bob Gunton and I on the set of *Judas*. Deep in the Moroccan desert, Father Kaiser was still looking out for us . . . and hoping we would give him some money. *(Photo courtesy of the author)*

When I worked with Reba McEntire, I didn't only get a singing lesson. I learned how to treat your fans and appreciate what your art means to them in a new way. *(Photo courtesy of the author)*

Virgin River really is the perfect place. They have a Renaissance Faire and the best colleagues anyone could ask for. *(Photo courtesy of the author)*

In *The Virginian*, I had a chance to ride almost every day. It was here that I first learned to appreciate how hard the stunt people and wranglers worked to make us "real" cowboys. *(Photo courtesy of Universal Studios Licensing LLC)*

Timeless love story. Even though Shakespeare wrote this star-crossed tale about two teenagers, I seemed to play it a lot as I was pushing thirty. *(Photo courtesy of The Old Globe Theatre)*

After the weirdest audition non-audition of our lives, Kurt Russell and I found ourselves playing brothers on *The Quest* to find our sister. It would still be on the air . . . if it wasn't for *Charlie's Angels*. *(NBC Contributor/© March 23, 1984 NBCUniversal/Getty Images)*

A newly married couple hits some trouble in *What Really Happened to the Class of '65?* Long before we could have dreamed of playing a married couple living happily in Virgin River. *(Photo courtesy of Universal Studios Licensing LLC)*

The story of *1941*: Californians fear that the Japanese are invading their state. My story: I fear that Brian DePalma will show up and prevent me from telling Nancy how I feel. *(Photo courtesy of Universal Studios Licensing LLC)*

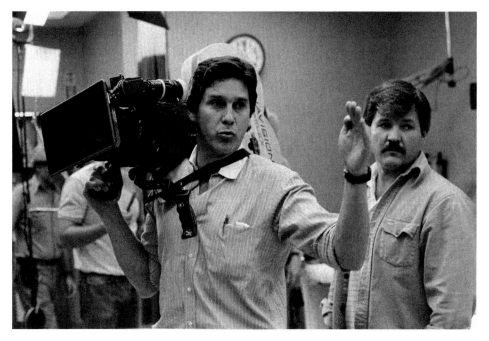

Directing in the OR at *St. Elsewhere*. This was the first time I directed episodic television. Thankfully for this shot, everyone stayed on set. *(NBC Contributor/© March 23, 1984 NBCUniversal/Getty Images)*

My scenes with Sunny were cut from the film, but we had known each other from a previous project and the feelings we had for each other went well beyond our acting. *(Photo courtesy of Universal Studios Licensing LLC)*

I was a little late on finding my love for Brian De Palma's wife—but I did get to kiss her in *1941*. *(Photo courtesy of Universal Studios Licensing LLC)*

I first met Jennifer Jason Leigh when she was a teenager at the start of what would be her fantastic career. I'm not sure why she tried to kill me in *Buried Alive*, but I got my revenge. *(Photo courtesy of Universal Studios Licensing LLC)*

On the first day of shooting *Fletch*, it was great to be reunited with Chevy. I had to fly back to L.A. from New York each week to hire Chevy to kill me for fake—even though Daniel Stern was in NY trying to do it for real. *(Photo courtesy of Universal Studios Licensing LLC)*

All those backstory pictures you see on a character's desk or wall in a movie all have to come from somewhere. One of the most fun weeks of my life was shooting a series of stills to create a backstory where Chris and I were College Football superstars. *(© Paramount Pictures. All Rights Reserved.)*

I was invited to be part of this iconic photo before I shot my stupid mouth off about the future of Westerns . . . but *after* I broke Lorne Greene's Mercedes. *(Fred Sabine/© August 28, 1972 NBCUniversal/Getty Images)*

This is how much fun Sam and I had on just the photo shoots for *Charlie Hoover*. Imagine how much fun we would have had making you laugh for more than six episodes. *(Charlie Hoover, photo courtesy of Sony Pictures Television)*

This is a picture of me and my kids that I cherish deeply. We moved away from Los Angeles so that we could enjoy being a family away from the "Hollywood" of it all. *(Photo courtesy of the author)*

I will always be proud of being asked to portray our 40th president. Reagan's legacy looms larger and larger as time goes on, and I hope that I did his legacy proud. *(Hopper Stone, SMPSP)*

TRIGGER TALK — Clint Eastwood, flanked by two fellow policemen, chats about the proper use of guns in this scene from Warner Bros.' "Magnum Force."

This was the first day of working with Clint Eastwood. I learned more that day from Clint about acting and the art of making a movie than any other single day in my career. Plus, it was a reunion with David Soul who didn't hide in the rafters this time. *(Photo licensed by Warner Bros. Discovery. All Rights Reserved.)*

One of the famous people I was fortunate enough to portray was Howard Hughes. Lucky for me, I played Hughes at the phase of his life when he was the king of the world. *(Photo courtesy of the author)*

Brief Tales of Hollywood Love

TALE 1: DAYS OF THUNDER

THIS ALL STARTED, AS SUCH THINGS DO, WELL ENOUGH.

Setting: New Year's Eve at the home of good friend Marty David-son, who had directed *Almost Summer*. There, I met a young woman, a film editor. Lovely, sharp. We hit it off very well, and I was already looking forward to our good-luck midnight kiss. "I'm here with my boyfriend," she finally clarified.

"Oh . . ." I said. "Well, okay." So it goes. "I'm sure we'll cross paths again someday." That "someday" was comin' quick.

"But, you know . . ." she whispered, "it's over. The relationship's over."

"He turns into a pumpkin after midnight, is that it?"

"We're breaking up." She doubled-down on her commitment to the idea.

"Then maybe we'll get our chance after all." I smiled my best New Year grin.

Days later, the film editor kept her word and we got our chance. Always running at 140-plus miles per hour, our relationship was hot, heavy, and passionate. Unfortunately, for me, by now I'd figured out who her turns-into-a-pumpkin-at-midnight boyfriend had been: Don Simpson.

The damned president of Paramount Pictures, one of the biggest film studios on the planet. Future megaproducer of little films like *Beverly Hills Cop* and *Top Gun*. A guy whose alleged habits included high-priced escorts, piles of drugs, and wearing black 501 Levi's only once before tossing them. A guy who, I now learned, was unaware that this editor was no longer his girlfriend.

In fear of her career, perhaps, she hadn't told him she wasn't exclusive anymore. For months. To one of the most powerful men in Hollywood, I'd officially become "the other man."

As the relationship is rolling ahead, I get a call that National Lampoon is making a new movie called *The Joy of Sex*. Based on the provocative bestseller with a script to be fixed by John Hughes, it is being directed by my pal Penny Marshall. Belushi already had a role. They wanted me to audition for the film. *Audition?* Surprised I had to test for a Lampoon film, and with a not-yet-great script, I was still interested. I needed the work. But something smelled fishy.

Then it finally hit me. Paramount Pictures was producing the film. My lover's ex-ish boyfriend would be my boss. Don Simpson would even decide if I got the job in the first place. No wonder they were making me audition. Payback's a dish served warm.

I called my agent and gave him the full, unedited background, I could hear him giggling as he tried to press the mute button. He promised me he'd discreetly get into it with Simpson. My agent called back days later. "Don says you're good," he said. "This was between him and her, and it's old news. You'll work at Paramount again. No problems. Guaranteed."

I'm fucking dead.

I came in for the screen test, and as I was settling in, one of the Lampoon staffers said, "Tim, just so you know . . . we're all on Team Tim."

What the hell is Team Tim?

"We really wanted you for this," John Hughes told me. *Odd tense to use before I'd given a single line.* "We would love you for this part."

The audition given and the screen test shot, Dennis Quaid got the part the following morning. There was never any real consideration of me doing that movie. Simpson just wanted to fuck with me. And, he had.

But at least I had the girl, right? Worth it, yes?

This was, without doubt, the most disastrous relationship I've ever had. Ever.

As for *The Joy of Sex* and Don Simpson: John Hughes quit the project, and Penny Marshall also dropped out. Quaid dropped out. Belushi overdosed before filming started. The new director, Martha Coolidge, was fired during editing after refusing to include gratuitous nudity. The National Lampoon paid a quarter of a million to have its name removed from the film. And the movie didn't even earn its budget back.

Simpson was fired as the president of Paramount.

Okay, fine, he went on to make some of the century's biggest films . . . But in 1982, he was just a petty, unemployed ex-boyfriend.

TALE 2: LOVE IN THE TIME OF TOMMY TUNE

Bruce McGill was on Broadway doing a hit show called *My One and Only*, a new musical built around various Gershwin tunes. Though disappointed he wouldn't be tapping out "He Loves and She Loves" on his throat, I still went a dozen times to support my friend.

His costars included Broadway-ubiquitous actor/dancer/choreographer Tommy Tune and a young woman named Lesley Hornby—better known to the world as Twiggy, the greatest supermodel of the era. The English model with the renowned narrow frame and enormous eye-lashed peepers ruled the fashion scene from 1967 well into the early 1970s. When I met her in 1984, she'd also won two Golden Globe awards, played Cinderella on London's West End, acted in David O. Russell and John Landis films, and been on *The Muppet Show*. Think Brooke Shields in her Jordache days or Farrah

Fawcett in her red-bathing-suit poster days, or Kendall Jenner (sans the TV shows)—Twiggy was *that* famous.

Living in New York on and off at the time, I'd often join Bruce and Twiggy after performances for drinks and NYC chitchat. One night, Bruce called and told me it would just be the two of us and that he had a story I wouldn't believe. He was right.

Hours before that night's performance, Twiggy's husband—an actor in westerns and episodic TV—had died of an unexpected heart attack. Michael Witney was just fifty-two. The only ones who knew this had happened, however, were the show's producers, as Twiggy had been in makeup when the terrible news came in. The decision, which Bruce now wincingly detailed to me, had been *to not tell* Twiggy until *after* the night's performance. The few who knew of Michael's death were ordered to keep away from her until final curtain call. The show, dear girl, must go on. (Hell of an industry.)

Many months had passed when Twiggy started coming out with us again after performances. She was more subdued than before, of course, and delicate. But I could also tell she *needed* to be out in the world again. And soon enough, I was being passed notes in geometry class that the recent Tony nominee would like to see more of me socially.

"She thinks you're fun," Bruce told me. "You cheer her up." He held out his hands to indicate all of this was beyond his doing or control. It seemed too soon—*"But two months dead: nay, not so much, not two"*—but I eventually assented and started dating a supermodel.

Twiggy, it seemed, only had eyes for me. At her urging, we began spending more and more time together. Every free minute she was claiming for Tim time.

She was smitten and so was I. It didn't matter that she was on skyscraper-sized billboards, we had great fun together and I loved every minute we had together away from the adoring crowds. That said, the more alone time we had, the more I could see that she was clearly still in mourning. Was it Tim Matheson she desired or merely the notion of being with someone, anyone, again? She also had a five-year-old daughter, and so, though younger than me by a few years, Ms. Lesley Hornby was still far more settled than I and looking to stay domesticated.

Perhaps to seduce me into the ways of domestication, she took a break from the Broadway show so the two of us could head to the Caribbean for several weeks. There, beneath all the palm fronds and mojitos, I now knew for sure: *It's just not right; we don't fit.* Twiggy was still staggering from the horror of her husband's unexpected death and looking to fill that dreadful void. I was the rebound romance, a place-holder, a bridge to the rest of her life. I just happened to be in the right place at the wrong time. Post-Caribbean, I quickly headed back to Los Angeles and was only in New York enough to see her every now and again. I figured I'd played my part well enough—been a fine shoulder to cry on—and hopefully, she'd move on.

She didn't.

When her run on *My One and Only* ended, she immediately flew out to visit me in Los Angeles and shared her plans to move west permanently so we could continue our "great love affair."

Shit.

We huddled in my car outside the place she'd just rented in L.A. and had the requisite heart-to-heart, and I told her it was over. That we'd had a lovely go but that she needed more time to heal. Twiggy still wasn't getting it. She was a terrific woman, and perhaps under different circumstances, I wouldn't have broken up with a supermodel.

"I'm in love with someone else," I told her. This was an unmitigated lie. I wasn't even "in like" with anyone else.

Those world-famous eyes examined my own for far too long. She knew I was lying. Poised, classy, and wise beyond her years. Twiggy finally smiled thinly. "Okay, Tim . . ." She kissed my cheek, stepped out of the car, and went on with her life.

Weeks later, she met Leigh Lawson, an English actor, director, and writer.

They've now been married for thirty-plus years.

(The fact that Lawson had a child with my dream girl, Hayley Mills, we'll just write off to romantic irony. It's a small world.)

Twiggy is now Dame Lesley Lawson, a Commander of the Order of the British Empire. And clearly, she quickly fell for and married the right guy.

I'm glad I lied and that she let me do so. I have zero doubts she's glad also.

TALE 3: TURN BACK TIME

I'd started seeing a gorgeous woman named Georganne—an actress building her résumé on various popular TV shows—and she asked me to pick her up at her sister's place in Malibu before a date. She ushered me into the house right on the beach, then led me back to meet her sister in the primary bedroom. We walked in where big sis was lying in her bed, reading. Her sister was Cher. *The* Cher. It's 1973—Cher has her own TV show, she has billboards up and down Sunset Blvd, and she is pumping out top-ten singles seemingly every month. Georganne had not bothered to reveal the identity of her sister to me. Imagine casually strolling into some room for a random hello and Cher is waiting there. It's startling, to say the least. And a more down-to-earth and genuine woman, and family, I've never met. Both sisters were wonderful, and Georganne and I dated on and off for several years. But much like many relationships in my life, work called me away from Los Angeles. I went to San Diego for a long run as Romeo, and dear Georganne went on to find her Romeo closer to home.

TALE 4: SCHLEMIEL SCHLIMAZEL

Penny Marshall had a crush. I was staying in Richard Drey-fuss's L.A. place (he was off in New York), which was a guesthouse behind Penny's house. She was in the third season of *Laverne &* *Shirley* as Laverne DeFazio on the number one show in America and was soon to be a pioneer director (not many women directors then, or now, and this Marshall was the first to direct a $100 million hit film) of *Big* and *A League of Their Own*.

We'd often go out with friends as a group, and, eventually, she made it known that she'd be interested in becoming more than friends. For weeks, I tactfully dodged the matter. This had to be handled tactfully—Penny was an amazing, amazing woman, but I just wasn't attracted to her. I didn't want to lose a friend, upset our social group, *or* piss off her big brother, mighty producer Garry Marshall (*Happy Days, The Odd Couple, Murphy Brown*, etc.).

She eventually cornered me on the idea, but I hadn't yet learned to tell the truth. To be direct. As I had done most of my life, from my mom and my sister to my adult relationships, I had carefully honed the skill of playing peacemaker. And I was still playing peacemaker—at any cost. This was not good.

After artful dodge upon artful dodge, I had used up all of my peacemaker's ammunition. We had even managed to fumble into a bed once but couldn't advance things too far, and my plan to save a friendship was now unflattering for both of us.

"I'm in love with somebody else," I said. *Look, if it works once . . .* "I just feel too guilty to . . . you know?"

Penny was not thrilled but—realizing that *both* of us had made a mistake—she accepted the routine enough so that we were able to slink out with some self-respect. Our friendship continued, but we quickly became acquaintances at best. I'd blown it. A lesson in good old honesty often being, just like they teach us, the best way.

Years later, Penny was asked to produce and direct a segment for the Oscars where various actors perform, and I'd been asked to film a bit for the spot. Another assistant director had come out to film me. That was my first hint. And when the Oscars ran, my bit had been cut from the segment completely. Any previous crush was officially over.

A few years later, I ran into the same issue with Margot Kidder (*Superman*, *The Amityville Horror*). We were doing *Bus Stop*, a play for television, where she struck me as a competent actor who had major personal struggles and excesses. She was looking for our characters to take their relationship into real life, but no thanks. I got out of there faster than a speeding bullet and didn't even break a sweat.

"I'm in love with somebody else," I said.

TALE 5: HAPPY BIRTHDAY TO ME (✖ 4)

Actually, it was on December 30, the day *before* my thirty-third birthday.

(Too old for all that's to happen next.)

My steady girlfriend, an Emmy-winning actress who I was wild about, was still in New York, having just finished a short run on Broadway with my old Faber College pal Donald Sutherland. I was in Los Angeles and all alone on my birthday week, poor guy.

At eleven o'clock in the morning, there was a *tap, tap* at my front door, and I opened it to find a woman in a negligee under an overcoat (all stereotypes come from somewhere). It was a woman I'd "spent time" with a few times before. The sheer cherry lace top and crotchless velvet panties, however, were new. "Hey, hey . . ." she said, grinning. "So . . . I know it's your birthday tomorrow. And . . . I wanted to give you an early present."

Opening the door fully, I'd decided it would be rude to send her away; we soon got amorous on the downstairs couch.

To be clear: I really did love this other girl three-thousand-plus miles away. I'd gone and fallen in love again. She was the only woman I was officially dating, and I saw a real future for us. Doesn't mean I wasn't a pig and an idiot.

Now it's 2:30 in the afternoon, my Adam & Eve paramour was long gone, and there's another quiet knock at my door. At my doorstep this time, a beautiful waitress I knew who worked a couple of blocks down the street. "I have to work all tomorrow," she said, pouting her puffy waitress lips. "So I wanted to wish you a happy birthday today."

"How sweet," I said. "What'd you have in mind?"

She stepped inside and reached for my belt.

Hours later, I'm settling in for the evening of some well-deserved rest with a glass of wine and listening to Eric Clapton's latest album, when the phone rings.

"Tim!"

"Who is this?"

"You know damn well who it is," the voice on the other end replied.

And I did. No one else in Hollywood had Kirstie Alley's voice.

Kirstie hadn't hit yet and was still two years from *Star Trek II: The Wrath of Khan* and five years from *Cheers* and a superstar career. She was also a few years from Scientology and, so, still in her fun Wichita-gal-now-in-L.A. partying phase. It was a good phase for her.

"I want to come over," she told me. "I'm out drinking with a bunch of phony assholes, and I just wanna hang out with someone real. Can I come over, please? I know it's late, but I really want to see you." She and I had casually spent some time together before but were usually dating other people and so never pursued anything seriously. It seemed this would be another night of that. *Screw it*, I figured. Let's get the triple play, and maybe someday I'll brag about it—or confess to it—in some kind of memoir.

Several hours later, and Kirstie Alley is naked and we're enjoying some postcoital conversation in my bed. I'm also now, literally, in my birthday suit and can suddenly hear something, someone, no . . . *something* . . . moving about the house downstairs. I spring up in my bed but sit crouched, frozen, calling on the listening skills of our primordial ancestors to hear what's going on below. It's a creaking, definitely creaking. I tell myself it's the cat. *Do I have a cat? Steps*, I think. Slow, soft steps up the stairs toward the bedroom. I squint into the waiting darkness.

My New York girlfriend now stood in the threshold of the bedroom. New York was still probably twenty-eight hundred miles away, but she unquestionably was not.

Kirstie stilled beside me, the sheet clutched in her hands and gradually sliding up to cover all but her eyes. (Days later, Kirstie would tell me that she'd "willed herself" to become invisible.)

My girlfriend, understandably, stood stunned. The first order of business was getting my girlfriend the heck out of my chamber of sin. The last thing I wanted, whatever was to come next, was the image of Kirstie and me together burned into this poor woman's eyes. I *had* to get her out of the room.

Lurching buck naked from the bed, I got to the doorway, and she was already halfway down the steps. I ran back into the room to pull some pants on and then followed her downstairs, where she was already outside with her luggage. I stopped her in the middle of the driveway.

"I flew out to surprise you on your birthday," she said. "I wanted to be here at midnight to be the first person to wish you happy birthday."

It was like Bruce Lee had gotten a running start and then kicked me in the heart. I could not have felt more like a complete asshole.

She was set on leaving, and I tried everything I could to keep her there. "It's midnight," I argued. "Just stay here. Sleep in the guesthouse. We can talk about this tomorrow." My begging went on for an hour. I'd gotten her to the guesthouse for some privacy and to give Kirstie a fighting chance for escape. "Let's just talk," I said and then tried every angle: I was drunk. Nothing really happened. I was so lonely. It meant nothing. You shouldn't ever surprise people like this . . . and so on. Nothing worked.

Meanwhile, I'm bleeding out inside because I realize *now* that I'm in love with her and I've really fucked this up. As this is playing out in real time, I have a flash in my mind: *This exact scene has happened before!*

Then I realize I am playing out in real life a scene I'd recently done for a film called *A Little Sex*. In the movie, the guy's caught cheating by his loving wife and it ruins everything . . . but, spoiler alert, she forgives him in the end. *How would this version play out?* It was now almost dawn, and she was calmed down enough to spend what was left of the night. "Let's just get to bed," I entreated with promises to fix things tomorrow.

By now, Kirstie had, magically, slinked out of the main house like she'd never even been there.

I led my girlfriend to the bedroom and began to tell her, honestly, how much I loved her. I tried calming her and caressing her—actions which weren't rebuffed and that started to lead to some promising makeup sex. The kind that might even open a newer and deeper level of our relationship. The realization that she was so much more important to me than I'd ever imagined drove me to open up more and increased my sexual ardor. She started to take *her* clothes off, and I'm thinking, *I've really messed this up and I need to make genuine love to this woman.*

That I'd been practicing all day didn't guarantee much.

It sufficed. We traveled together back to New York, and for a while, it seemed like we'd gotten past my atrocious behavior. We even took a little vacation in the Caribbean. There, we fell back into our old loving ways, as if my infidelity had never happened. I was like the character in my movie and couldn't be happier; I'd dodged a bullet.

But just a few weeks later, when I went to visit her in New York, she greeted me at the door with the opposite point of view. "I can't see you anymore," she said. "It's over."

I was heartbroken and ashamed. I'd been such a fool, never realizing what I'd had. This was real karma, deserved, and I was paying the ultimate price. All I could do was hope that time would heal the rupture of trust. For the next ten months to a year, I kept calling to see how she was, to ask for forgiveness, and to tell her how much I cared for her. "Let's make this work." I made every promise there was, looking for a fresh start. Finally, she declared she was coming out to L.A.

"I *do* need to see you," she said.

"Great!" I was so excited. "Listen, we'll go to dinner at Musso & Frank and . . ." thinking maybe there's a recovery here, maybe there's hope for me if I get her back in one of our regular haunts and remind her how great we are together. For the first time in a year, I'm optimistic.

At dinner, I waved my hand like James Bond, and the waiter brought us champagne as planned. While working the muselet free, my ex says, "I've fallen in love with Bruce." Bruce was a New York director and one of my former best friends. "We've been together for months."

She'd wanted to see my face in person when she told me this. She'd teed the whole thing up to see for herself a smidge of the hurt I'd seen in *her* face in the early hours of my thirty-third birthday.

I'd lost her and thrown away a chance at happiness by being weak, selfish, and dishonest. This is when I finally learned: *You don't ever screw around.*

She and Bruce eventually married and had three kids together.

Kirstie Alley remained a good friend and nothing more. She'd willed herself invisible.

"Ifs and Ands and Peter Pans"

It's an expression I learned from Kurt Russell. The roles just missed, the ones turned down, the scheduling bottlenecks that *might* have meant Tom Cruise was Ironman or the Beatles filmed *The Lord of the Rings* with Stanley Kubrick. Both were almost true.

My almost-true stories:

The fantastic *Hardy Boys* pilot you did as a teen that isn't picked up.

Landing a major role at twenty-two in *Johnny Got His Gun* for Warner Bros., working with legendary writer Dalton Trumbo—only for Warner Bros. to cancel the project and another studio pick it up, demanding a complete recast.

Drinking with John Huston, the legendary director of *The Maltese Falcon*, *The African Queen*, and *The Misfits*, when I was only twenty-five. He's making a boxing flick called *Fat City* about a kid boxer in Stockton—often ranked the most dangerous metro area in California—and casting is in the final round. "You're a good actor," one of my heroes tells me in his renowned sage voice. "But I don't quite see you in this part." The knockout blow is coming. Huston smiles, "If *you* lived in Stockton, *you'd* leave."

Being offered to play ex-fighter pilot Ted Striker in some small comedy called *Airplane!* but having to pass when the dates conflicted on Spielberg's airplane comedy *1941*.

Entertainment is filled with tens of thousands of these almost-happened stories, and Kurt's view was always to treat them, especially your own, with as much interest as your next eye blink. That said, now's a perfect time to share a few you might find interesting.

AFTER *ANIMAL HOUSE*, ALL THE STUDIOS WANTED TO MEET ME. Not necessarily to offer me a job, but just to have lunch and feel me out, looking to see if I *could* be the next John Travolta or Richard Gere. *Who is this guy?* they were all trying to figure out. *What can we put him in?*

The problem was that even I didn't know the answer to this question at the time. I couldn't seem to get a grasp on what I should play. *Who am I?* Cary Grant? Rock Hudson? Spencer Tracy? "We'd love to do something with you," executives would say. "But what do you particularly *want* to do?"

Being earnest turned out to be the wrong answer. In my idealistic stupidity, I told people how I'd just gone off to do Shakespeare and was looking to expand as an actor. It was a very sincere answer but hopelessly vague and not what they wanted to hear.

For example, I'd been invited to the Beverly Hills manse of megaproducer Robert "Bob" Evans for just such a meeting. Evans had produced *Rosemary's Baby*, *Love Story*, *Chinatown*, and *The Godfather II*. Sitting beside him was Irving Azoff (CEO of Ticketmaster, manager of the Eagles, and producer of *Fast Times at Ridgemont High*), and C. O. Erickson (*Rear Window*, *To Catch a Thief*, and *Vertigo*). These three could make me a major movie star *if* they wanted.

They had a project barely starting and "just wanted to talk." All their questions were about my career and goals, but they, like the others, were really just sizing me up again. (In this industry, everyone is sizing up everyone else 24-7, part of why I moved to Santa Barbara for a no-sizing zone.) They finally got to the project.

"The script's based on this great *Esquire* article," Evans beamed. "It's like *Saturday Night Fever* . . . but with *cowboys!*" He'd gone full-on jazz hands.

"Some great music, I bet," I said, and smiled, not sure I was ready for cowboys again.

"The best," he said. "You ever ride one of those mechanical bulls?"

"Of course. I've done work with Larry Mahan, the rodeo champion."

Evans eyed me curiously as the other two looked on. Ultimately, the three decided, literally, that *Urban Cowboy* should be *Saturday Night Fever* with cowboys and nabbed Travolta for the part.

But there were a hundred other projects to discuss across town. Taking meetings and having power lunches was now a full-time job.

Whether that job or lunch ever paid off was another matter.

———

IN 1983, I'D JUST FINISHED FILMING A YEAR OF A TV SERIES CALLED *Tucker's Witch*, where Catherine Hicks and I run a private detective agency in L.A. and she has supernatural powers. Yeah, yeah. It was a clever show and I mostly enjoyed working on it. And, I got a season of much-needed salary. When we were canceled, a call came in quickly for a new show.

"I can't," I said. "I'm tired. I just want to go camping for a couple of weeks." I was exhausted and needed a break. Plus this new program was *also* about a couple flirting at a private detective agency. The rafting and camping gear was already piled into my truck for my drive to Utah. "You gotta read this script!" my agent begged. "A really good pilot, a great writer."

"You'd be great!" the studio promised me. "The part's already yours. Cybill Shepherd will play Maddie!" Loved Cybill, but no thanks. Not another TV series right now, and certainly not another detective agency. "I'll pass," I told them and went to find my trustiest hiking boots.

I spent the next three weeks floating on a river in Utah, gathering my steam again. And *Moonlighting* spent the next five seasons on ABC. Sixteen Emmy nominations. A top-ten show. Was Bruce Willis the secret sauce to all that success? Most probably.

But it might have been fun to find out.

That same year, Henry Winkler took me to lunch to offer me the chance to play a secret agent working for the shadowy Department of External Services. The character, a guy with extraordinary scientific resourcefulness, could solve any problem using everyday materials at hand. Each week's episode was a new science experiment as our hero saved the day. In one episode, some jumper cables and two quarters become an arc welder. In the next, a car muffler, seat cushion stuffing, and a cigarette lighter became a working bazooka. Personality-wise, the character was totally in my wheelhouse. But all the rest sounded silly to me at the time. I passed. *MacGyver* ran on ABC for seven years.

Film School Boot Camp

Who's Who?

The most important part of a project, besides the script, is casting. It's the magic sauce. Get it right, and things work easily. Get it wrong, and it's never going to work.

When I signed on to do *Dreamer* (the bowling movie), we met with every actress in town to play the romantic female lead. My favorite was a young, relatively unknown actress named Debra Winger. She was sexy, raw, vulnerable, and such a good actress. Putting her in that movie would have made it more real and visceral, like the film they had told me they wanted to make. *No. No. We want a bigger name.* They cast Susan Blakely. Lovely and talented, but no Debra Winger. That was the beginning of the end of *Dreamer.* They wanted a "cute" movie, not a "real" movie.

As an actor/producer on *Just in Time*, I was told—after shooting the pilot—by the network and studio I had to fire a young actress named Annette Bening, making the casting process begin anew. One actress came in and wowed us all. She was so fun, sexy, and unique that I was bowled over. If we have to replace Annette, this was the actress we should use: Frances McDormand. But we got resistance from the studio again, and finally they and the network said no. "She's not 'right' for the part. She's not a conventional leading lady" was their explanation. A dagger to the heart—and to the project. (Bening + McDormand have, combined, eleven Oscar nominations and three wins.)

Would *The Godfather* have been the same if James Caan had played Michael? Would *Friends* have worked with someone else paying Ross? Would *Moonlighting* have worked without Bruce Willis? Would *Star Wars* have worked with Christopher Walken as Han Solo? And . . . perhaps the Indiana Jones franchise wouldn't have worked with Tim Matheson. This is the alchemy of Hollywood. Respect it—it's magic.

A decade after turning down *MacGyver*, I was offered the dad role in *7th Heaven* on a new network I'd never heard of: the WB. It looked like a wimpy show to me, very *Ozzie and Harriet*; the guy's a minister, very white-bread, middle America. Catherine Hicks was already cast in it. (She didn't even have supernatural powers in this one.)

"It's going to series," they told me. "Two years, guaranteed."

Two years of steady pay always sounded good, but I was holding out for film. I had just done two pictures for Paramount—*Black Sheep* and *A Very Brady Sequel*—and thought maybe this was my moment to be back in the movies. Foolishly, I said no. Adding insult to injury, it was about to get worse.

At this time, managers had come into vogue in Hollywood. The business had shifted to a place where agents really focused on information and making deals, and people were bringing on managers to guide their careers and take care of them. Where agents had fifty or more clients, managers might have six. I'd decided to meet a bunch of managers and eventually hired Beth Cannon. I expected my agents to have two dozen actors and directors just like me; they were in the numbers game. But with a manager, the whole point is that, in their world, you're not just a number to get off the call sheet so they don't have to deal with you. Instead, the manager is supposed to help you make the right choice with the next ten years in mind, not the next six months.

But after nearly ten years with me, Beth signed a new client: an actor named Stephen Collins. Actors are a small community, and it was no secret that Stephen had always envied my career; he'd joined Beth for exactly that reason. "I don't like it," I told her when I learned she was putting him *and* me up for the same work. "We're the same kind of actor; I see him at the same auditions all the time."

"Oh no," she assured me. "You guys aren't the same at all. This is a nonissue." Naturally, after I'd said no, Beth pitched Stephen to *7th Heaven* and he got the job. (Not so dissimilar after all.) The show ran eleven years and was a huge hit. I was pissed and let Beth know it.

Soon after, I'm working at USA Studios and Universal as a director, and they want me to direct a TV movie called *As Time Runs Out*. Okay, great. "We're thinking Steve Collins as the leading man. Can we make the offer?" they ask me. I took a couple breaths and then took the high road. "Yeah," I said. "That sounds fine." I'd decided I had no problem with Stephen. Beth's still with him *and* me; we'll work this out.

Then Collins has Beth declare, "Stephen won't be in this movie if Tim directs it." Stephen, she explained to the producers, wanted an old pro instead. Having never seen anything I'd directed, he wouldn't even take a meeting with me; he just killed it and got me fired. Beth stayed silent to me throughout.

I fired her as my manager. *As Time Runs Out* got its old pro director.

In a 2014 interview, Stephen admitted to "inappropriate sexual conduct" with three female minors. His IMDb has been empty since.

———

I READ FOR *AMERICAN GRAFFITI*, LIKE EVERYONE ELSE IN TOWN. I was studying acting at the time, and before I did my screen test, I asked George Lucas, "George, what are you looking for here?"

This was for the yellow-deuce-coupe-driving character John Milner, eventually played by Paul Le Mat. "This guy's a young John Wayne," Lucas told me. This was of almost no help. Should I toss one hip out and dangle my hands? "Whoa, take 'er easy there, pilgrim." I was hoping he'd give me some kind of action to play. I did an okay audition and, obviously, didn't get the part. Every actor has hundreds of similar stories.

Two years later, I read for *Star Wars*, again like everyone else in town. A general meeting and then a meeting with the casting person. Too old to play Luke and too young for Han.

Three years later, it was *Raiders of the Lost Ark*.

I knew I looked too young for the part of the roguish archeologist. Thirty-four and still couldn't grow a mustache. With my Danish Matthieson heritage, I could go days without shaving. "What can you do?" I asked the makeup people at Lucasfilm, and they added a couple of lines to my face and darkened what stubble they could find.

Great luck, my screen test was with Karen Allen. Getting into a fight at a fraternity house has a way of bonding people forever. She alone set me at ease for the next few hours. I did what Henry Fonda had taught me as a teenager: stood very still, hit my marks, and "told the truth." That's who I thought Indiana was, and it proved a pretty good audition. One of my best, actually. Indiana Jones was definitely a character I understood. Still, three days later, I got the "we're-going-another-way" call.

"Understood," I assented. It had been an interesting what-if.

"But George wants you to come in," they added. "He wants to talk to you."

I was on my way to a play rehearsal and stopped in at the studio to see Lucas. Still kind of heartbroken, knowing it would be a massive movie—with Steven Spielberg *and* George Lucas—it was as close to a sure thing as Hollywood had ever conceived, and every actor in town knew it. Instead, I was on my way to some play thousands of miles away from Broadway.

George Lucas is a quiet man, almost shy. You could tell he was more comfortable with gadgets and story and film than actual people. "It was a tough choice," he finally got out. "We're really sorry."

"That's how these things go. It's okay." Saying all the right things. "I appreciate the opportunity." (Thinking now of Kevin Costner being cool when director Lawrence Kasdan called to tell Kevin he'd been completely deleted from *The Big Chill*; Kasdan was so impressed with Costner's classy reaction, Kevin got his first starring role in the director's very next film.)

"You really did the strongest test." Lucas now looked at me directly for the first time. "Yours was the best audition." He's either screwing with me, I now assumed, or worse: It's like someone breaking up with you. She says that she loves you and you're a great lay but that she's still gonna suck Harrison's dick now.

I looked George Lucas in the eyes. "Oh, George," I said. "Thank you. Don't worry about it. We'll work together again." I'm now consoling *him*. (He *is* a genius.)

We're "still looking" for that first film together.

The Fall Guy

IN MINNEAPOLIS, PLUGGING MY LATEST FILM, I ARRIVED AT A LOCAL TV station for the customary morning new-movie interview. The receptionist eyed me curiously. "What are you promoting?"

"It's a film called *A Little Sex*," I explained. A rom-com with Kate Capshaw (*Indiana Jones and the Temple of Doom*, *Black Rain*, Mrs. Spielberg).

The receptionist shook her head, disappointed.

"A 'little' sex?" she grumbled. "Why not *A Whole Bunch of Sex*?"

She had a point, and the movie earned less than a third of its budget back.

It was the start of a string of failures and disappointments I'd be a part of. But going into a project, you rarely know it.

Bruce Paltrow (director, *The White Shadow* creator, and father of Gwyneth) was salt of the earth, quick, funny, and talented. He wanted me for his next film. *A Little Sex* had a good-enough script but not, I thought, right for me. I just wasn't taken with it and was holding out for something special.

What I really wanted was *Police Academy*. Don't laugh. The script was great, the best comedy I'd seen since *Animal House*. The part that ultimately went to Steve Guttenberg was funny and perfect for me. But I couldn't even get a meeting with the producers or director.

The *Animal House* lift was fading fast. Then, the actors strike of 1980 hit Hollywood, and everything shut down. Within six months, I'd gotten into, and ended, a disastrous relationship with a psychotic editor, was running out of money fast, and I was flat-out feeling stuck. I needed to do *something* . . . When the strike ended, I decided to make *A Little Sex* with Paltrow.

The movie failed to "find its audience."

Next up was *The House of God*, a United Artists comedy based on a massive best-selling novel. The script was terrible, but the book was a hit and the movie had a good cast: James Cromwell (*Babe, L.A. Confidential*), Sandra Bernhard (*The King of Comedy*), Howard Rollins (*Ragtime*), Joe Piscopo (*SNL*), and Michael Richards (*Seinfeld*). As a comedic ensemble, we all figured the poor script was savable. The director, however—who'd had a recent hit with *Ice Castles*—wasn't funny, wasn't decisive, and now spent most of his questionable energy banging, by most all accounts, the leading lady. The shoot was scheduled for eight weeks, and when we reached that, we'd only limped past the halfway mark.

Adding to all of this, my father was going through major health issues (which we'll get to later) and I was about to bury another good friend.

———

As an actor and director, the pros I never question are the stuntpeople. Lighting and cinematographers are a close second, but stuntmen and stuntwomen literally put their lives on the line for our entertainment. In my experience, they consistently understand the best pathway to a great shot, how to maximize a budget, how to boost audience enjoyment, *and* how to do it safely.

A close buddy of mine, Albert John "A. J." Bakunas, was a stuntman. A. J. had worked on movies like *Dog Day Afternoon, Hooper, The Bees*, and a dozen more. The license plate on A. J.'s car read FALLGUY. (His particular talent was performing high falls—one of the most perilous stunts.) He had so much flair, he'd recently been a guest on *The Tonight Show*, and Johnny Carson loved him. A. J. was that big a personality.

We'd met on *The Apple Dumpling Gang Rides Again*, where I'd foolishly pressured the director and stunt team into letting me do a dangerous stunt on a moving train. My character was supposed to do an epic jump onto A. J. and, clinging to my twenties by a bare fingernail, I figured, *Yeah, I can do that!*

My stunt double in that film was Joe Stone (Joe had been doubling me since *The Quest*), and he pulled me aside to explain things more clearly: "Tim, when you jump . . . If you miss your mark by a foot or jump one second late, *one second*, you will go right past A. J., over the train . . . and then over the cliff on the other side of the train. There are nine things you have to do *exactly* right, or you're going over that cliff."

This, for me, was eight things too many. Joe did the jump for me.

But A. J. had noticed how sincere I was about trying, and he proved kind enough to offer his services. "It's mostly mathematics and physics, man," the guy with the FALLGUY license plate assured me. "And a bit of balls, which you seem to have."

He invited me to his house, where he had—should we be surprised?—a top-of-the-line stunt airbag rigged in his backyard with a thirty-foot high-fall scaffolding. "We'll start you at eight feet," he said, judging my abilities, and then he showed me several methods to land safely. Then ten feet, twelve. Fourteen feet.

I was like a little kid again in my Superman cape, flinging myself from my bed. "See," A. J. assured me, laughing, "it's easy." Over the next few months, I was doing different stunt falls from twenty feet. A. J.—who'd grown up in New Jersey and been a high school gym teacher before heading to Hollywood—was hilarious and easygoing, and we quickly became good friends.

A breather in the fun came only when I'd flown to Philadelphia to shoot *The House of God* and A. J. headed to Kentucky to shoot *Steel* with Lee Majors. A. J. and another stuntman, Dar Robinson (who I'd worked with on *Magnum Force*), were engaged in a good-natured pissing contest about who could do the highest stunt falls. A. J., who'd held the high-fall record, learned that Dar had just done a fall out of a helicopter from 300 feet, shattering A. J.'s record by 50 feet. A. J. had already shot a nine-story fall (90-plus feet) for *Steel* but now convinced the director and Lee Majors to let him jump again from the *top* floor—323 feet.

"Are world records worth the risk?" Majors asks in a promotional video made minutes before the stunt was filmed. "It's obvious to A. J. Bakunas, it is. We'll see."

We'll see . . .

It just so happened that I'd called the *Steel* production office trying to get a hold of A. J. that same day. We hadn't spoken in a few weeks. "There's been an accident," they told me. The airbag had ruptured. "He's at Good Samaritan Hospital."

I couldn't believe it. This was one of the smartest, funniest, most personable guys I'd ever met. The next Lee Majors, maybe. There was no way it ended like this. "He's going to be okay then, right?" I asked.

"We don't know," the voice on the other end admitted.

My friend died early the next day.

A. J. is one of the greatest might-have-beens I've ever crossed paths with. His death, in 1978, was also the first time I knew of a contemporary, a young man like me, who had died. It gave a guy something to think about, for sure.

Years later, his friendly rival Dar Robinson was also killed when his motorcycle smashed through a railing and went over a cliff while Dar was filming a scene for *Million Dollar Mystery*, a forgotten comedy.

He'd missed his mark by one second.

———

THE HOUSE OF GOD HAD GONE WAY OVER BUDGET AND WAS OFF the rails, so the rewrites started, to try and rein the mess back in. *What could be done to the plot so that it ends shooting in a few weeks for the least amount of money?* Never a good way to write a screenplay.

I expected to be playing golf with a chimpanzee any minute now. They ordered us from our location in Boston back to L.A., where the movie was to be finished on the old MGM lot, which didn't match anything we'd shot in Philadelphia *or* Boston.

Diagnosis: terminally shitty.

Remedy: the film was stuck up on a shelf and never released. You can find it on the internet, but that's the problem with the internet: Some things weren't meant to be shared.

This movie, along with *Dreamer* (*Rocky* with bowling), constituted several "Tim Matheson" stinkers in a row. The "Otter Lift" wouldn't last much longer—and was probably already gone; I just didn't want to admit it yet.

Genuine worry started creeping in again.

Then, a break.

———

Like everyone else, I started my reading of *Daily Variety*— Hollywood's bible from 1905 until the internet fucked things up— each day by turning to "Just for Variety," Army Archerd's canonical column. He was reporting on a recent interview with Mel Brooks regarding *History of the World: Part I*. Mel was talking about the next project he was planning.

"I've got this movie I wanna do," Mel explained to Archerd. "*To Be or Not to Be*. It's a remake of the 1942 Jack Benny movie directed by Ernst Lubitsch. A comedy set in Nazi Germany about a theatre troupe. I'm gonna get Tim Matheson from *Animal House* to star, and it will be him and me and Anne."

Anne was Anne Bancroft, Mel's wife. Also the Oscar, Emmy, and Tony winner for stuff like *The Graduate* and *The Miracle Worker*.

Holy shit! This was the first time I'd heard *anything* about this project.

Rereading the article carefully to make sure I hadn't just imagined my name, I called my agent immediately. "I've already called them," he said. Naturally, he'd also seen the article. "Mel's people say it's going to happen."

Blazing Saddles, *Young Frankenstein*, *High Anxiety*—the hottest comedy producer in Hollywood had picked me out of the heap. My shooting star still had some light left in it!

Any intimidation of Ms. Bancroft—for which I held much—disappeared almost immediately. She was full Italian and had grown up in Little Italy in the Bronx and was as real as it got. Someone once asked her at a party why she, international icon who had conquered stage and screen, was with a low-brow comic like Mel Brooks. Without missing a beat, Anne yelled out, "Hey, Mel. This guy wants to know why I'm with you. Show him, Mel!" as she waved her hands nonchalantly at Mel's crotch.

Shooting one scene with Anne and Charles Durning (*The Sting*, *The Best Little Whorehouse in Texas*), Mel came in the middle of rehearsal and started redirecting the scene. The film's actual director was Alan Johnson. "Oh, look, everyone!" Anne said, and stopped her husband immediately, hands on her hips. "Mel Brooks is trying to tell Oscar winner Anne Bancroft and Oscar nominee Charles Durning how to act!"

The crew's laughter broke all the tension.

"All right, all right!" Mel retreated quickly. "Do it *your* way!!"

All my improv lessons were paying off on this one. In the first take, not easy, the three of us successfully captured a scene with no cuts and all dialogue, Anne and me firing back and forth with Mel caught between us throwing out random "What?!" and "Hey!" and "Howwwa!"

It was a really special experience to stand toe to toe with this pair of legends. Plus, I got to get into bed with Mel, his character thinking I was his wife. How many others have been able to cuddle with Mel?

At the cast party, Mel threw an event with the best food and booze I'd ever seen. Bob Hope would have approved; it was a celebration fit for Caligula's Rome. There, Mel called out and personally thanked every single crew member by name without any notes. It blew my mind. From the wardrobe supervisor to the techs in the lighting department, he knew 'em all—and shared something specific they'd done to help make the movie better and usually tossed in a little joke about them.

By the time he got to me, I was curious to hear the roasting I might get. Something about my dedication to the craft or unknown physical-comedy skills. "And Tim Matheson . . ." Mel waved his hands and smiled ear to ear. "A fine young actor. What a good-looking guy, isn't he? Jeez, he looks good and he's fun to work with too. But really I want to thank you most of all . . . for not fucking my wife."

TO BE OR NOT TO BE BARELY MADE ITS PRODUCTION COSTS BACK and probably lost money on distribution. It was a rare Mel Brooks flop. A faithful remake of a 1942 black-and-white film about Nazis. Brooks's next film venture was *Spaceballs*, another hit. But despite the perfect fit, I didn't get Mel's call to play Lone Starr.

It was too many misses in a row, and the career was rapidly, shockingly, stuttering out. If I didn't get a couple of *W*s fast, it might never start up again.

Chance Encounters

"WHO IS TIM MATHESON?"

"Get me Tim Matheson!"

"Get me a Tim Matheson type."

"Get me a young Tim Matheson."

"Who is Tim Matheson?"

A cycle in entertainment. Like something out of the Bhagavad Gita or my own ancestors' tales of Ragnarök. You slog to get known, enough that you might even get some calls from people named Huston or Spielberg. And then one day, an actual call goes out into Hollywood that a casting agent is looking for an actor *like* you—but not you.

My agent called a studio one day: "You're looking for a 'Tim Matheson type'? How about Tim Matheson?!"

The final step in the cycle is back where you started—forgotten again.

The early 1980s had not been kind, careerwise.

Fortunately, 1985 was a year for two major victories.

Each had been *years* in the making.

Entertainment is mostly discussions, plans, and toil that lead to nothing. Most projects started never actually get done. Most partnerships and encounters soon dissolve to nothing.

But, you never know . . .

"DO YOU OWN RUBBER GLOVES?"

Soon after *Animal House*, I was invited to test for a film by a director named Michael Ritchie. He'd recently directed *The Bad News Bears* (a huge hit) and Robert Redford's *The Candidate*.

It was just him and me. He'd put up a little video camera, and we shot a couple of scenes. Just me talking to Michael. This was for a film called *An Almost Perfect Affair*, a romantic comedy about an affair between a filmmaker and a film producer's wife, set during the Cannes Film Festival.

Michael was funny, kindhearted, articulate, and sharp. Brilliant, even. I liked him immediately. He was so sincere and knew where the comedy was. Ultimately, I didn't get the part, which went to Keith Carradine (*Nashville, The Duellists*).

But Michael called me a few years later with a movie he wanted me to do and invited me out to lunch. "You gotta do this movie," he told me over salads at the Hotel Bel-Air, but I didn't really love the script or think it was a fit for me at the time. "You want to sign on to this movie, Tim." He kept pushing.

"I'd love to work with you, Michael," I told him. "But I'm not sure this is the film for it. The script is—"

"I hear what you're saying," he said. "But trust me. I'm telling you: You should do this movie. Just sign on . . . and we'll see how it goes."

I thanked him for lunch, and we went our separate ways again.

A year later, we were next-door neighbors, and I asked about the film.

"The movie never started shooting," he admitted. "That's why I kept telling you to take the job. I knew you'd get paid anyway, but I couldn't, in good faith, come out and tell you that."

This gesture had been entirely based on my "failed" audition for *An Almost Perfect Affair* years before. And he was just getting started.

"YOU'RE A SHITTY ACTOR," I TOLD CHEVY CHASE. "*SNL* GOT BETter when you left." "Bill Murray's the funny one. You make Dan Aykroyd look talented." "Do you have any idea what you're doing?" "Aren't movie stars supposed to be . . . attractive?" "You know everyone just tolerates you, right?" "*Having* a small dick is the leading cause for *being* one, Chevy."

This went on for hours during close-ups. Hollywood's current leading comedian asked me to antagonize him from off camera whenever I could, to get spontaneous reactions. He did not need to ask me twice.

Burt Reynolds, Jeff Bridges, Charles Grodin, George Segal, Richard Dreyfuss. Even Mick Jagger. They all had a shot at it, but it was Chevy Chase who had finally nabbed the role.

"Just throw crap, Matheson," Chevy told me. "Anything you can think of."

We were filming *Fletch*, Michael Ritchie's next film.

I'd been cast as Alan Stanwyk, who offers Fletch $50,000 to kill . . . me. Chevy was coming off *National Lampoon's Vacation* (National Lampoon had another hit!), and *Fletch* was going to be something.

And despite the fact that I'd let Chevy down after Doug Kenney died, he still wanted me for Stanwyk. We'd built a connection over the years. And despite the fact that Michael and I had whiffed on a couple of projects, the director still wanted me for Stanwyk. We'd also built a connection over the years.

I was doing the *True West* play in New York (being mauled nightly by Daniel Stern, as described earlier), and it didn't look like *Fletch* was going to happen when I first got the offer. In hopes of reenergizing my career, I was currently looking to do something different and interesting, and I was afraid that *Fletch* was just another comedy.

But I also wanted to work with Michael Ritchie, so I agreed.

To help make the schedules work best for me, Michael flew me out on a private jet after the Sunday night *True West* show each week with promises I'd be back to work in New York by Tuesday (when the play started again). I was doing my best Belushi imitation going back and forth. The first week, we had to stop in Kansas City to refuel, and I got maybe two hours of sleep before standing beneath the Santa Monica Pier filming my opening scene with Chevy. By the time I arrived on set, the film had been in production for weeks, and the director and film's star had already worked out the thorny dynamics of how to make a film with Chevy Chase.

There is no denying Chevy was and is a huge talent. He could steal the proverbial show in seconds and *could* carry a movie on only cruise control. There are few performers who can go big and still feel natural: Farley, Belushi, Jim Carrey, Kate McKinnon, Melissa McCarthy, Tina Fey, Ryan Gosling . . . and Chevy.

But two Chevy films—*Under the Rainbow* and *Modern Problems*—hadn't done so well. As the comedic star of *SNL*, *Foul Play*, and *Caddyshack*, he'd assumed, via star power, almost total creative control of those projects. Not always a good thing.

For *Vacation*, he'd trusted director Harold Ramis to take control a bit more, and the results were obvious. It was a massive hit and the arrival of an indelible character. Clark Griswold will live forever. So, for *Fletch*, Chevy was again putting his trust in a talented director who could rein him in and even help him grow as a performer. The interesting thing about Chevy was that he didn't really consider himself an actor. He was a comedian, an incredible performer for sure, going on pure talent. Now he wanted to stretch as an actor, to learn the craft more, and to go to different places. On this film, Chevy wanted to engage on a real visceral level with whoever he was playing a scene with. It was a new path for Chase, one I recognized myself, and I tried to support it in any way I could.

Michael Ritchie had challenged him to create a character again . . . to act. Fletch wasn't just personality and quips. He could play fearful and curious and contented. To help with all this, Chevy and Michael had developed a compromise and partnership that was, when I was on set, working. The improv prodigy would have all these ideas on how to do a scene, and Michael would calmly say, "Let's film it *my* way first and then we'll try a couple of your ideas. Whatever you'd like." Chevy played along and the scenes, as written, got done—with most all of the original script making it into the final product.

Michael used a simple trick to make sure that the movie got what the movie needed. He would often shoot the end of the scene first. That way, we (Chevy) would be locked into how the scene had to *end* in the edit room, allowing Chevy more freedom to play during the scene but also making sure that this freedom resulted in a movie and not a mess.

Film School Boot Camp

Learn to Relax

One of the hardest parts of being an actor is figuring out how to make the most of the time when you're on location or at the studio and not actively working on set. These make-or-break times can get you in trouble with your fellow actors, the producers, and the director if you don't manage this time wisely. Hollywood invented "hurry up and wait." It's the *wait* that's the hardest part.

Over the years, I've picked up some tricks from other actors and developed some myself: I worked with an actor named Jack Elam on *Lock, Stock and Barrel*. His thing was a game called Liar's Poker. Jack was the best player around, and he always won. He would bring his own dollars, bills he had stashed with five 7's or eight 6's—it led to wild bluffs and huge laughs. It was only a dollar and always fun, but that was Jack, and everyone appreciated the game and the levity he provided.

George C. Scott and Stanley Kubrick played chess together during downtime on *Dr. Strangelove*. It's a quiet game with no chatting, it requires intense concentration, it didn't distract from the work at hand, and it kept them in the zone when they were called back to set. I was also inspired by Brian Cox (*Succession*, *Troy*) when we worked together on a film called *The Etruscan Smile*. He kept an iPad with him tuned to Turner Classic Movies, and he'd watch classic movies all day. This practice kept him in the zone, inspired by the work of other great actors. It also had the side effect of protecting him from being dragged into chatty conversations when he wanted to conserve his concentration and energy, without his being perceived as rude. He'd arrive on set relaxed and always deliver the goods.

I use all of my time off set getting ready for my time on set. I like to run lines with a recording on my iPhone, leaving my character's dialogue out of the scene as I prepare. That way, I can run the scene over and over, hearing the other actors' words, locking in the dialogue so I'm ready when I go on set. I also listen to music that keeps me in the mood of the scenes that I am doing that particular day. I have discovered that the music calls out to a part of my brain where emotions are stored and helps me access them. It works for lighter scenes as well as more dramatic ones. I once did a quick-paced comedy filled with rapid banter that played super fast. Off set, I listened to fast-paced music to give me the rhythm of the dialogue in the scene. It helped me tremendously. Take a nap at lunchtime. Even for ten minutes, it helps me. That way, I'm not slowing down and getting exhausted in the afternoon or latter part of the day, but I'm as fresh and strong as I was first thing in the morning. I also learned a trick from a director: Change your shoes at lunch. It gives you a fresh start on the day and kind of recharges you.

The bottom line is, you need to have a hobby or something else that interests you and that you can dive into when you're not on set. Not only will it keep your mind busy, but you will also find that it makes you a more interesting member of the team, which has all sorts of positive benefits. Sir John Gielgud said, "I act for free. I get paid to wait." He could have added, "What I do when I wait is how I get paid."

For the most part, the whole *Fletch* experience went by in a blur for me as I shuttled back and forth in a whirlwind between L.A. and New York. Throughout, my task was to play the straight man. Following in the footsteps of actors like Bud Abbott, Dean Martin, Desi Arnaz, and Margaret Dumont. I just had to play Stanwyk as a real person and let Chevy do his thing around me. Now, I was in the Dean Wormer role.

When shooting was done, I celebrated by taking my mother and sister to Hawaii for a vacation. The call from my agent came two days into our trip. "They need you back," he said. "Michael needs to reshoot your final scene. They had a technical issue."

My final scene had been filmed in the Marion Davies and William Randolph Hearst mansion—the one in *The Godfather* (with the infamous horse head scene) and *The Bodyguard*—at the cost of $15,000 a day ($40,000 today)! These guys were serious.

"I can't," I explained carefully. "We barely got here, and I can't just leave my family."

My agent said he'd take care of it and did. He told the producers and Michael that I was on some small island in Hawaii and couldn't be reached. This was an excuse that still worked in the mid-1980s, back when it was still possible to be unreachable. Remarkably, the producers understood and agreed to push the reshoot aside for another week. When I arrived on set, I had to keep up the charade that I'd been stranded on some remote island for eight days.

FLETCH IS A TESTAMENT TO BOTH RITCHIE AND CHEVY CHASE. Like *Animal House*, *Fletch* had a wonderful script, and these two got it done using the talent on set. I was out of town for the premiere and my only thought was, *I hope it works.* I didn't know anymore. Again, no one does in this town.

Fletch went on to become one of the top ten grossing films of 1985. So I got married.

———

TINY DANCER

LIKE *FLETCH*, THIS PRODUCTION WAS MANY YEARS IN THE MAKING.

Right after filming *1941*, I'd flown to New York and borrowed the empty apartment of my *1941* costar Treat Williams. It was on the Upper West Side, a subterranean apartment with more crossbars and padlocks than a medieval castle. Being from the Valley, I was thinking, *Holy shit! Why does anyone need this many locks?*

But the young woman dropping off Treat's keys gave the place some promise. A cute little dancer with the Eliot Feld Ballet.

Friendly, wholesome, real. She was just . . . different than the women I knew in Hollywood. An Air Force brat who had grown up all over and a total straight shooter, no airs.

For years, I'd wanted to get married and have kids. I wanted to fall in love and have a family. The ghosts of my chaotic childhood pined for normalcy, whatever that was. And so, I went from one horrible relationship to the next. I kept trying to make it happen. Every woman I slept with, I'd think, *She's the one!*

They never were.

And by the early 1980s, I'd given up. I'd finally said to myself, *You know what? If I never get married . . . if I never have kids . . . the world will carry on just fine. I'll carry on.* I'd surrendered and finally removed that pressure from the situation.

Naturally, this is when the New York dancer shows up in my life.

Megan Murphy and I became friends only; she was living with some guy anyway, another dancer. It eventually got sexual between us but still very casual; she was still living with "some guy." And I'd quit on the idea of *the one.*

No one's getting married, no one's falling in love.

I shot *A Little Sex* in New York, and Megan and I spent more time together. We had become good friends who would see each other *if* she was free and *if* I was free. This dynamic went on for years. But when she came to Los Angeles to dance in the 1984 Olympic Arts festival, she stayed with me, and other than for work, we were largely inseparable. Nearly six years had passed since we'd first met. The longest relationship I'd ever had.

My next trip to New York, at dinner, I told Megan, "I think I love you." I had never said anything like it to her before. The truth just slipped out. And it had surprised both of us. She looked at me differently after that. After dinner, we went back together to my hotel. Sex had been a regular part of our relationship for years, but this love-talk wasn't. Lying in bed in the deep of night, the oddly romantic sounds of New York drifting up from the streets below. "*Would you ever considering marrying me?*" I asked half-jokingly, trying to ease the new awkwardness I'd created.

Big pause, then: "I don't know. Maybe . . ." Megan replied.

"Maybe" is definitely not "no."

Pushing to close the deal, in the morning, I took her to Tiffany's, bought her an Elsa Peretti necklace, and casually browsed the world's most famous engagement ring counter. The discussion continued through the fall. She wouldn't live with me until we were married. She also wanted to make sure her career remained just as important as mine. That sounded great. "Maybe" became "yes."

We married in June 1985. A year later, we were expecting our first daughter.

But if I was going to afford baby food or make the next house payment, it was time to re-create myself again. *Fletch* had been a nice résumé bullet, but I'd only had a supporting role. Whatever bonus points I'd gained as part of *Animal House* had all, it seemed, been spent.

My career needed an overhaul. It was time again to show the industry *another* new side of Tim Matheson.

It was time to kiss and murder on cable TV.

Kiss and Tell

KISSING OTHER GUYS' WIVES HAD BECOME MY SPECIALTY.

Kevin Kline, Michael J. Fox, Steven Spielberg, James Keach, über-producer Mark Burnett, Robert Urich, William Macy, and Tom Cruise. I kissed, pecked, snogged, necked, smooched, bussed, and made out *sometimes for hours* with their brides. Got to first base; sometimes, was even told to go to second.

To be fair, all their wives were successful performers—Phoebe Cates (Kline), Tracy Pollan (Fox), Kate Capshaw (Spielberg), Jane Seymour (Keach), Roma Downey (Burnett), Heather Menzies (Urich), Felicity Huffman (Macy) and Mimi Rogers (Cruise)—and we'd only been acting.

To keep my leading-man roles, to keep finding work, I'd shifted from young prankster to middle-aged lothario. Mirroring my real life some, I'll admit.

It was the golden age of cable television. (In 1981, some 25 percent of households had cable; by the early 2000s, that figure rose to 90 percent.) USA, TNT, AMC, FX, TBS, Bravo, E!, the Hallmark Channel, TLC, and Lifetime were *all* playing catch-up with HBO and the major networks and needed original movies, miniseries, and TV programs on skintight budgets.

Cable TV movies were cheap and quick to make, and more to the point, people loved them. The cable networks had discovered the formula of movies that weren't quite silver-screen-ready but would be great for a binge on Sunday morning or to wind down on a Thursday night, many years before anyone had suggestively uttered the phrase "Netflix and chill."

Obsessed with a Married Woman, The Woman Who Sinned, Dying to Love You, Shameful Secrets, A Kiss to Die For, Harmful Intent, Midnight Heat, An Unfinished Affair, Buried Secrets, Little White Lies, Second Honeymoon, A Holiday for Love, Forever Love, At the Mercy of a Stranger, Sleeping with the Devil.

Made 'em all, and others, for the next ten years. As Michael Caine reflected when he accepted a Golden Globe, "I made a lot of crap . . . and, a lot of money." But doing cable TV movies allowed me not only to keep the lights on but also to eventually dip my toes into directing and producing (more on that later).

There were the feature films *Black Sheep* and *A Very Brady Sequel* mixed in, but for the most part, it was cable television that kept my career and family afloat. I'd swallowed my pride enough to go where the work was.

During these years, I also made creepier cable films like *Sometimes They Come Back* (written by Stephen King), *Buried Alive, Bay Cove* (about newlyweds facing a secret coven of witches), *Twilight Man, Tails You Live, Heads You're Dead,* and *Quicksand: No Escape*—another film with Donald Sutherland, who farted in every scene we were in together trying to make me laugh. But even *these* somehow always had a lot of kissing.

Long before murder podcasts and murder shows, cable TV knew what it was doing. Sex and bizarre murder were a perfect, and now proven, combo.

I'd started rehearsing for these roles in 1959—the kissing part, not the murder part.

———

My first kiss was in San Bernardino during the magical time when my mother had vanished for a year and we lived like a

TV family with my aunt and uncle. I was in the sixth grade, and my sister, a grade older, had a friend.

While I was a bit of a goof and trying to find my social footing, my sister always ran with the most popular crowd in the school—no matter which school we went to. She was popular, dated the most popular guys, and had, if you polled the schoolyard, the coolest friends. One of these was a girl named Virgie.

My sister said, "Virgie wants to make out with you. Whaddya think?"

Like any sixth-grader I thought, . . . *I guess.*

Virgie came over, and we climbed into the bottom bunk bed.

At the time, I was still more of a peck-on-the-cheek kind of guy. I had a "girlfriend" named Monica Dominowski and we'd kissed maybe three times, but these were little air kisses at the side of her face like I was meeting an Italian butcher.

This older woman (fourteen) was another story entirely. We started kissing, and she immediately slid her tongue into my mouth. French kissing wasn't even a term I knew yet; I just knew this teen's tongue was swirling around my larynx. I was twelve and still rather innocent, but my head and hormones were sent off a cliff.

There wasn't another girlfriend or kissing opportunity until I was in the eighth grade and back in Burbank. I was horrifyingly shy and had disastrous luck with girls. One girl I liked was part of the in crowd, and I'd gone over to her house with plans to kiss her, maybe try some of the moves my sister's friend had taught me. We made out a bit, but I got a hunch I was awful at it and canceled the mission. I mostly just wanted to hold hands and walk down the hallway together—a total square. She moved on quickly, probably to some guy who could properly French kiss.

This is around the time Janelle Penny informed me I needed to be six feet tall. So I moved on to Nancy Montgomery, who had fewer height prerequisites, and she and I actually spent a whole summer together. When we went back to school, however, it was like *Grease* and I was Sandy *before* the leather pants. Nancy fell back in with the cool kids, broke up with me, and started going out with Kevin Burkett, one of the guys on the basketball team. *I guess she did have a height requirement.* I drove around alone in my car for hours at night, trying not to cry. A week later, I started watching the basketball team more often, for hints on how to dress, act, and talk.

A forward named Ken Strathearn became my new role model. He was tall, athletic, and admired; he had the world on a string. I used to take *Jonny Quest* money to buy clothes like his. I had no idea how to be cool, but I knew that if I imitated Ken, I was on the right path.

Nevertheless, I was still hurt by Nancy's dumping me. I swore I'd never let a girl or woman do that to me again. And for the next few years, I kept my vow and mostly avoided such entanglements.

When Jennifer Leak pulled me into bed at nineteen, I was still pretty naive. It wasn't until after our divorce—*yes, also a bit during our marriage*—that I actually started exploring sexuality and started to get good at it.

I probably should have called my sister's friend.

———

THESE DAYS, THERE ARE INTIMACY COORDINATORS ON SET TO NEGOtiate every action and make sure everything is on the up-and-up. But for decades, it had been up to the actors to work things out themselves. I experienced two extremes from my professional kissing years.

In the first tale, Jane Seymour is naked.

We are making *Obsessed with a Married Woman*. The world knows Jane from *Live and Let Die*, *Somewhere in Time*, and *East of Eden*. It will soon know her from *Dr. Quinn, Medicine Woman* and as the smoking-hot mom from *Wedding Crashers*. She'd be stunning even in a winter coat and sweatpants. Jane arrives on set, tosses her robe to the costumer, and now she's mostly naked, in bed with me.

Neither the director, nor anyone else to my knowledge, has asked her for this level of commitment. "I just think it'd be better for this scene," she casually explains.

This was like my sister's friend all over again. *Who was I to argue?* My shirt was also off, right? But this isn't a power move on her part, I quickly realize, or a come-on. In the scene, I'm supposed to be overwhelmed with attraction and passion. *I can't get enough of this woman* kinda thing. She's just a smart actor able to distinguish reality from make-believe. She knows she'll look better on film, more natural, *and* I'll look more natural if I have to do less acting.

Mission accomplished. I've never acted "overwhelmed with attraction and passion" better in my whole career.

IN THE OTHER TALE, SHANNEN DOHERTY SAYS, "DON'T EVER PUT your tongue in my mouth." *(Where was this girl when I was twelve?)*

We've barely been on set for an hour. I've just met her. *How long has she been waiting to get this out?* Not too far from twelve-year-old me, I'd had zero plans to go for any tongue business. I don't even wanna hold hands.

In real life, Shannen (*Beverly Hills, 90210*; *Heathers*; *Charmed*) is twenty-five years younger than I am, but our characters fall in love in *Sleeping with the Devil* because I'm a billionaire in the film and, also, it's Hollywood. "My boyfriend says you only French kiss in feature films," she tells me. Her boyfriend is a producer; it's the kind of things producers say to their girlfriends, I guess.

She's a young actor, and though I'm a charming bastard, she's likely weirded out by the age difference. I'm no Luke Perry. (I don't tell Shannen that her *90210* cast-mate Jennie Garth had hilariously used Band-Aids to make smiley faces over her nipples for *our* filmed love scenes a year earlier.)

"I have the same rule, Shannen," I promise. "We're good."

"Oh, okay . . . Awesome."

Every time we kiss while filming, she's as rigid as one of Brandon Walsh's surfboards. I suspect she's, like, totally thinking: *Grody! Gag me with a spoon!*

For both of us, an actor's job is never done.

———

MY MOM HAD BEEN FORCED TO RETIRE AT SIXTY-FIVE FROM THE Los Angeles County municipal court system—and had, of course, reinvented herself again. Sally Matthieson—all of five feet—had started *another* career as a liaison between bail bond companies and the L.A. County courts. She'd work for *another* fifteen years. When she was around eighty, however, my sister, Sue, and I began to notice that Mom, usually defined by her determination and wit, wasn't always the woman we'd known anymore. Now that she was sober, this change wasn't the ravages of booze but was simply the ravages of time. Mom had been getting more forgetful and was becoming lost on the streets she'd known since her teens.

My life was such that I could be called out of town, or the *country*, for weeks or months on end, so my sister took up the mantle of caretaker. We moved my mom up to Walnut Creek (outside San Francisco) so she could be closer to Sue. My sister was a saint; she would visit my mother every day after her work as an attorney in San Francisco to make sure Mom was doing okay. I made regular trips to see Mom when I could.

In the summer of 1998, I had a break between directing gigs and I'd arrived to visit my mom for breakfast, but she was nowhere to be found. After I called Sue, who'd seen her just the evening before but who didn't know where she was now, panic set in. The car was gone, and Mom didn't have a cell phone. We scoured the streets of Walnut Creek and even traveled into San Francisco. We called credit card companies and the police; still, she was nowhere to be found. Writing these words today, I can still feel the empty pit in my stomach from that night. When the phone rang, it was the police, and my sister and I braced for the worst. But it wasn't the Walnut Creek police—it was the Burbank Police Department, and they had found Mom. She'd made her way 350-plus miles to her last condo, in the city she always called home. Mom was confused about the people "living in her house," and the new owners had called the police.

My sister and I now made finding Mom a safe place to live our main job, a home with the professional support she now clearly needed. For those who have gone down this path for their own parents, you'll agree it's not an easy task. What place was possibly good enough to put a woman who'd slept on a couch and worked two full-time jobs so that my sister and I could eat?

After misses and frustrations, we eventually found a safe assisted living facility for her. It wasn't the Burbank home she still clearly fancied. But it was a start.

———

I'D SUCCESSFULLY GOTTEN HOLLYWOOD TO REIMAGINE ME AS another type of leading man. The work on cable was steady, but I knew that nothing lasts very long, a lesson from childhood that has served me well for decades. Like many jobs, these roles had just become work. I was making decisions based on what I needed to do to keep up with the lifestyle I'd built for my family. The work I *wanted* to do wasn't being offered to me, and I felt myself withering away.

To break out of the doldrums, I knew I'd have to orchestrate projects and opportunities myself. It was time to make my own breaks without relying on the whims of others.

My plan was simple: I'd become the money.

I'd produce films. I'd publish a magazine. Buy a cable channel. I'd build a Matheson entertainment empire. It was a fine plan, as plans often are.

I soon learned that while actors often get stabbed in the chest, the money guy usually gets it in the back.

Master of the Universe

"JUST SIGN RIGHT HERE," THE GUY SAID. HIS NAME, I THINK, WAS Enzo. Or Lorenzo. Or Luca Brasi. There were five more guys just like him with names like Angelo, Frankie the Chin, and Jimmy Soprano.

We were all in a cramped dark room in a tumbledown building somewhere in lower Manhattan; we'd oddly *or predictably* used the back steps into the building. My business partner, Dan Grodnik, and I were seated at a long table with two of the six investors. He and I slowly looked at each other, confirming our shared goal without words: *getting the hell out as soon as possible.*

"Sure, sure," I said. "I think first we should—"

"It's a great deal," another guy chimed in from behind me. He was chewing on the nub of an unlit cigar. "We love it."

Dan and I had come to pitch the notion of these guys investing in the company we had just bought: the National Lampoon. It was a pitch we'd given fifty-plus times to investors and banks across the country. Nothing. These New York guys, however, had said yes five minutes into the meeting and started pushing papers at us. I quickly got the sense it would be our brains or signatures on the contracts.

"Let's do the deal," said Enzo pushing the pen across the table at me again.

"Gentlemen," I stalled. "The Lampoon has a board of directors we need to consult with first."

"*Hai voluto la biciletta? Adesso, pedala!* Know what I mean?"

I didn't.

"Forget the board," the guy clarified. "Let's just get this deal done today, and we can all get rich starting tomorrow." His colleagues all chuckled knowingly, and I applied all my acting skills to join them.

But I still held strong. "Sounds great," I said. "But we should all do our due diligence first and—"

"Love the deal, Tim. Let's just get this signed." He stared at me and then down at the pen. *Bada bing!* I turned again to my business partner, who now just stared straight ahead. We really needed that five million to keep the Lampoon afloat, to build it into what we'd first imagined. But I also understood who these guys were, where their money came from, and that they'd squeeze the Lampoon completely dry in less than a year if we signed. We needed to get out of this meeting, this building, this town, without signing shit.

"Here you go, Tim," he now picked up the pen and held it inches from my face. "Sign the papers."

How long, I wondered, *before Tim Matheson sleeps with the fishes?*

———

ALL OF THIS STARTED, AS MOST THINGS DO, WITH A SMALL IDEA: I was tired of being at the whims of Hollywood studios. I wanted more leverage. More of a chance to have influence over my path. *Basic actor stuff.*

"Look," I told my agent, "I'm a good actor; everyone knows who I am. If I were a middle-level second baseman in the majors, I'd be pulling in eight million a year. There's gotta be some opportunity somewhere we're not going after."

He agreed and got to work. Months later, after what felt like a thousand meetings, I had a two-pilot development deal with ABC. My chest felt puffier that week as I set up my office. It was my responsibility now to find a show, some writers, a director, a cast, and a production company to make the first pilot. My first step to becoming a Hollywood mogul: total control of my art *and* the path to success all in one.

What could go wrong?

I found and picked a romantic sitcom called *Just in Time* about a guy who's an editor at a magazine where he and his colleagues get into hijinks. It was another *Moonlighting* rip-off but good enough, I thought, that we could do something special with it.

For casting, I'd play the main character and, after an exhaustive search, including Sharon Stone stalking us to get the job, we hired newcomer Annette Bening (*The American President, Bugsy, American Beauty*) to play opposite me as the romantic lead. We shot the pilot, and I loved working with Annette. We had a ball on the shoot, and I immediately welcomed her obvious talent—she *does* have five Oscar nominations.

I was about to deliver Warner Bros. Television and ABC a hit show. A show I felt had the rhythm and feel of classics like *His Girl Friday*—a romance between two equals. Garry Marshall, Aaron Spelling, James L. Brooks, even Michael Douglas . . . these guys had better watch out. There was a new hit-producer in town!

ABC loved the pilot, which was good news. The bad news was, they felt Annette was wrong for the part. After many heated arguments, they forced another actress, Patricia Kalember, on me instead. Patricia is great, and I respected her work, but they had fired Annette Bening, for God's sake.

Here comes the splitter. Our writer, Fred Barron, had come up with the show idea and was writing the first few scripts. But he wouldn't write. After he got paid, his emotional well-being became a daily roller coaster. He'd need to spend hours on the phone with his therapist in Boston when we desperately needed him writing in Los Angeles. Actors weren't getting completed scripts until 12:30 a.m. for scenes to be shot the next morning. "You can't do it like this, Fred," I told him. "It's not fair to the actors." I tried talking with him, but he didn't want a partner; he just wanted an actor who would shut up and never challenge him.

"You can't tell me what to do, fuck-head," he grumbled back. "I'm an executive producer." (Which on this deal, as creator, he was . . . but so was I. It was *my* deal; I'd hired *him*!) In a meeting with the heads of Warner Bros. Television about the show, Fred suddenly went off the rails and launched into a heated diatribe about me. The studio heads were wide-eyed and utterly silent in response to the sudden, childish—and inappropriate, timing-wise—personal outburst.

"Okay, Fred . . ." I said, trying to salvage the meeting. "Why don't we keep our personal stuff out of this meeting, and we'll get together later to talk about it man-to-man. Back to the show . . ." The room breathed an awkward sigh of relief, glad to have me as the adult on our side of the table. Strike two.

Fred seemed to dislike jokes. He thought dramatic irony and punchlines were beneath him when I'd sold this show to ABC as a sitcom. "We're supposed to be doing a comedy," I pleaded. "Where are the jokes? The setups?"

"This guy and his jokes," Fred would mutter, shaking his head at me. We were now making *The Mary Tyler Moore Show* without Mary Tyler Moore or any laughs.

The show lasted six episodes before ABC pulled the plug.

I still had my office and an assistant at Warner Bros., but no more work to do. The execs spent another year-plus finding reasons not to do the shows I pitched them. Total disaster.

Fine, I decided. *Screw TV. I'll just make a movie.*

That's only one episode, right? No problem.

———

YEARS BEFORE I MET MEGAN AND BECAME A DAD, I'D DATED A JAPanese dancer who had worked with Hollywood royalty herself and got us into some swell parties at the homes of pals like Sammy Davis Jr. and Dean Martin.

The relationship was short-lived, but my love of the Asian films she introduced me to lasts to this day. Already a Bruce Lee and Toshiro Mifune fan, I was now introduced to Shintaro Katsu, a Japanese actor playing Zatoichi, a nomadic blind masseur and swordsman who fights for justice every time he stops somewhere new. Zatoichi could cut a buzzing bee in half with the sword hidden inside his blind man's cane and keep a baby sleeping soundly or extinguish all the candles and lanterns before a night battle with twelve guys in the final scene, evening the odds. The most successful series in Japanese cinema, the Zatoichi series included twenty-six films and one hundred TV episodes. It was *Kung Fu* with a blind guy, in the perfect combo of adventure, action, and comedy. I unequivocally adored them.

Zatoichi was the film I wanted to start with as a producer. I recognized that we, like the Japanese, could make three or seven or twenty more if ever called on. I dug deep into my own savings and acquired the rights.

A writer I'd known for years, Charlie Carner, and I worked on the pitch and story outline for our film based on the 1967 *Zatoichi Challenged*, by Ryôzô Kasahara. In this terrific story, Zatoichi is tasked with marshaling a spoiled orphaned child across the country while assassin samurai are after the kid. Our film was titled *Blind Fury*. Pitch and outline done, Charlie and I now needed a salesperson to act as producer and help us get the movie set up at a studio. Charlie brought in a producer named Dan Grodnik.

Dan had been a producer of such films as *Terror Train* and *Up the Academy* (*Mad* Magazine's *Animal House* attempt). In high school, he'd set up local concerts, high school dances, and ski trips to turn a buck. After studying film at the University of Southern California, he decided the same skills would prove handy. He knew a good thing when he saw it, and he said he'd love to join as a producer. Our glib front man, he was sure we could sell this project.

And he was right. Both Tri-Star Pictures and Interscope Communications got on board. Dan and I selected fledgling director Phillip

Noyce and Don Burgess, a great cinematographer who would go on to shoot *Cast Away* and would be Oscar nominated for *Forrest Gump*, while Charlie finished the screenplay. When we couldn't convince Jeff Bridges, Mickey Rourke, *or* Don Johnson—all who were more right for the part—we landed on Dutch actor Rutger Hauer (*Blade Runner, Ladyhawke, The Hitcher*) to play Vietnam veteran Nick Porter, our Americanized Zatoichi. Hauer was, at least, the perfect combo of a known name, within our budget and someone the studio would greenlight the movie with.

I set up a screening, with popcorn and everything, to show Noyce and Hauer a few Zatoichi movies and to get them as excited about this character as I was. I hoped to share the subtle tone that, by mixing unforgettable action with humor and heart, would make our Americanization of this character a hit. I discovered that neither had much interest in watching the original hit films. *Actually, no interest.* Neither man cared. Eventually, when my suggestions became more passionate, they both openly refused. They didn't want the original films to somehow over-shape what they were imagining. Out of supercilious artistry or just laziness, these two were going to create a hit film series from scratch—even though it wasn't from scratch.

I'd thought being a producer meant you could work with the director to help create *your* vision and, since I was an actor, I could also convince Rutger to make the film as I'd imagined it. Wrong. Director Noyce was always threatening to quit whenever we tried to convince him to shoot scenes a certain way. (He wouldn't shoot enough footage for his action scenes, where you're supposed to capture multiple angles and shots to edit later for a more dynamic visual experience.) And Rutger insisted that his character should have a Walkman cassette player around his neck and wear headphones to listen to music all the time—taking away what should be the blind character's superpower—despite our whole pitch being "Zatoichi can hear better than you can see."

As an actor, I'd always hated producers who swept in and cut the director off at the knees, so I wasn't going to do that. I still had my day job as an actor to do on other producers' projects, and I ultimately took these acting weeks as a great opportunity to detach some from *Blind Fury*. I would just have to trust both Noyce to make the right decisions and my partner, Dan, to keep things moving along nicely. Hemingway once quipped, "The way to learn whether a person is trustworthy is to trust him." Hemingway should have just said, *My two partners were assholes.*

As soon as I was out of the way, director Noyce began swaying Dan to the notion that *his* ideas were better than what was in the approved script that Charlie and I had sweated over for more than a year. Dan, with an opportunity to increase his influence, would agree. Noyce had also been going around both Dan *and* me to get directly to the studio heads at Interscope and Tri-Star. During these chats, he always failed to mention that he'd never before done an action flick or that he spent hours on set arguing with his own stunt crew and camera department.

"I'm going to do it in a single take," Noyce would say. The stunt team would warn him about film coverage he'd need later when editing, and they suggested advantageous areas to shoot from. "No, we're good," he'd answer, promptly dismissing the suggestion. "Let's set up the next shot." He'd say this to guys and gals who had helped shoot these kinds of scenes hundreds of times. He just didn't care. "We're making something new here, not the old, worn-out shots."

Film School Boot Camp

ABL: Always Be Learning

A journeyman director named Jack Sholder was the first director we hired on *Blind Fury*. He came on for development and worked with us on the script and the beginning plans for production. Or I *thought* he was working with us. As it turned out, he was just using his demands for rewrites, new screenwriters, and the time it took to change names of characters so that he could get a screenplay credit as a way to stall. What he didn't tell us is that, all the while, he had been using our project to leverage a better deal for himself on another movie. We had to pay Jack, we had to pay his screenwriter (we had to throw out his lousy rewrite), *and* we had to find another new director. (I never saw Jack's movie . . . you probably didn't, either.) Jack was using us all along, and I hated how this made me feel as the producer. I learned as a director to always give my producers 100 percent of me—I never wanted anyone to accuse me of giving them the "Sholder."

After Sholder left us, we hired Phil Noyce. Before directing the film *Dead Calm*, Phil had mostly been a TV director, and I believed that he'd be able to elevate his game as we called him up to what I believed was the big time. Phil made mistake after mistake on *Blind Fury*, from messing up the ending to having the main character who is blind dull his sense of hearing with a pair of headphones to what I saw as his biggest mistake: refusing to watch the original source material.

I never thought that Phil was using us as Sholder had. But I did feel the fool when *Blind Fury* wasn't the movie that I knew it could be. But I applaud Phil Noyce. He used our movie as a way to learn and took his lessons and his talent to great heights. He'd go on to direct some of the biggest action films of the 1990s, including the megahits *Patriot Games* and *Clear and Present Danger*, based on the Tom Clancy novels. I've never asked Phil, but my guess is he watched *The Hunt for Red October* and read Clancy's books.

I went through the rest of the production trying to be optimistic, but I was distraught and felt betrayed at every turn. Me, the guy who'd first seen Zatoichi and brought the project to life—I had been sidelined.

When the first cut of *Blind Fury* was shown to the studios, they hated it. It was nothing like the original vision that I had sold them. It also hadn't been well acted or staged. The action sequences had been almost impossible to edit (because of the missing coverage). And there was no ending, just a whimper.

"My" director and "my" partner had completely removed the final battle scene in the script while I was away on an acting project. The final scene was a great set piece, too, worthy of the original Zatoichi, where our hero battles two dozen bad guys in the dark.

"You have no ending," the studio executives warned. *No shit.*

Back to the drawing board, writer Charlie and I worked desperately to do a quick patch job on the ending. But too much had changed from the script during shooting that we couldn't go back to the original idea. We wrote about five new scenes that could be shot in the mere three or four days we'd been given, to give the movie a fitting ending. Instead of an epic battle with ninjas in the dark, there's now a single assassin who's electrocuted in a hot tub. Then Rutger Hauer walks off into the sunset with a toy dinosaur. *Blind Fury* held together. Barely.

The studio guys said print. And I hated it.

While I was still detesting my first film, Gene Siskel and Roger Ebert gave it two thumbs-up. Promising. But the public wasn't adding its thumbs to the count. The film cost just under five million to make but earned about three. The math was simple enough.

Most people would have gotten the hint by now. But for almost thirty years, I'd had far more people telling me "go away" than "you're hired." It was time not to retreat but to expand. I just needed a home base from which to do so.

Zero idea I'd soon find the home base back in Delta House.

———

THE TV SHOW HADN'T WORKED; THE FILM HADN'T WORKED. BUT that, Dan assured me, was from our lack of total control. To get that control, it was clearly now time for us to have our own money to make the kind of movies we knew how to make. Of course, Dan had a money guy.

"You're never going to get that kind of money," advised David Batchelder, a towheaded funds guy who's worth several billion today. In 1988, he'd worked in oil, entertainment, banking, and risk management and knew a lot about getting big deals done. (He'd recently advised T. Boone Pickens, a world-renowned hostile-takeover king and corporate raider. Now he was advising us.)

Dan Grodnik and I were still a team. Despite how our film had played out, he was a salesman and always hustling, and I thought I needed someone like that as a partner. Plus, Dan had found us Batchelder. And I still had that dream of being the pie maker, not just another ingredient. Maybe now Dan could help make it happen. So, for a while, he and I tried raising *fifty* million, half what it would take to start an actual production company. Same results.

"You don't have the reputation or credentials for that," Batchelder told us. He clearly hadn't seen me in *Fletch* or Dan's *Up the Academy*. "Here's what you *can* do," he said. "Buy an existing company, one that's struggling, and right that ship so it becomes a cash cow for these film projects of yours. Find a business in entertainment with a legit operating history that you feel is undervalued in the marketplace. Then take, say, ten million and turn it *into* a fifty-million company. Now you've got your films. Find a company, and I'll find you the money to buy it."

This guy was the renowned expert, so we looked for companies teetering, names where the bloom was definitely off the rose. In 1988, *Playboy* made that list. Crown International Pictures. *Spy* magazine.

Eventually, we added the *National Lampoon* to our roll of possibilities.

The magazine still existed and had, of course, its movie division. But this was a decade after *Animal House* and five years since

Vacation. The Lampoon company had now been losing money for years. Magazine subscriptions were down from one million to less than a quarter million. Most of the great writers had moved on, and the *National Lampoon* founder, Matty Simmons, had replaced key staff with members of his own family. There were a lot of Simmonses running around that office when we first showed up, uninvited.

"Go to the major investors," Batchelder had explained. "Show them, 'Your stock is going down and you're getting killed; we have a plan.' Get control of the board, and then we'll move in on Matty Simmons and *his* shares."

In December, we approached the board and the Lampoon's biggest investors. The stock was at $2, and most of these folks had bought their shares at between $7 and $8. They were desperate for ideas, for hope. We showed them our plan to revitalize the magazine and boost film production, to bring in outstanding writers again, and to reestablish the National Lampoon as the number one source for American satire. Nine mega-stockholders liked what they heard and assigned us their voting rights. Dan and I bought another 3 percent of the company ourselves. (Rather, *I* bought 3 percent, since I'd cosigned the loan that Dan had taken for his shares.) He and I now controlled 21.5 percent of the Lampoon. A lot. Enough to get Matty's attention.

Matty Simmons called me a "failed TV actor" and was both surprised and furious that "Otter" was attempting a hostile takeover. Simmons compared me directly to my *Animal House* character: "Charming, but not very smart." Simmons couldn't believe that Dan and I had already amassed more than 21 percent of the voting shares. With this number, we demanded to become part of his management team. And the board, now on our side, demanded the same. We made it clear to Simmons that we weren't going away and that things, starting with his nepotistic hiring, were going to change. By January 1989, Dan and I were seated on the board.

By March, Simmons had conceded to where this was always headed—that he'd lost control of the Lampoon—and he sold us all his shares at an exorbitant, but worth it, price of $6 a pop. He cleared close to a million and would still be a producer connected to the company, already tasked with managing *Christmas Vacation*. It was as golden a parachute as you could get.

With deeper pockets and a better line of credit, I'd signed things and guaranteed Dan Grodnik's portion of the money to purchase Lampoon stock and to buy out Simmons. Dan and I now controlled 31 percent of the company, more than enough to call the shots moving forward. We were co-chairmen and co-CEOs.

Batchelder took some cream off the top for his services and was now tasked with using the clout of the Lampoon to pull in a quick $5 million investment we'd first been looking for. We talked to everyone.

"Don't worry," Batchelder said. "I'll set up all the meetings, and we'll get you out there." We met with every big brokerage house— Bear Stearns, Paine Webber, Deutsche Bank—one meeting after another. Lunches with angel investors and private equity moguls. Eventually, as the more traditional routes said no, we ended up in a cramped room with the cast from *Goodfellas*. (A meeting we'd escaped with careful, unkept promises to keep in touch.)

DURING ALL OF THIS, I WAS FAIRLY NEWLY MARRIED, WITH TWO baby girls—Molly (1986) and Emma (1988). We'd gotten an apartment on New York's West Side on the Hudson River, to support Megan and her return to dancing, and I was flying back and forth between L.A. and New York for meetings and acting. The phone rings; it's Batchelder: "I got you a meeting with Michael Milken."

This is *before* Milken (eminent financier, high-yield-bonds trailblazer) faced ninety-eight counts of racketeering and fraud and served a ten-year prison sentence. This was, instead, when Milken could raise money like Michael Jordan dunked basketballs and was making $100 million deals every other day.

Meeting Michael was like going into a prestigious doctor's office. There were four or five conference rooms filled with entrepreneurs hoping to be blessed with a few moments of Milken's attention. While we were in one room, he was across the hall meeting Wolfgang Puck, software startups, and leaders of small nations. When it was our turn, Mike listened to our pitch and couldn't have been nicer.

"I like it," he concluded. "Let me think about it." Two days later, he called and said, "I need you two to come over to my house at six o'clock Sunday morning." (I wasn't going to *anyone's* house at 6:00 a.m. on a Sunday. I'd been around long enough to know, *If we take that meeting, he owns us.* We met Monday at 11.)

"I'm not crazy about the *Lampoon*," he told us. "But this sister magazine, *Heavy Metal*, has some potential." (*Heavy Metal* was a popular adult sci-fi and fantasy magazine that was a subsidiary property under *National Lampoon*.) "*This* is the future," Milken said. "I can do business with this in Japan and the rest of Asia. I'll guarantee my money back from that alone if nothing else."

We had our deal! I went off to shoot a sci-fi film called *Solar Crisis*, and I left Grodnik and Batchelder to cross the t's and dot the i's with Milken. Our new company was already gasping for cash, and we needed to get this closed quick. His money would save the day.

But my buddy Dan Grodnik wanted a better deal.

So while I was pretending to fly into the sun to save the planet, he was still taking meetings. He'd gotten into GE Capital and worked his way up through the middle echelons to the top five guys. "I don't want to do the Milken deal," he told me. "GE Capital is the best deal for us. All I need is one yes from this final guy and we're done."

While he worked with GE, however, we needed to stall Milken. Weeks passed by as Dan tried and tried to cajole that final yes from GE. Eventually, Michael said he was tired of waiting and passed entirely. Then GE Capital also said no. And adviser Batchelder had seen—and earned—enough.

"It's easier to borrow fifty million dollars than five million," he now told us. The man who had orchestrated our whole business plan and led us down the takeover path was now interested in bigger fish with bigger paydays. He vanished as Milken and GE had, taking all his other possible money connections with him.

Dan and I were now co-chairmen of a broke National Lampoon company, and it was an utter shit show. The business was losing money faster than we'd ever imagined. Subscriptions had fallen off, advertising dropped, and there was no longer a creative force like Doug Kenney behind the *Lampoon* magazine. We didn't have enough money to hire the writing talent we wanted. Our plan had always been to raise the money to set up a new Lampoon (Lampoon 2.0, if you will) with this money and move the business to L.A. Get eight or nine creatives to do the magazine and then go do movies and TV with them—the way it was in the 1970s.

The more we got into the nuts and bolts of the company, however, the more we realized Simmons and Lampoon Inc. had been cash-strapped for years. They had been selling off everything. John Hughes had written *Uncle Buck* and *Vacation* originally as short stories for the *Lampoon*, but Lampoon Inc. didn't own these; Hughes did. To save money, Matty Simmons had let the artists and writers retain control and ownership of their work. The company owned very little material at all for us to develop or leverage.

To make matters worse, when we attempted to approach the studios for an overall *Lampoon* movie deal, we finally discovered that Simmons had sold off those rights for quick cash years before. And we were suddenly also being sued by Crédit Lyonnais, a major

French bank connected to massive loans to *Heavy Metal* magazine. These loans from years before hadn't been disclosed prior to the buyout.

Our only hope, a total Hail Mary, was a golfer named Dorf.

J2 COMMUNICATIONS AND JAMES P. JIMIRRO APPEARED. THIS WAS the guy who'd figured out how to turn *Dorf on Golf* (those straight-to-home videos of Tim Conway on his knees playing a diminutive golfer) into a multimillion-dollar company. He was interested.

At our first meeting, we stood around Jimirro's desk. There were no chairs; it was like going to the principal's office in junior high school. I also immediately noticed five pencils carefully stacked right next to each other on his desk, erasers all lined up, the first pencil the longest, the second the next longest, and so on. The last pencil was no more than an inch long, and each had been sharpened to the finest point. This stingy multimillionaire with bizarre compulsions was the cheapest man I'd ever met. He always had to be in control of *everything*. His employees had to pay to park and handed over a quarter for every cup of coffee they drank. There's an old saying, "Cheap is expensive," but Jimirro didn't care.

This wasn't promising, but unless I wanted to find out what size cement shoes I wore, it was our only deal, as we'd lost both Milken and GE. The Lampoon company would close in a month if we didn't get an influx of new cash.

Instead of a Lampoon office in L.A. as we had planned, Jimirro had a different suggestion: "You guys will set up in our offices. You can take this space over here." We did as told and set up shop in the J2 offices. To make long-distance calls, you had to get in line to get on some strange trunk line to New York first. There could only be one long-distance call at a time from the J2 offices—all to save a couple hundred bucks a month. "What century are you in?" I grumbled. He made it impossible to get any business done. Our new magazine was headquartered in New York, for God's sake!

Jimirro started licensing the *Lampoon* name immediately. If you were a wet T-shirt contest in Myrtle Beach or some beer fest in Bugtussle, Texas, you could pay $10,000 to become the National Lampoon Wet T-Shirt Contest or the National Lampoon Beer Fest. Meanwhile, he kept reworking our deals, using lawyer after lawyer to find ways to back out of things we had agreed to when we brought him on as a partner.

We labored hard and landed New Line Cinema to make *Loaded Weapon 1*, a *National Lampoon* film. Jimirro immediately put the deal in jeopardy by demanding that J2, instead of New Line, which was financing and releasing the actual movie, would produce and sell the VHS tapes directly, as he had with *Dorf.* This is not how Hollywood worked; studios always maintained home video rights to be sold in Best Buy and Walmart. "No," Jimirro told us. "I have to own the video rights."

"Nobody's gonna make that deal," I warned.

"Well, fuck them then," he said. "No deal." The *Loaded Weapon* arguments continued, and Jimirro ultimately made some backroom deal: New Line kept the video rights, J2 got a little off the top, and Lampoon got nothing. He just wanted us out and did everything he could to get us out.

I engaged Marty Singer, the renowned L.A. litigator.

"This guy's extorting us," I told him. "He keeps changing the deal and is threatening to blow up the whole thing *after* we're in bed with him. He's cutting back and back and back, and we're running out of cash again already. Promises were made, papers signed. Isn't that extortion or something?"

Singer pointed his finger at me. "Not until you go broke."

"How's that?"

"You have to take the company all the way bankrupt. *Then* you can sue him for 'extortion or something' and seek damages."

"But . . . I don't want to bankrupt the company," I said.

Marty Singer, Hollywood's brightest lawyer, shrugged. "That's how this works," he said. "Sorry, Tim."

OTHER THAN GOING HOME EACH NIGHT TO MY WIFE AND DAUGH-ters, 1989 featured the worst eight months of my life.

What had happened on *Blind Fury* was happening again. My partner Dan wanted to be in charge and always felt he knew better about every discussion or decision. Each night, I'd lie awake and try to figure out how I'd been stupid enough to get myself into this situation a *second* time.

There's a story about a frog and a scorpion, both of which want to cross a river. The scorpion says, "Let me get on your back, and you can swim us across." And the frog replies, "No way! You're a scorpion. You'll sting me." And the scorpion promises, "No, I won't; that's crazy. Then we'd *both* die. Let's just get across." So they go into the river, and halfway across, the scorpion stings the frog. "What the hell?" screams the frog as they start to sink. The scorpion shrugs and says, "What did you expect? I'm a scorpion."

I absolutely wanted to get out. Life was too short. I didn't want to drive to an office every day to find out how I'm being fucked over. It was like quicksand: nothing and then up to your knees and moving a little slower, but it just keeps getting a little higher, and one thing goes wrong and the next thing goes wrong and then the next thing.

Despite best intentions, the Lampoon quickly fell deeper into the dumpster. I'd just moved west to an apartment on the beach with my wife and two kids and I'd drive into Westwood every day to Jimirro's place and then back to the beach. I'd get home to sit outside in the sea breeze and maybe have a cocktail and just sit out there and think, *This is what life should be like. Not this bullshit I'm going through every day with these idiots. It's just a nightmare.*

More than anything, I felt shame and hurt. Hurt by my partner Dan. By vanished Batchelder. By Jim "Dorf" Jimirro. I just couldn't be around people like this anymore. I couldn't, clearly, be a Hollywood mogul.

My wife agreed and supported me through it all, always a shoulder to lean on. Producer pal Jerry Weintraub (*The Karate Kid* and *Ocean's Eleven*) was another person I could come to with my business woes. "You're not a scorpion," he basically told me. "And you're in a land of scorpions now."

As soon as we officially paid Matty Simmons off, I said *I'm fucking done* and just quit. I was heartbroken. And I was out.

MY AGENT, JOHN GAINES, SAID, "WE'LL GET YOU WORK, TIM. DON'T worry." I'd been gone from acting for most of the year now, a lifetime in the business. There was nothing in the pipeline.

I don't think Matty Simmons ever spoke to me again. He was furious we had taken his company away from him and, in hindsight, rightly so. J2 Communications couldn't keep up with the publishing schedule. We'd planned a monthly issue of *National Lampoon*, but only nine issues were published that first year. Then two issues hit the stands the next year, and in the last three years of its existence, the magazine was published once a year.

But I couldn't worry about Simmons or the *Lampoon* anymore. I had my own problems: suddenly cash-strapped, equity-strapped, and now with a family depending on me back at home. I couldn't produce; the work offers were drying up.

In retrospect, I realize that as bad as Dan and Jimirro and the scorpions were, I was digging my own grave throughout this time. My internal desperation drove me to security and had me doing too many things at once. I kept piling stuff on and being absent from important people in my life. I couldn't be a good business partner to Dan, because I was running off making movies. I couldn't be a good father to the kids, because I was running off with the *Lampoon*. I couldn't be a good husband, because what precious little—albeit distracted—time I had at home, I spent with the kids. I had put myself on a treadmill where everyone, especially me, was bound to be disappointed. And patently bitten off more than I could chew.

It was time to accept my new Hollywood and fully enter the world of TV movies. I was headed back again to cheating murderous spouses.

If entertainment's goal—which many days it seems so—is to make performers and other creatives feel humbled and horrible, it was doing one hell of a job.

The Other Big
Terrible Things

NOW A MARRIED MAN WITH CHILDREN, IT WAS TIME TO PUT AWAY all my own childish things. I quit my infamous Fun Club, a group of guys from various walks of life who enjoyed a life of excess. This act alone would get rid of about fourteen vices.

As in actor in the late 1970s and 1980s, I did cocaine. *Everyone* did coke.

Executives, the props department, your costar, the girl who had just delivered the pizzas. We snorted it the way people devour avocados today. It was cheap, no one was yet lacing it with poison, and it was everywhere. Once, I was invited to a party at a high-ranking politician's place in Utah—complete with string quartets, everyone in tuxedos, and Mormon prayers being offered from everyone you met. The son of the host came up to me and offered his hand. I was prepared to pay the proper amount of respect to him and his beliefs both political and otherwise when he pulled me close and asked if I wanted to do some blow in the other room. Coke was *everywhere.*

My first experience was, no shock, with a stuntwoman. She'd invited me to her cabin, brought out coke like it was potato chips, and asked if I wanted to try it. And admittedly, you felt like you were on top of the world for a while. Bruce McGill had a friend in the coke business who had nicknamed the drug "the only thing that matters."

But by 1984, I'd quit. I'd seen what it had done to John Belushi, Doug Kenney, and many other friends and colleagues in the industry. Actors who I'd worked with and who couldn't hold it together enough to get parts anymore. Superstars whose careers were on three-year breaks while they tried to get off this shit.

It had worn off its welcome for me pretty quickly. The first problem with coke was that it was never as good as the first time you took it. Never once. People spent years, careers, lives, chasing that first high. Your second martini tastes as good as the first. Not coke.

I'd also just gotten sick of it and wanted foremost to get rid of all people I was doing coke with. One night, I looked around and realized the only reason I was hanging out with most of these people was because we were all doing coke together. Sober, I wouldn't have spent five minutes with most of them.

So, I found a book cleverly titled *How to Quit Coke*. Within its pages were allegedly a guide to all the over-the-counter vitamins and supplements I needed for a proper detox. I purchased everything the book recommended and gulped down wild concoctions every day. It was a bit of a mad science experiment. But two months later, I was clean, and me and coke were done.

Pot was as pervasive as it is today, except back then, we were just breaking the law to do it. I smoked pot, which, sans therapists, provided good emotional treatment for me. Trying acid a few times, I soon gained a new perspective. Whether it was an actual out-of-body experience or merely the freedom to realize that I wasn't in touch with my feelings, these few times helped me realize that I had a core personality flaw. I avoided confrontation like a diabetic does Dunkin' Donuts.

For decades, I'd been in several one-sided relationships. People would do things, but I wouldn't call them on it. This avoidance had become a real issue, weighing on me in the places I couldn't see. These breakthroughs mostly came to me while I was high, to be worked on when I was sober.

That's part of why acting class became so important to me. Exploring different roles and getting in touch with feelings—without depending on narcotics. The greatest thing about being some other character is that you get to leave yourself behind. No one else in life really gets to do that unless you get stoned or drunk or you're an actor—most people never get to stop being who they are. Playing *other* people, I could get a perspective on my own shortcomings, and I used acting to augment (or to mask) my own connection—or lack thereof—to myself.

All of a sudden, these feelings would emerge—feelings I didn't even know were in there. Whether you're with Stella Adler or taking an acting class at Kim Dawson Agency today, it's all powered by escapism.

Now to deal with the one escapism my family knew so well: alcohol.

———

BOTH OF MY PARENTS HAD BEEN ALCOHOLICS MY WHOLE LIFE. AND if I was going to successfully handle my own drinking, it was first time to finally take on Mom.

When drinking, my mother had a way of going after people. She could just, you know, *get in there.* I've never seen my sister so upset as one night after Mom got drunk and attacked her verbally and *very* personally. And for me? She'd cook up something different. She never went after me directly. She always took aim at the things I cared about most:

In the early years: my friends.

As a young man: my girlfriends.

As a young adult: my wife.

As an adult: my kids . . . which, obviously, were also her grandkids.

An incredible grandmother. Truly. Unless she drank.

After years of her drinking, I finally sat her down. "Mom," I told her, "we're not going to see you anymore when you're drinking. Drink whatever you want when on your own time, but if we're together, there's going to be no drinking around my children. You turn into a mean, mean person, you know?"

"Well, fine," she agreed." I'm just . . . Then I guess I won't see you guys."

And she didn't. For almost two years.

I'll never know if it was for me, herself, or Molly, Emma, and Cooper, but after two years, she quit, and to show my gratitude, I quit with her. The removal, for the last time, of that demon made time together wonderful for everyone. I'd bring her back with me to Santa Barbara to spend the weekend with my family. She again became a—full-time—loving and supportive grandmother.

I'll drink socially now. You cannot expect the guy who played Otter to turn down a bicchiere of vino when visiting his wife's family in Italy, can you? But for years, I haven't felt any reason to jeopardize my family or career just to be a fun party guy on a random Saturday night. From my own childhood, I knew that *boozing just doesn't have any place in family life.* Such vices were no longer worth it, and I set them aside.

The last drug to kick off was the hardest.

Fame.

———

CELEBRITY, POWER, HOLLYWOOD "JUICE." ONCE YOU'VE GOTTEN A taste of this stuff, it can be a hit you seek all day long, every day. To the detriment of family, friends, and your own sanity.

I'd go to dinner with my wife and be pissed about being at table C when I could clearly see that another actor was at table A, the "best" table. It was far too much Hollywood algebra to process, and it was making me miserable. Another actor would tell me about a show he'd just gotten or something he was producing, and I'd feel terrible, a total failure, if in that moment I had nothing equal (or better) to talk about. I knew this sense of competition was ridiculous. I had a blessed life and was fretting over stupid things.

But in entertainment, those stupid things matter. It's how we keep score. And I, more often than not, felt I was losing.

One morning, I'm dropping our girls off at school. I park the car, and as I walk them in, I spot the head of a studio across the way. His kid also goes to the school. "I'm just gonna say hi," I tell my kids, and scurry over to play politics. It's a company town, you know, and I was always working.

The studio head and I exchanged pleasantries, and, my job done, I turned back to find my kids.

They were gone. I'd lost them. It had been no more than five minutes, but they'd vanished. After confirming they'd just gone on to class without me, I stood alone in the lot by my car for a long while. Decisions on where to send our children to school, who their piano teacher was, what sports they played, and where they played them were being determined by who the *parents* of the other kids were, not whether it was the right school or matched my child's interest in an activity.

I was ashamed. I felt like such a heel, such a terrible dad. Working and hustling like I had since I was ten, but now I had other people to look after.

Hollywood was too tempting for me. There was nowhere to turn without the lure and intoxication of a new project, a new connection that *might* lead to the intoxication of a new project. I couldn't find the balance. This was not a drug I could just stop.

I needed to get away from the dealers and other addicts.

In 1994, I moved my family to Santa Barbara, two and half hours away from Hollywood. The American Riviera. Snuggled warmly between the glorious Pacific Ocean and Santa Ynez Mountains. Lush wooded suburbs in a climate often described as Mediterranean.

My neighbors were suddenly software engineers, airline pilots, and insurance salespeople. None of the parents of my kids' classmates could help me professionally in any possible way, and I loved it. None of my kids were ever lost when I brought them to school. Topics of entertainment only came up when I picked up the phone or drove into Hollywood.

How big a star I was or wasn't didn't matter to anyone in Santa Barbara.

And it quickly mattered less to me.

For years, I was away from all that Hollywood hustle bullshit.

Then Rob Lowe moved into town. *(There goes the neighborhood. Ha-ha-ha . . .)* The rest of Hollywood, it seems, had also discovered the quiet joy and exquisiteness that is Santa Barbara. And keeping score was about to matter again.

Finding a good game to play will do that to you. As I introduced Rob around Santa Barbara, there was little way to know we wouldn't be there for long.

Rob and I were both headed to 1600 Pennsylvania Avenue.

Hoynes for America

The West Wing

MY NEW NEIGHBOR ROB LOWE WAS BRAGGING ABOUT A NEW PILOT he'd just done for NBC. At the time, I was the assistant coach for my son's T-ball team; Rob's son was on the team too. The kids were six, so the coaching stakes weren't very high.

In the pilot, Rob played Sam Seaborn, a young speech writer working in the West Wing, and the show was all about the behind-the-scenes staff who keep the White House humming every day.

"That's great," I lied. "Congratulations."

It sounded like the most boring show ever.

Civilian Tim is fascinated by the machinations of politics in real life, but I couldn't imagine talking about that as entertainment on network TV.

"Aaron Sorkin wrote it," Rob went on. A not-so-humble humble brag.

I loved Sorkin's show *Sports Night*. Funny, smart. *A Few Good Men* and *The American President* were already favorites of mine.

"Tommy Schlamme directed," Rob added. His eyes twinkled, no doubt enjoying the professional jealousy I was failing to conceal.

"Well . . . sounds like a great team," I demurred, still thinking the concept was horrible. How could the administrivia of 1600 Pennsylvania Avenue possibly entertain?

Thankfully, others thought differently. The pilot was picked up by NBC.

A month later, I was the one sitting in a room discussing *The West Wing* with Sorkin and Schlamme.

My agent had called to say Sorkin wanted to meet me for the role of vice president. I was at a point in my career where I didn't audition for guest-star roles. I'd basically graduated from AA Ball to the majors, and now they wanted me to go back to tryouts? This would have been an instant pass for anyone except Aaron Sorkin. "I'd like to see the script," I said. *Where's the harm in that?*

"Can't," my agent replied. "Sorkin won't let anybody see it."

"You're kidding."

"I'm not."

"That's . . ." I imagined Tom Cruise shouting about the truth. "Okay, how about the sides, then?" These are the excerpts used for auditions, a page or two. "He's gonna let us see those?"

Sorkin did. And they were good. Really, really good.

"Hold on . . ." I said after reading these pieces. "He won't cast *anybody* who *doesn't* audition?"

"Nope," my agent swore. "Everybody auditions for Aaron Sorkin." I could tell he was quoting some new Hollywood mantra.

"Then," I said, "I've got to audition for Aaron Sorkin." *Fuck it,* I decided. *I'm not going to stand some imaginary ground and wait for Sorkin to call me when he's not gonna call me.*

It proved one of those magical meetings. Just Sorkin, Tommy Schlamme, John Levy (head of casting), and me. "He's the kind of guy who plays a lot of golf," Sorkin explained. The dramatist was in a light blue sweater-vest, his familiar boyish blond wave swooshed over the top of his tortoiseshell square eyeglasses.

Vice President Hoynes, Sorkin continued, was a career politician who *could* have become president, *should* have been president, but this new guy Josiah "Jed" Bartlet had grabbed the brass ring instead.

I was Lyndon B. Johnson to Martin Sheen's John F. Kennedy; we'd just swapped the ages.

For the audition, I was having fun with the material, keeping it light and quick. It was, apparently, exactly what Aaron thought this guy should be. I'm cracking jokes and then Aaron says, "Read it *this* way," and shifted everything forty-five degrees. I made the adjustments to play with it, and it proved just as good in this new way. The words were masterful.

On the way back to my car, I passed Corbin Bernsen going in to audition for Hoynes right behind me. And that's the nature of these gigs; you just know all the usual suspects are going to be there (Bruce Boxleitner, Gary Cole, Robert Urich, Treat Williams, Harry Hamlin).

Ultimately, I didn't know if Sorkin saw what he wanted in me. Like a zillion times before, I'd done my best and started the drive home to Santa Barbara. Halfway home, I got the call. There was no showbiz BS with Sorkin and Schlamme. My agent called to say I was *The West Wing* VP if I wanted the role. A recurring character, five or seven episodes a year, with no guarantee beyond that. Basically, whenever Sorkin needed me.

I raised my hand and took the oath.

I'D MISSED THE CHANCE TO WORK WITH SHAKESPEARE BY ALMOST four hundred years. Aaron was a worthy alternate.

You'd sit and do a read-through for a new *West Wing* episode and think, *How does he do it?* Because the *last* episode, I'd always conclude this is as good as it gets. The dialogue was just . . . perfect. Smart, precise, original, authentic, always meticulously character-driven. I was working with an actual genius.

But, it was always check-and-raise with this Bard of Burbank. Aaron constantly elevated the bar for the next episode. And it started from day one. At the first table reading for my character's introduction to the series, the scripts were being passed out and Sorkin grinned at me. "In Hoynes's first scene," he said, "you're speaking French."

"Yeah . . . Yeah right . . ." I said, laughing along. But Aaron wasn't joking. I quickly read ahead, and Hoynes is giving a press conference with the French ambassador in French, at the same time both showboating and displaying how smart he is.

Okay, I realized. *This show is really gonna be something different.*

It was the most brilliantly crafted dialogue. Stylized in its own way, like a classic romantic comedy almost because, to me, it played like a *His Girl Friday* or *Pat and Mike*—smart dialogue that was clever, funny, wise, rich, smart, and really fast.

Sorkin comes from the theatre and has a virtuoso ear for the sound and cadence of people talking as performance. His instincts were always right. A few times, I've come across other writers obsessed with their words and fight to keep every word for ego alone. Sorkin wasn't that. His words, his careful choices, were . . . art. They were always the right words in the right place at the right time. He wrote with a meter and rhythm for the characters that informed everything on screen.

You might throw an idea out in the very first rehearsal, but, by God, if he said no, that was it. But as careful and precious as he was, if you became the character and you made it better, he was not afraid to let it be better. For one episode, I did a little pause in the middle of a speech during blocking very early in the rehearsal process; Aaron and Tommy hadn't, I thought, even come down yet. I had this long speech, and instead of just rattling through it to a group of reporters, I got to the middle of the speech and added a kind of "ahhhhhh" sound before making my turn from one reporter and delivering the rest of the speech to another bunch of reporters.

As I walked back to my trailer just after rehearsal, Aaron was shouting my name from behind me. "Tim?! Tim!!! Hi . . ."

"Hey, Aaron." I'd stopped and turned. "How are you?"

"Keep the 'ahhhh,'" he said. "That works."

Then he sped off, *our* walk-and-talk complete.

He knew exactly what he wanted to see . . . and *hear*. Once rehearsals were done and we started shooting a scene, if you deviated a single word from the script, they would do the scene over. To help, the show atypically had *two* script supervisors, one for continuity of things like wardrobe, props, and the actions of the actors during a scene. The other, more of a dramaturge, was just for language. "You said 'status' instead of 'position,'" she'd correct.

Once, I shot a scene and was advised, "That's a semicolon . . . not a period." His team would literally correct our *punctuation*.

Meanwhile, many guest actors would misguidedly come in like it was a regular TV show, kind of knowing their lines, expecting some give, expecting some line feeds or room to improvise. But the regular cast was at a whole other level, and these guest actors were left professionally staggered. The regulars had learned quickly to always bring their A game.

Arriving one day to shoot scenes with Martin Sheen and John Spencer (Leo McGarry) and heading to the set, I ran into both Allison Janney (C. J. Cregg) and Richard Schiff (Toby Ziegler). They weren't even scheduled on the call sheet, were not expected at all that day. Yet both Allison and Richard had come in on their own time. To rehearse alone.

Allison was standing by herself at C. J.'s podium. Richard was in a room talking to himself and to an assistant who helped him nail his lines.

These two did this for hours. They wanted to get Aaron's words *exactly* right. That year, both Allison and Richard won the Emmy as best supporting actress and best supporting actor. (She'd win four *more* as C. J. and was nominated six times; Richard was nominated three times.) Awards aren't everything, but it's a fine nod to the extra work this extraordinary cast was putting into every show.

Because of this, I was often a bit nervous when I came in to shoot my scenes. And I'm someone who had taken the craft and learning his lines seriously for decades. Still, to get Sorkin totally right, you needed Allison Janney's dedication. I was only being brought in for a couple of days at a time here and there; it was tougher for me to get in the zone.

I didn't want to fuck this up. I'd seen firsthand how *The West Wing* people reacted when another guest actor wasn't utterly prepared, and I knew I needed to up my own game to keep up with the main cast.

My first step there was to learn more about Vice President Hoynes.

———

WASHINGTON POLLSTER PATRICK CADDELL AND FORMER WHITE House press secretary Dee Dee Myers were two of the main political consultants on the show. They immediately started feeding me information on life as an American vice president.

I read bios on every VP I could get my hands on: LBJ, Adams, Humphrey, Rockefeller, Agnew. The more I read, the more I understood the old joke, often told *by* vice presidents: "A man had two sons; one was lost at sea, and the other became vice president. And neither of them was heard of again." No wonder Aaron Burr killed a guy.

Research done, I now identified with John Hoynes of Texas better. The shame of coming in second, of being the country's spare tire. Of watching some other guy in *your* Oval Office. Daniel Webster turned down the vice presidential job offer in 1839, commenting, "I do not propose to be buried until I am dead." To help add to this feeling of being on the outside looking in, I leaned into the fact that I was only ever a guest actor.

I never got my face in the opening credits. Never got in any of the staged *Entertainment Weekly*–type group shots as *The West Wing* became a national phenomenon and started winning more Emmys than any show before.

I'd do maybe five or six episodes a season at most. A "special guest star." The third kid through the door, again.

Bradley Whitford (Josh Lyman) always joked, "The vice president's a heartbeat away from the office of the president, and Tim Matheson is a heartbeat away from being a regular on *The West Wing.*" It was a great line.

Did it really bother me? No. I had a great role on a hit show. The regular cast was phenomenal. NBC had given Sorkin and Schlamme carte blanche to make the show great. If they needed to spend X to reshoot Y, they did. This was unheard-of in television. (This was early "prestige TV.") There's a good reason the show looked so great.

Would I have liked to be a more permanent player? Of course. But so would Al Gore, Walter Mondale, and Dan Quayle.

Ironic, then, that Martin Sheen (President Bartlet) is the one cast member I never got to know too well. There was very little personal chitchat; we'd do our scenes and move on to the next thing. Bartlet and Hoynes truly spent as much time together as they had to, no more. Just like in real life.

JOHN SPENCER, ON THE OTHER HAND, PROVED TO BE MY ROCK, a mentor, and a friend on this show.

In my first scene with John (Leo McGarry), I was nervous. Despite my twenty-plus years in the business, the obvious excellence of *The West Wing* still had me on edge. I was saying all the right words but just not connecting to Hoynes as a character, as an actor. It's like dancing and suddenly losing the beat of the song; you keep doing your moves but you just *know* you're half a beat off.

In this case, keeping with the dancing metaphor, I just looked at my partner. I focused on John, really started listening to him deliver Leo's lines. There was a self-assurance and sincerity with John's delivery that was tangible. You couldn't help but be pulled in, and I was instantly grounded. It allowed me to perform at a level more on par with what John was doing.

For the remainder of my years on *The West Wing*, I could, and would, always look to John to center my own performance. And by what I'd gathered later from Allison, Richard, Bradley, Rob, and others, I wasn't the only one.

John and I developed a special bond for the same reason our characters did: both characters struggled with alcoholism. In the show, Leo is an alcoholic who Hoynes invites into a secret West Wing Alcoholics Anonymous group. It's one of the few times the show allowed my VP to clearly be a good guy. While prepping for these scenes, John confided to me that he himself had been an alcoholic most of his adult life. That a particular scene in *Presumed Innocent* with Harrison Ford, where John is dumping evidence off a ferry, was the "first time I'd shot a scene sober." He'd been clean for the ten years since, but he offered me his experience as I, in a rare act of vulnerability, divulged information about my own childhood, being raised by an alcoholic, still having a front-row seat to alcohol's destruction, and experiencing some recent battles with Mom. This moment of art imitating life shaped our characters and bonded us, in real life, as friends.

I was humbled by his openness and vulnerability and felt emboldened to speak honestly about things for the first time. He'd made me as close as family—to help me as an actor, to help the show be better. And that new bond would become the center for my time on *The West Wing*.

Not that John was always a bastion of sageness and harmony.

One of the funniest things I've ever seen on a set was John trying to get drops of something called Collyre Bleu, one of many secret elixirs actors have used for decades, into his eyes. This particular potion clears up tired eyes, but it's also a tad toxic and is banned in the United States. It's only available from France via Hollywood or, now, online-store backchannels. A little secret they don't tell you when you're acquiring illegal eye drops—this stuff will dye your skin Smurf blue if it lands anywhere but straight into your eyeball.

We were in the makeup trailer, and John was trying to get a couple of quick drops into his eyes before the next scene. But nothing was coming out of the tiny bottle that John was having a full-blown battle with. He was grumbling enough that I'd turned to watch just as he squeezed harder, then harder again. John won the battle but at what cost? A gush of liquid from the bottle splashed over his face, chin, and chest. One mislaid drop could stain your skin for two days. He was now drenched in this stuff.

John was too stunned to move, to talk, to scream. I demonstrated the appropriate amount of concern while exploding inside with laughter. When the makeup crew broke out laughing, I could only join them. For the next fifteen minutes, John was pampered like an Egyptian king while the makeup artists got to work. When they were done, he looked as good as new. His eyes, even more so.

———

THE WEST WING HAD BECOME THE MOST IMPORTANT SHOW ON television.

The show swept the Emmys its first year. It was nominated eighteen times. *Eighteen*. And won nine, including best drama series. It would win the top prize its first three years.

It was a perfect merging of talents: actors, directors, and writer. It revealed how good television could be. And in many ways, it also altered our view of what *could* go on in the White House. The show did go hand in glove with the Clinton administration and the ideals and optimism of many people in the country at the start of his presidency. Personal scandals eventually derailed some of Clinton's hopefulness, but that spirit lived on in Sorkin's White House.

All of the show's many successes changed my own life almost overnight. Even as an irregular guest star, I'd be walking through some coffee shop and someone would shout out, "Hey, Hoynes!" *The*

West Wing was one of those instant hits, and more acting opportunities started coming in again for the first time in years.

I started working on a series called *Breaking News*, which was pitched as *The West Wing* in a newsroom (basically, Sorkin's later series *The Newsroom* . . . and I was the same character Jeff Daniels played; more on this fiasco soon). Fans who had long forgotten *Bonanza* and *Fletch* would recognize me as Hoynes and run up to say hello. "You're such an evil guy," they'd also say about Hoynes.

Comments like this always caught me off guard. *I don't play a bad guy,* I wanted to assure them. But Hoynes was certainly a nemesis of sorts to Bartlet and his staff.

My only assignment was just to keep up with whatever Aaron was doing.

"Toby, the total tonnage of what I know that you don't could stun a team of oxen in its tracks": I saw that dialogue on the script page, and I went, "Holy shit." It was one of my favorite Hoynes lines, but there was never a shortage.

Everyone was happy and riding this wave—everyone but my T-ball shortstop's father. Rob Lowe was miffed.

Originally, the show had been pitched (to the studio and to Rob) as a show about Sam Seaborn and *his* colleagues. Then it quickly became an ensemble show with Martin Sheen as the recognized star.

Between years one and two, after all the success, the rest of the main cast pulled the so-called *Friends* gambit and demanded a substantial raise in tandem: They *all* got raises, or the show was over. Rob hadn't been part of this, because he'd started—as the original lead and a bona fide movie star—as the highest-paid actor on the show. They all got raises with this great success; he didn't.

One of the last times I came on set to shoot an episode with Rob, something was clearly amiss. It seemed as if Rob was kind of on an island by himself, and it couldn't have been fun. Other than Sheen, the rest of the cast were hardworking character actors who had made livings on TV or film wherever they could. Rob, meanwhile, had been the lead in *About Last Night, The Hotel New Hampshire,* and *St. Elmo's Fire.* He'd been on the cover of *Teen Beat* magazine countless times. Maybe it was that; maybe it was the raise thing. Maybe something else. He never said.

But halfway through Season 3, he was done. He'd quit. Sam Seaborn was given a storyline of a failed congressional run in California, and Rob went with him. And he and I never once talked about it.

——

BEFORE WE SAY GOODBYE TO ROB, IT'S A GOOD TIME TO TALK ABOUT the time Rob Lowe stole my nanny. (Or, did he?)

A good nanny is hard to find, especially in Montecito and Santa Barbara. You need to find the perfect balance of worldliness, adaptability, desperation, trustworthiness, *and* someone who's not going to ruin your marriage. In L.A., such a person is easier to find. There are many younger people looking for a side hustle to go with their budding careers in Hollywood. In Montecito, ninety miles away, it takes some doing to secure someone.

We'd been living in Montecito for months, and after half a dozen failed trial runs, we had finally discovered a local young woman who proved great with our three kids. (By this point, Megan and I had welcomed our son Cooper to the family.) This young woman had no experience as a nanny, but she tried hard and made us feel that the kids were safe. We liked her and the kids liked her, so we nurtured her along. Everything was fine.

Then Rob Lowe showed up.

He and his wife and young family had also recently moved north to quieter Santa Barbara. (I like to think of myself as a Phase 2 pioneer in this trend; Jeff Bridges and Christopher Lloyd were two of the original trailblazers. Now, half of Hollywood lives there.) Rob looked me up to get the lay of the land.

I'd first met him years before in L.A., when I was helping Friends of the River, an environmental group that protected free rivers (rafting and camping were my life at this point). Rob was a major star and gracious enough to work with us to help raise money for the cause.

Later, my wife and I welcomed his family to the north and introduced him to our community. We hung out. Our families hung out. Our nanny and kids hung out with his wife and kids for playdates.

Before we know it, my nanny is standing in the kitchen.

"I have to quit," she tells us forlornly. "My boyfriend's band just got signed to a record deal, and I need to be there for him. We're moving to L.A. and would like to move there as soon as possible." We didn't know she had a boyfriend, let alone one in a band. But what could you do? We accepted her two-week notice with great disappointment and started looking for her replacement.

Two weeks and one day later, I got a call from my pal Rob. "Hey, Tim, I'm over here in Wales doing a TV movie, and we need a huge favor. Can we borrow your nanny?" I explained that she'd just quit—out of nowhere—and was moving to L.A. to be with her boyfriend's band. "It's only for a couple weeks," Rob said and begged me to give him the number, which I did. But in hindsight . . . *The boy doth protest too much, methinks.* How odd that our nanny up and quit so quickly. And then Rob calls so soon thereafter from Wales, where they'd practically invented nannies. But he needed *mine*.

A week later, we learned that our nanny was in Wales with the Lowes. And she stayed with their family for another five years.

I never found out what happened to her imaginary boyfriend's band. Sometimes I pretend he is one of the guys in Maroon 5.

If it was all very innocent, then I've spent fifteen years laughing about something that wasn't all that funny; sorry, Rob. If he did snake my nanny, I'm still laughing about it. Well played, sir. Well played.

BECAUSE OF *THE WEST WING*, I'D BEEN OFFERED A STARRING ROLE that proved the weirdest television deal I've ever been part of. This was the series *Breaking News*. What should have been my parachute when I was ejected from *The West Wing* wasn't. *Breaking News* was made for Warner Bros., which had just scooped up TNT, CNN, *and* Turner Broadcasting including TBS.

I was playing an edgy Dan Rather–like character who, after he left CBS, starts a cable network that resembles CNN. It was a smart ensemble program. Written in the vernacular of *The West Wing*— smart and fast—it had a lot of style. Clancy Brown and a bunch of other good actors were also on board. Actor-turned-director Ken Olin (a role model, for sure) was producing and, along with some other good directing talent, directed the pilot and a couple of the other episodes. I loved playing this character and was looking forward to playing him for years. We shot thirteen episodes.

Tommy Schlamme, the most important TV director at the time, got a sneak peek and benighted it "the best pilot I've seen this year." High praise, indeed. It looked like I was in another hit. I began shadowing one of the directors, because when we came back for the expected Season 2, I was going to direct an episode.

Suddenly, even before our pilot ran, AOL (America Online) bought Warner Bros. and, along with it, everything in the Warner Bros. empire, including *Breaking News*. Some bean counter at an internet provider quickly determined AOL could take a gigantic tax write-off for our show *if they never aired it*. So that's what they did. They just stuck all thirteen episodes in a vault and let it go away. It was one of those things. Show business, right? (Ask Brendan Fraser or Michael Keaton or Leslie Grace about the 2022 *Batgirl* movie. Incidentally, also a Warner Bros. project.)

What the absolute fuck? I felt like I'd been hit with a phone booth. A mediocre tax deal had eclipsed the creative work of hundreds of people for nearly a year. These suits, these heartless corporate take-over lizard people, didn't give a shit about artistic endeavors or the way watching a show can make people feel. The business decision was pitiful and so very disappointing. It was the first foreshadowing I remember of what the business looks like today and what was behind the strike of 2023.

Even at this phase of my career, things still happened that surprised me. Surprising in a way that rips your heart out. Like being told "I'm in love with somebody else" out of nowhere. You invest your life and heart into something for months, and *everybody*—the studio, the network, Tommy Friggin' Schlamme—loves it. Then AOL accounting says, "It's *not* going to happen. No one's ever gonna see this. 'You've *not* got a series. You've *not* got mail.' We've got a tax break!"

Film School Boot Camp

Hollywood Changes
You never know what will happen in show business. Even when you think you do, you don't.

In 1991, I did a pilot for Fox TV called *Charlie Hoover* with Sam Kinison. We were told that it had sold and that we were flying in a private jet to New York City to announce the show at the upfronts (big presentations made by the television networks to an audience of advertisers, with the hopes that they'll want to invest their advertising budget in certain shows). This trip was a huge deal. The studio sent a limo to drive me to the private jet where every star on Fox at the time was on board. Ed O'Neill, Katey Sagal, Christina Applegate, and even Buck the dog from *Married . . . with Children*; Jim Carrey, Damon Wayans, and Jamie Foxx from *In Living Color*.

Sam and I boarded the plane to a chorus of "congratulations!" on our new show's getting picked up. It was a great flight. On landing in New York, I found maybe twenty messages on my phone;

agent, agent, manager, agent, lawyer, agent, manager, lawyer, lawyer, agent—*What the hell?*

I called my agent, who informed me, "They're still going to make the show, but . . . it's not coming on in the fall. It'll come on in midseason." *Ouch.* A steep demotion for sure. So in the span of a five-hour flight, the "hit show" we had on the air became a backup show for a midseason slot. Everything had changed, and all I had done was sit on an airplane.

Ask anyone who's been in this business for more than a few years, and they will have similar stories—I have a dozen. It happens to everyone. The thing you have to do is keep moving forward. Our business is not only about the *show* in *show business*—sometimes it's about the *business.*

When people ask me, "How has the business changed since you were a kid?" I often tell them the cameras have gotten smaller, visual effects have gotten better (see *Star Wars*), and fewer shows shoot in what is physically considered Hollywood. Today, filmed entertainment is produced worldwide. What has also changed, with the most ripple effects across our art, is that many of today's studios are offshoots of other businesses and only a sideline of giant companies.

Movies and TV shows often become line items on spreadsheets, and in that world, there is little room for artistic understanding, compassion, or support. The studios used to be run by people who were once filmmakers themselves or who appreciated and supported what filmmakers do. They believed in the magic of telling stories and telling them as well as they could. On a spreadsheet, the contribution of a great story makes little sense. Gone are people like Robert Evans, Walt Disney, Sherry Lansing, Alan Ladd, and the greats like David O. Selznick, Louis B. Mayer, and the Warner brothers—all of whom built Hollywood.

But just as filmmakers have always done, they keep finding ways to sneak good shows—ones that entertain, enrich, and move audiences—past executives who don't understand the process or the craft. And hopefully, we can keep making shows that can move these executives and accountants to tears and enrich their souls. Then they might understand. Movies are one of the last handmade products in the world. Machines and computers make cars, clothes, food, and appliances. But film is still made by groups of people who collaborate from twenty different departments and come together to tell a story created by a person out of thin air and performed by actors assuming the characters from the script. All of this is led by one person: the director. No two directors would ever do a scene the same way, shoot from the same camera position, or most probably even use the same actors. Movies are a one-of-a-kind handmade thing. Despite the enhancement of computers—real creative people are still the ones at the controls.

It was another month before I was back on the set of *The West Wing*. Still licking my wounds from AOL's decision, I needed to be back working on something creative that people might actually get to see.

Before shooting my first scene, I strolled around the empty soundstage.

The "Oval Office" was largely made up of props from *The American President* and *Contact*, the Jodie Foster film. I skated my fingers across Bartlet's imitation *Resolute* desk and couldn't help but reflect back on when I'd discovered that the fireplace on *Window on Main Street* was totally fake. Now, standing in the middle of the Oval Office, which was framed in lighting scaffolds, monitors, and boom stands, I knew that despite the constant setbacks, this magical world called Hollywood was something I still wanted to remain part of.

My mom passed at ninety-one while I was working on *THE West Wing*.

Both my sister and I were at her bedside when she, a force of nature, took her last breath. We buried her in Forest Lawn Cemetery on a hill overlooking Burbank, where the three of us had all lived together for so long. I visit her grave often, to remind myself and our family of her indomitable spirit.

Film School Boot Camp

There Are No Small Victories

Whether you're working in traditional Hollywood, acting on stage in your local area, or making art and other content for your own social media channels, making things is *hard*. Always make sure to celebrate even the smallest accomplishments. All too often, we score ourselves on how big a hit something is or how many likes it got. But even if your role ended up on the cutting-room floor, you did the work to get the part, and *that* is something to appreciate.

My mom was great about this. When I was a young man and even into my later adult years, my mom, who was often too busy putting food on the table to stay at auditions or visit me on set . . . or who sometimes had to show up late to a performance, clipped out everything in every paper that ever had my name on it. Each time I would visit her, the stack would grow. As a kid actor, it was fun. But as I got older, I started to find it kinda ridiculous. In the 1980s, she started having everything laminated and would put even the smallest clippings up on her wall. She kept pinning things to the walls, filling boxes with articles, and managing multiple scrapbooks filled with things that weren't so meaningful to me. Boy, was I wrong. When she died, and I went through her things, it finally hit me that she knew what I didn't. While I was focused on the next job and the next thing and the next reinvention, she knew the value that was in each and every accomplishment.

It's hard to do while you're in the middle of things, but my advice to you is this: Appreciate each opportunity to love what you're doing. The success of things is what you make it—whether it's a hit or not is out of your control.

———

Aaron Sorkin was on the phone.

Jed Bartlet, Martin Sheen's beloved character, had the catch-phrase "What's next?" as the president dealt with each day's many challenges, missteps, and victories. It was a phrase I'd lifted easily and gladly whenever the latest Sorkin script arrived. The scripts just kept getting better. The writing hit an almost-unthinkable standard as the show wrapped up its fourth season, our best, in my view. Aaron's hit show was a virtual lock for the record-breaking *fourth* Emmy for Best Drama Series Emmy. (*Hill Street Blues*, considered the TV-drama gold standard, had been the only show to ever win four total.) We remained on an unprecedented roll.

I'd also been nominated for an Emmy, my first, for my role as Hoynes. I put on my best tux and visited the Shrine Auditorium in downtown Los Angeles with six hundred of my closest TV friends. I didn't win, but I was excited to have been recognized for my work. At the after-party, Gary Goetzman hugged me and asked what I was doing there. "I got nominated for an Emmy!" I said, laughing. Which he was very much aware of. "Not at the Emmys, Tim. . . . At the *after-party*? See all these people carrying around, and showing off, their Emmys?" I looked around, and sure enough everyone else *did* have a shiny trophy in their hands. I smiled sheepishly, and Gary patted me on the back as he went behind the bar and made us both martinis. I'm still learning from Gary.

Hopefully, there would be time for another after-party done right. Word around town was that a repeat nomination and tux appearance for my work on Season 4 was looking pretty good. After almost a decade in made-for-TV movies as the adulterous husband or middle-aged stalker, I was back!

Aaron had already added so much to my Hoynes character. *West Wing's* VP had started as the golden-boy Texan senator who the Bartlet gang reviled and distrusted, a necessary, loathsome political ally. Then he'd gotten an interesting back story with Josh Lyman's Bradley Whitford, the connection of a recovering alcoholic with Leo McGarry's John Spencer, and more scenes going toe to toe with the president in a complicated political relationship that was both real-life government *and* human.

I couldn't wait to see what Aaron's plans were for Season 5. To hear "what's next?" directly from the modern master of storytelling.

"Aaron!" I said as I picked up the phone, grinning.

"Tim," he said, "I've got Tommy on the phone also!"

Okay . . . Schlamme was still Aaron's creative partner and the producer of the show. This phone call had taken on more weight in a hurry.

"Listen . . ." Aaron got right to it. "I got some news for you."

My stomach did that thing that comes with phone calls and meetings in the entertainment world—something I'd still not gotten used to in decades of doing this stuff. Knowing that the next sentence could be either triumph or doom and that there wasn't much you could do about it either way.

"Tommy and I are leaving the show after this season," he said.

"Wow . . . no . . ." I tried processing the information. It didn't make sense, because they had a monster hit on their hands. It also made perfect sense: They had a monster hit on their hands. They could go and do *anything*. New programs, more money from other networks. Also, what had started as a network with total support had now grown (predictably) into a financial squeeze by NBC (the network) and Warner Bros. TV (the studio footing the bills).

I remember shooting a scene in the Oval Office in the first season, and they'd dropped a piece of coverage—filming the scene from multiple angles to weave into editing later—so five of us all went back and shot a few additional angles. Nobody does that. It's very expensive, and a television audience probably wouldn't even notice the difference of the extra shots. But Sorkin and Schlamme had a standard, and they believed that the audience *would* notice, even if they didn't know why, and so the two men didn't compromise. Not compromising for your art . . . costs big money. Warner Bros. TV (of the mighty AOL empire) had yet to turn a profit on the show. Or so claimed Warner Bros. After four years, the execs had decided the studio could do it for a lot cheaper if the team didn't go to such extremes. Historic awards and enormous growing fan base notwithstanding.

"I appreciate you calling," I said. "I know you guys—"

"We're leaving," Aaron said, interrupting me. "And so are you."

Me? *What was that?* There was that feeling again . . .

"Hoynes . . ." I said.

"There's going to be a scandal of some kind," Aaron explained. "Hoynes will step down, and soon after, President Bartlet will have a major MS relapse . . ."

"Then Goodman can take over the White House," I said, realizing where this was going.

"Then Goodman takes over the White House," he said.

John Goodman played Glen Allen Walken, Speaker of the House and a Republican mainstay from Missouri—archrival and counterpoint to the Bartlet administration and its young staff. With Democrats Hoynes and Bartlet out of the way, it was the speaker's constitutional role to assume control.

It was, admittedly, an ingenious cliff-hanger to end Season 4. Sorkin had raised the story bar once again. Damn, why couldn't he write with a little more mediocrity?

At least they weren't forsaking Hoynes and me to "Mandyville," the now-notorious land (thanks to Moira Kelly's Season 1 character Mandy Hampton in *The West Wing*) where TV characters simply vanish without any explanation.

"Tim . . . we really appreciate all you've done for us," Tommy said, already wrapping things up. I knew they both had other calls to make that day. Announcing their leaving, but no characters other than mine were being sacrificed for an exciting finale.

"No, me too," I managed to say. "I can't thank you two enough."

Other polite things were said, and they hung up.

I sat in the room alone staring at the phone as if someone were still on it. The most success and recognition I'd had in, honestly, years. Gone. One story line; one phone call. The unemployed actor again.

The West Wing had been one of the highlights of my television career. It was the best writing ever and the best cast I've worked with on TV, and Tommy Schlamme's direction was top-notch. Just one of those special things. But now it was over.

I thought about my suddenly former fictional TV boss. Knew exactly what *he'd* say. Echoing my mom.

"'What's next?'" I said out loud.

The Other Time I
Wore a Toga

"WE WELCOME CHANGE AND OPENNESS FOR WE BELIEVE FREEDOM and security go together. . . . General Secretary Gorbachev, if you seek peace, if you seek prosperity for the Soviet Union and Eastern Europe . . . Mr. Gorbachev, tear down this wall!"

The face in the mirror stared back at me as I spoke the words aloud. My hair was artfully parted into a pugnacious pompadour, sheathed in Brylcreem. I had been transformed into the Great Communicator, the Jelly Bean Man, the Gipper, Dutch.

Nancy simply called him Ronnie. (He called her Mommy, for what it's worth.)

While my time playing Vice President Hoynes was over, the role had evidently, and quite successfully, opened up a new typecasting opportunity: the authoritative man. Within a few years, I'd been invited to play Howard Hughes, JFK, Ronald Reagan, *and* Pontius Pilate.

THE FIRST TIME I'D PLAYED SOMEONE ELSE, A *REAL* SOMEONE ELSE, was in 1976, smack-dab during my I'm-a-serious-actor theatre phase. I'd landed the role of a young Ernest Hemingway for a play to be filmed and shown on public television. The play featured Hemingway facing himself at various periods in his life, and I was the "just-out-of-WWI Hemingway." In this role, I began the habits and routines that would last another fifty years.

First, I read everything I could about, and by, Hemingway. Research has always been my favorite part of preparing for a role or directing a project, and that is doubly true when taking on the responsibility of embodying someone's real life. Investigation becomes even more important. Leading up to production, I ripped through *A Farewell to Arms*, *The Sun Also Rises*, and *For Whom the Bell Tolls*; biographies and writings by A. E. Hotchner, who was a close friend of Hemingway's; and history books about a soldier's life during World War I. I arrived on set with a comprehensive—dare I say "earnest"?—view of young Hemingway.

Helping me learn how to play "Hem" was Norman Lloyd. How to possibly capture Lloyd's career? He played tennis with Charlie Chaplin. He was on Broadway with Orson Welles in the Mercury Theatre Players. He was in Hitchcock films and played Amy Schumer's dad in *Trainwreck* at the age of 100. Lloyd was blacklisted in Hollywood as a Communist (which he wasn't) during McCarthyism in the 1950s. Alfred Hitchcock demanded Lloyd be hired to produce episodes of *Alfred Hitchcock Presents* in 1957. The studio wouldn't touch Norman, knowing the backlash that would come because of the political nonsense. "I WANNNNT HIMMMM . . ." demanded Hitchcock. It was not a debate. Norman became Hitchcock's producer. Resurrected, Lloyd worked for another fifty years.

For *The Hemingway Play*, Lloyd was technically a producer but would also become the director every night for us when the official director—a bored old-timer who proved far less dedicated than the rest of us—departed home early each night. As soon as he left, we'd all turn to Norman Lloyd.

"Okay," he'd say. "Here's what we can do." Then we'd re-block and rehearse for another two hours. Each morning, the director would come, see how far we'd gotten, and assume *he'd* done a great job. *Ah, Hollywood.*

While I wrestled with the best ways to embody Hemingway aged 20ish, a *real* person, Norman Lloyd, taught me as much about entertainment as anyone before or since. He and his wife, Peggy, would invite me and Megan to dinner, where he'd share stories for hours about the history of our town and his own turbulent journey as an entertainer. It was admittedly comforting to confirm the industry had *always* been the industry. A full-contact sport.

—

EARLY INTO MY VP HOYNES RUN, I WAS INVITED TO PLAY JOHN F. Kennedy in *Jackie Bouvier Kennedy Onassis*, a TV film for CBS starring Joanne Whalley as Jackie O. Once again, I raced to the bookstore and loaded up. I also worked on the notoriously challenging-to-master Boston-Kennedy accent. A Boston Brahmin. An affected New England accent associated with Harvard and New England's upper social class in the 19th century and early 20th century but essentially extinct since the 1960s.

Except I was going to bring it back.

What was JFK without that distinct delivery?

Martin Sheen had also played Kennedy a decade before, and he counseled me on how he'd handled the late president's accent, including the tones he'd lifted from his own mother, a lass from Tipperary, Ireland. As a kid, I'd loved characters with accents because I could step away and there was an even greater mask, a shield, between me and the audience.

I'd been so focused on nailing Kennedy's voice and mannerisms, I'd focused less on motivations, passions, convictions, and heart. We shot during a Montreal summer, and when I watched the film on CBS months after filming, I hated my performance. I saw myself doing an impression of JFK—but not *being* JFK. I was disappointed in myself. It was fine on the surface but lacked passion and vulnerability. Joanne Whalley, meanwhile, was great as Jackie—she'd focused on the elements she was supposed to. I have a great picture of us laughing and dancing at a staged gala during the production. She's glowing like I remember the real Jackie O, and in this one still moment—I, at least, *looked* like JFK beside her.

Like Kennedy, Reagan is also known for his distinct voice, vocal patterns, and delivery—and I did not want to make the same mistakes I'd felt I made with Kennedy. My job, in *Killing Reagan*, was to portray an actor who had become a politician with fixed convictions and who loved his country and trusted his second wife completely. From the JFK experience, I'd learned that the voice wouldn't be enough. If I tried to mimic Reagan, the production would fail.

I read multiple books about, and by, Reagan: his acting, his governorship, the candidate Ronnie, and, ultimately, the presidency. I'd learned he always led with a joke, no matter who he was talking to or meeting with, from heads of state to everyday people. But one small thing helped me a great deal to get the spirit and feel of the man: going for a ride on a horse. I'd head out every weekend and spend several hours in the Atlanta woods. As Reagan always said, "There's nothing better for the inside of a man than the outside of a horse." You can't worry, get distracted, or be self-involved when you're riding a horse. I'd learned this truth already in my younger days on the various western shows.

I also knew this truth: you can't act politics.

That's how Cynthia Nixon and I both approached it. Ours was a love story between Ronnie and Nancy. We had to be the Reagans.

We'd meet in the morning and go to the makeup trailer together; sit side by side for hours as the artists in hair and makeup morphed us into Ronnie and Nancy. The second we walked out of that trailer, we were only addressed as Mr. President and Mrs. Reagan. (This was the only time I'd ever had a director do that.) And Rod Lurie, a wonderful writer and director, made sure that the fine young actor Kyle S. More, who played John Hinckley Jr., never met or crossed paths with the "Reagans" during production. Lurie kept us focused on *our* story and not the would-be assassin.

This time, my performance was nominated for a Critics' Choice award, and *People* magazine decided the lead actor "captures the essence of the Reagan persona." Mission accomplished. Now, *there's* one for the Gipper!

Film School Boot Camp

Thou Shalt Do Research

Research, if you're lucky, can tell you everything you ever wanted to know about a character. I once played outlaw Emmett Dalton in the TV movie *The Last Day*, about the Dalton family's fateful end in Coffeyville, Kansas. I found an autobiography written by Emmett Dalton himself. It told me practically everything I needed to know. He was even kind enough to write about what he was thinking in certain moments of our story. *Fantastic!*

Doing Shakespeare was also full of research: you almost have to look up every word in the plays because the words might have a different meaning and context in the 400-plus years since they were written. You have to research the period of the play, its history, the country where it is set, and the real people it was written about: Henry IV, Henry V, Richard III, Richard II, Julius Caesar, and so forth. The most revealing thing about Shakespeare, his plays, and the actors at the Globe Theatre was when I found out about the nature of the troupe of actors Shakespeare wrote all of his parts for. Will Kempe played the comic parts; Richard Burbage the dramatic leads like Hamlet, Othello, and King Lear; and William Sly and others were the models for which Will Shakespeare wrote. This helped me understand the parts as I read them for the first time and then tried to play them on stage. With the classics, it has

> never hurt me to listen to recordings of other great actors playing
> parts that I was going to play. "Steal from the best." The more you
> immerse yourself in the research of the story and characters, the
> easier it is to act or direct it.

A final real-life character I'd played was Pontius Pilate, Roman governor of Judea, best known, of course, for presiding over the trial and crucifixion of Jesus.

The film was a project of Paulist Productions, a Hollywood production company built by Catholic priest Ellwood E. "Bud" Kieser and the Paulist Fathers, an evangelistic Catholic order. I'd done several episodes with Father Kieser in the late 1970s for his anthology program called *Insight*, which ran for twenty-plus years.

Father Kieser was a unique man. He'd recognized that Hollywood could help spread a moral message, and to that end, he had successfully built a production company from scratch. You could call him "Father," but he preferred it when you called him "Bud." He hardly ever talked religion or preached at you; he just wanted to make some good TV shows that had a moral center. And he did it on a shoestring budget. CBS gave him studio space for nothing. Bud focused most of his production efforts during the *hiatus*, the time that used to occur *between* TV seasons, when top-notch writers, directors, and actors were unemployed and wanted to work. When you worked for Paulist Productions, you worked for a "special educational rate," which meant we only were getting a couple of hundred dollars for five days of work, a much lower rate than normal. Even so, everyone wanted to work for Bud. The scripts were good, the directors strong, and the shows filled with wonderful actors. The list of actors who worked on Paulist shows includes Brian Keith, Martin Sheen, Bob Newhart, Ed Asner, Harvey Korman, Patty Duke, Carol Burnett, John Ritter, William Shatner, Cicely Tyson, Paul Sorvino, Donna Mills, Marlo Thomas, Rosanna Arquette, Barbara Hershey, Albert Brooks, and so many others.

On my first episode, I ran right into a classic example of how good a producer Bud really was. On the final day of shooting, he personally handed out paychecks with a grateful acknowledgment of the work, time, and passion we'd just invested in his show. He then went person by person and—this was his signature move—Bud grabbed your right hand as he thanked you and pumped it warmly. In his left hand, he held your check and raised it toward you. When you took the check, Father Kieser didn't let go of either hand for perhaps twenty seconds. He wanted to see if you'd donate the reduced paycheck back to the show. I needed the money, so I held on to the check as firmly as he held on to my hand. Laughing all the while, Bud finally let go. He engendered much affection and love from all who worked with him.

Bud Kieser and Paulist Productions had sold the idea of a Judas movie to ABC. Sadly, Bud passed away just before production started. Sans the Father, we all flew out to Ouarzazate, Morocco, to film in the same location where *Star Wars*, *The Mummy*, and *Lawrence of Arabia* were shot. It was, no surprise, hotter than hell, and the production was run on another shoestring budget.

This time, there had been no time for serious research or preparation. Besides, there are not a lot of recordings of Pontius Pilate's accent. The shoot was only five days for me, in and out. My plan was to pull out the old Henry Fonda card again: I'd make Governor Pontius as simple and real as possible. The approach worked, and the scenes played honestly.

On our last day, to get to the filming location, we had to drive down desert roads for hours; one long dusty road led to another smaller road and then another road even smaller still, until they weren't really roads at all. By the time we got to the set—a centuries-abandoned casbah village as remote as any I have ever been to—I was dehydrated and delusional and thought I *was* C-3PO wandering the sand dunes looking for R2-D2.

For authenticity, the production had flown in a team of costumers from Italy. This team was expert at "sword and sandal" wardrobe and spent an hour making sure I looked as authentic as possible in Pontius Pilate's toga. One look, and I realized all we needed was a striped tie slung loosely around my neck and I was Otter again. An older one, surely. Jokes were made. And it was likely the first time a film crew burst into "Shout!" in the Moroccan desert.

After wrapping the last day of shooting, we started the two-hour drive back to civilization. The barren desert in all directions, nothing but endless ribbons of undulating dunes stretched out as far as the eye could see, golden crests of sand rising like frozen waves. It was easy to lose yourself in reflection here. I found myself wishing Father Bud Kieser were still around to give me one of his famous handshakes or pep talks. It was the only thing missing from the experience, and it weighed on me.

After thirty minutes of bouncing along a narrow sand path, we arrived at a cross section to the main dirt road back into town; our driver slammed on the brakes as a giant semitruck came bounding down the main road. As we made a right turn to follow the truck an hour-plus toward town, the large truck reduced speed and was now showering us with a tornado of dust. It was going to take *several* hours to reach town at this speed, and we urged our driver into attempting to pass, not an easy task on a one-and-a-half-lane road in the middle, literally, of nowhere. With a deep breath, our driver told us to hold on, and he gunned it. As we pulled left to pass and the backwash of dust no longer blinded us, we all saw it! Written not in Arabic or Moroccan Berber, but in English.

Emblazoned on the rear of the truck was a sign: KIESER TRUCKING.

I could almost hear Father Bud Kieser laughing. And laughing back myself seemed the only thing to do as we continued across the desert. From somewhere beyond, I was sure that Bud had sent this truck as a way to say thank you and to remind me to donate my earnings back to the church.

Ready for My Close-Ups

<u>EXT. ST. ELIGIUS HOSPITAL (A.K.A. ST. ELSEWHERE)—DAWN</u>

Boston's South End is waking from another night of Boston
stuff.

<u>INT. DOCTORS' LOCKER ROOM—CONTINUOUS</u>

Doctors/actors DAVID MORSE and HOWIE MANDEL and DENZEL
F'IN WASHINGTON are dressing for the day's work. Legend
director/actor and personal mentor NORMAN LLOYD, who was
a regular cast member on *St. Elsewhere* (take that Senator
McCarthy), is watching from the side. Rookie TIM MATHESON
is directing his first television show ever—a lifelong dream—
but despite weeks of preparation and decades spent on film
sets, he seems nervous and disorganized. It is time to shoot the
first scene for a new episode of a celebrated TV show.

                    DIRECTOR TIM
          Okay, everyone . . . What I'd like you to do
          is . . . you guys kind of be doing your morning
          chitchat, not too much, and putting on shoes

and lab coats. You're already anticipating a long
hard day at work, right? We're going to do a
slow sweep of the room and then slowly come in
on you, David.

The cast and crew look at DIRECTOR TIM and then each other
and then collectively walk off the set, shaking their heads and
muttering. Leaving DIRECTOR TIM alone on set.

This is the kind of thing that happens in nightmares but is
now actually happening in real life. DIRECTOR TIM stands
nearly alone on the set. Only his first assistant director hasn't
deserted with the rest.

                   FIRST ASSISTANT DIRECTOR
           Well, that didn't go too well.

———

I'D ALWAYS WANTED TO BE A DIRECTOR, EVER SINCE I GAZED UP AT
Witness for the Prosecution in wonder, trying to figure out how to get
into that world.

Studying film became my main hobby. Directing and storytelling
held my interest as much as the acting. The TV series *Million Dollar
Movie* would show the same movies over and over all week, the old
black-and-white classics, Howard Hawks movies like *Bringing Up
Baby, Sergeant York, His Girl Friday*. I'd watched *The Wizard of Oz*
two dozen times and all the Disney films I could find. Spending
more and more time thinking, *How did they film that? And who were
they?* After I'd see a movie, I was always the last person in the theater; I wanted to read the names of all the people who had made it
all seem so real.

MILLION DOLLAR MOVIE WAS PLAYING DOUBLE INDEMNITY WITH Barbara Stanwyck and Fred MacMurray, and I was on the shag carpet, focused on the TV. The film opens with MacMurray arriving at a mammoth office building on location in downtown Los Angeles. As he moves from the crowded streets into the lobby, he is greeted by the elevator attendant, who escorts him to the elevator. The camera is already in the back of the elevator. They enter and the doors close on the walls of the lobby. The shot remains on these two men's backs as they make small talk and the elevator lights ping one floor to the next as we, the audience, rise with them. The camera is us and just like in real life, it hasn't cut once. To me, as a kid, all this looked just like another Hollywood set. Then the doors open, and my eleven-year-old jaw drops. What was just a modest lobby moments ago has opened into a massive two-floor workspace—*no way was this a soundstage.* Fred MacMurray exits the elevator, and we follow him as he strolls the catwalk, looking down on what seems to my young eyes like a hundred desks in an office that seems to stretch for miles.

I practically sprang from the floor. *Oh my God, I know what they did!*

Billy Wilder had carefully *planned* this shot with his cinematographer and crew and actors. They were *always* on this giant office floor, but when McMurray first comes in the elevator, there was a set flat that made it *look* like the lobby. When the doors were closed, the crew wheeled the flat (or "Hollywooded it") away from what the camera could see. Then, when the doors open, it *seems* like the men have traveled up ten floors. It was like the fake fireplace but taken ten steps further! Very clever and ingenious shot. Yet also simple to do.

I was so charmed, enamored, with the smartness of it all and was always looking to spot more of the same in other films. I also wanted to learn *about* Billy Wilder and to see as many of the director's other movies as I could find.

WHEN I WAS A TEENAGER, STANLEY KUBRICK CAUGHT MY ATTEN-
tion when I first saw *Dr. Strangelove*. Sitting in that cinema, everything was fresh and new. I'd never seen anything like the cinema
verite mock documentary shooting style that Kubrick had learned
from French filmmakers. Peter Sellers playing three different parts.
The well-known shot of Slim Pickens riding the atomic bomb—the
camera-dolly pullback to make it look as if Slim were dropping and
then the shot of nothing but bright light as the bomb goes off. *Who
does this stuff?* Director Stanley Kubrick. It was transforming. It was
just new cinema to me. I knew I wanted to somehow make a film
like that, and I tracked down his *Lolita*, *Spartacus*, *Paths of Glory*,
and *The Killing* and started taking notes.

Director Tim's Favorite Shots in Film

Lawrence of Arabia: *Profile of Peter O'Toole holding a burning
match. As he blows it out, cut to desert sunrise.*

2001: A Space Odyssey: *The hominid apelike creature throws his
bone weapon into the air. The bone spins up and out of frame. The
bone enters another frame and continues up, stops and starts to fall.
Cut to a space shuttle dropping out of frame, revealing the moon in
the distance.*

Taxi Driver: *Robert De Niro standing in front of the mirror in his
dingy room. "You talking to me? You talking to me?? I'm the only one
here." Gun emerges from his sleeve and he squeezes trigger.*

Psycho: *Janet Leigh in shower. A figure enters, seen through shower curtain. Curtain pulled aside, knife slashes, a terrified Leigh, blood
swirling down the drain, knife keeps slashing, ends with Leigh sliding
down the wall into the tub.*

Apocalypse Now: *Robert Duvall on the beach with war all around
him. Choppers fly through, jets drop napalm behind him, mortars*

going off. Troops march across the background. Duvall speaks to a spooked soldier: "I love the smell of napalm in the morning!" All in one uncut take.

Steamboat Bill Jr.: 1928 silent film starring Buster Keaton. In a ferocious storm, Keaton stands dazed in front of a two-story house. The front of the house falls away from the home's frame and falls toward Keaton, who is unaware. The second-floor window opening falls right around Keaton as the house front smashes into the ground around him. All done in one take.

Long before I got serious about my acting, I was hooked with the artistry and mechanics of filmmaking. I'd started studying European filmmakers, who worked in the same medium but from a different point of view than their Hollywood counterparts. François Truffaut, Jean-Luc Godard, Ingmar Bergman, Federico Fellini, and Vittorio De Sica were auteur filmmakers using the camera to tell stories that were not as straight ahead as what we were making in the United States. It took me several viewings to understand each film, and each time, I fell more and more in love with their art.

In my twenties, I went to see the rerelease of *Lawrence of Arabia* in a great long-gone theater at the corner of Wilshire and Beverly Boulevard. It took director David Lean nearly three years to make the film, and it showed. The film was stunning. At the start of the film, when Peter O'Toole blows out the match and the movie cuts to the desert and the sun—*this* was magic, real magic. The best movie I'd ever seen to that point; like I'd felt about Kubrick's work, this was a totally different kind of movie.

When I was put back under contract by Universal after *The Virginian*, I talked the studio into giving me a small editing room. I shot and edited numerous movies and submitted two of them to the California Institute of the Arts for admission. I wanted to go to school and finally become a director.

The first film I submitted started with an ant and then the shot pulled back, back, back, back, back, back until it was in outer space—one giant pullback. The other was a lot of visuals and cinematic effects.

Kubrick. Bergman. Matthieson.

My application was rejected.

———

It was disappointing. Very.

I slowly realized that, when I was acting, I didn't have to just play my scenes and return to my trailer to wait to be called. I could stay on set and take lessons from the actual directors and cinematographers. Everything I needed to learn to be a director was happening right in front of me. Hollywood is a classic town of learn by apprenticeship! I was prepared for people to tell me, "Hey, actor, stay in your lane." This could not have been further from the truth. Everyone I asked was willing to help. Just like the wranglers before, the people in the business were proud of what they did and happy to share it with someone genuinely interested.

There was a director at Universal, Alexander Singer, who stuffed scripts, notes, and storyboard sketches in his leather holsters like a gunslinger. He also wore a vest like he was on safari, filled with all sorts of gadgets like a viewfinder and anything else he might need while filming.

"Any advice for a young filmmaker?" I asked the gunslinger one day.

"Wear comfortable shoes," Singer said. "And sit down every chance you get."

I took notes and checked out his shoes. "Anything else?"

"Always fire someone on the first day." He wasn't joking, either. Another director taught me to always do one of the toughest shots on the very first day to show everyone what the expectations were.

Another unexpected mentor was Walter Doniger, who directed me in an episode of *Ironside*. In the first day, I hated his directorial style. I was accustomed to having some room to bring what I thought the character would do, not just be told exactly where to stand and how long to stand there. I was frustrated and came in early the next day to try and talk to him. What I saw him do amazed me. Before any of the actors were called to set, he would meticulously work out the scene with intricate camera moves on the dolly so that during his master shot, he would also have executed numerous close-ups—or coverage, as it is called. It was a tremendous lesson to learn. After these master shots, Doniger only had a few shots left to complete the scene—so despite the long setup and the limited space left for actors to "help stage the scene," he'd always finish the day early, and studios and actors loved him for that.

Me, however? The cast of *St. Elsewhere* walked out on me after my first attempt at directing. Shit.

———

BRUCE PALTROW, MY FRIEND WHO HAD DIRECTED ME IN *A LITTLE Sex* two years before, was executive producing *St. Elsewhere* and had, daringly, taken me up on my "I really want to be a director" speeches. He'd given me an episode to direct.

With my cast vanished and me with nowhere to go, I searched for Paltrow for emergency aid and found him hiding in the shadows with Denzel, Howie, David, and Norman. I still have nightmares punctuated with the howls of their laughter when they saw my panic-stricken face. Bruce had gotten me the gig but had also made sure to prank me at my most vulnerable. As soon as I caught on, I joined them in laughing, then got everyone back to work.

We spent the rest of the day shooting and, with some minor hiccups, I got through it. *St. Elsewhere* still did dailies (which aren't really done anymore). During lunch, the director, producers, writers, and select actors would sit in a projection room and watch the selected takes from the previous day's shooting. It was like watching game film on the sidelines *during* the game—an opportunity to discuss what was working and what needed help. I wasn't sure of myself and so mistakenly told them to print almost everything. Now we were watching it all together and the heckling and wisecracking started immediately.

This time, regrettably, it wasn't a Paltrow setup.

"Why the hell did you print that take? It's exactly the same as the first one . . ."

"Jeeeesus! Why the fuck did you shoot that?"

"At this pace, we're never gonna finish this episode."

I had learned the hard way that my forty-five minute daily session was three times longer than normal and that the writers wanted to get out of dailies and into the lunch line. With all of my footage, several of them were getting hangry and it started to get ugly. It was like a Dodgers game, getting the play-by-play called out on my directing. All the while, I had to sit quietly with all my directing deficiencies on full display. A grown man, I was almost in tears.

Then, the next day, one of the older lead actors took umbrage with the episode's storyline—some golden-years romance his character was supposed to have. "I'm not doing that," he told me. I tried explaining that the scene *was* in the script and that I wasn't a producer who could resolve such matters. "Then find me someone who is," he said and walked off the set.

On top of the regular cast, *St. Elsewhere* had weekly guest stars, and my episode was no exception. Our guest star, a well-known film actor, didn't want to shoot and stalled and stalled every time she was asked to work. I didn't want to hurt anyone's feelings. I'd only just learned how to be good cop as a director and didn't yet know how important a skill being a bad cop is. Per Whitey Sacks, "sometimes you gotta kick the dog." I would hide so the guest star couldn't filibuster me between takes with her neurotic riffs to stall shooting a take. On her final day of shooting, she came to work a total basket case, confused and straitjacket worthy: She said she'd been up all night, her dog was sick, and she hadn't slept. She asked for the studio medic to give her a B-12 shot to help energize her, an old Hollywood trick. But there was a slight twist: She didn't want the doctor to do the injection; she just wanted the needle to do the injection herself. *Oh my God! She's (possibly) a drug addict too! There goes my day!* I joked with Howie Horowitz, the assistant director, "Hell, if you think it's an upper and not a downer, then give her the damn needle and we'll race through the day." Thankfully, she finally allowed a real doctor to come down and give her a real B-12 shot, and we went on with our day. *Crazy, crazy, and crazier!*

It was like taking Melson's pugil stick over and over again all week long.

Throughout the week, the cast worked around my limitations. Denzel was like a master studio musician—efficient, exact—he did his scenes spot-on and then went home. David Morse was intense with his own preparation and commitment to making it a great show, and while that approach can sometimes be complicated and time-consuming, Morse's performances were worth it. Both David and Denzel couldn't have been more supportive.

When the episode aired, I got my first official directing credit. But I hadn't been ready. After over twenty-five years on sets, I'd thought I knew what a director does, but I only saw directing from the limited view of an actor. Producers never see the hours of prep an actor does, and directors don't really see the hundred spinning plates a script supervisor has to keep in the air. Everyone is focused on their own job and only half appreciates, at best, what everyone else in a production is doing.

If I was ever going to direct again, there was still a lot of work to do.

It was another ten years before I directed episodic television again.

———

IT WAS THE 1980S, AND CABLE TV WAS LOADED WITH WHAT WE called MOWs, movies of the week. And directing these was great! As the director, you got to make a ninety-minute movie on a multiweek schedule, and it was *your* vision for the film. Very different from the episodic work, where the days were limited and you were stepping in to execute someone else's vision. MOWs were staples well into the 1990s and I directed cable thrillers like *Breach of Conduct*; *Tails You Live, Heads You're Dead*; *Buried Alive II*; *In the Company of Spies*; and *Hell Swarm*.

Getting a job as a director is much like getting a job as an actor, except no one cares if you're good-looking. When projects need directors, agents send out the material, and you, as the potential director, have to campaign (i.e., audition) for the work. This often includes making storyboards, pitching location ideas, thinking about how you want to make the movie, all before your first meeting, and knowing that, as with actor auditions, they're interviewing twenty other directors or more for each job.

It was slow-going. You learn from your mistakes.

Working with actors came naturally. (I'd once had a director who gave me ten notes for a single line. Ten. It was about eight notes too many. I wasn't going to be that kind of director.) Mostly, it was technical skills I needed to learn.

I'd campaigned and won the job as director on a mostly terrible sci-fi movie called *Hell Swarm*. I worked for months to get the job because I wanted to learn how to make an action movie. And to that end, the most exciting part in the movie was a huge action shootout.

Only afterward, in the editing room, did I realize I'd made a cardinal mistake in filming the gunfight: I didn't film the bullets actually *hitting* anything. I'd gotten all caught up in the *pew-pew* flash of the character's guns without showing the cuts and consequence of their bullets striking cars, windshields, and walls in tiny explosions of wood, glass, and drywall. That's something every filmed shootout needs, and I'd simply *fucked it up*. To solve this, I frantically rifled through the Paramount library to grab stock footage of bullet hits and things exploding to manufacture the shootout after the fact. Not the right way to do it, but I guess I got away with it.

Film School Boot Camp

Action Speaks Louder than Words

On *Hell Swarm*, I broke down the huge shootout scene. I made shot lists and worked out every detail of all the action and stunts. I choreographed every camera I had so that I would have everything I needed in the editing room. What I didn't know but learned the hard way on this shoot is that stunts take longer to shoot than "normal" scenes. Every high fall, person on fire, motorcycle jump, fistfight, knife fight, car chase, car crash, gunfight (you get the idea) has to be methodically rehearsed and discussed, first at one-quarter speed, then at half speed. Not until everyone is on the same page can you speed it up to the pace you want to film it. There must be safety meetings with all members of the crew so that everyone knows when and if a speeding car is coming through the set, or where explosions will take place and how big they'll be. For safety, you must move slowly and not rush anyone into doing anything before everyone is comfortable and knows what to do. If there are any firearms on my sets, I go over each one, check the cylinder, make sure they are empty, dry-fire them to make sure they are empty, then *and only then* do you load any blanks into the weapons with a loud warning on set: *HOT GUNS ON SET!* No one should ever have any doubt about whether it's safe to have a gun on the set. Growing up on westerns and wearing a real gun every day, I learned that you can't be too safe or too careful with a real weapon. Even blanks will maim or kill you. Always treat every gun like *it is loaded*.

Action sequences aren't just about the big parts. You also need to film many little pieces (a fist making contact with a cheek, for example) to put the scenes together. That means a camera move, resetting the lighting, often a makeup or costume adjustment to ensure continuity. This takes a lot of time, but it's worth it . . . and that is where I messed up on my huge virgin action scene. I didn't get all the shots on my shot list when the sun went down, but it was merely some inserts, I thought, so not too bad! Wrong! So I learned this lesson the hard way: Directors have to manage multiple things that are in their control (or at least that they influence) on set—camera locations, blocking, performances, and so forth—and the one thing you have to manage (that the assistant director and producer will constantly remind you of) is *time*. Whether the concern is the time allotted by union rules, the costs associated with overtime, or simply the sun going down on your set—at some point if you don't time manage properly, you won't get what you want as the director.

Such mistakes on *Hell Swarm* were what compelled me to dig deeper and learn how to direct. Just like with acting, I'd force myself to investigate how to make this work better in the future. How to go home at night *not* feeling like an ass. Which, I guess, is basically the driving force behind my whole life.

To understand action scenes, I studied John Woo for hours and, thankfully, had a new tool for learning: laser disks. These were record-sized DVDs that included additional footage and, most importantly, director commentaries. I could now hear John Woo and other directors discussing how and why they'd shot a scene the way they did.

Someone once told me that Picasso had said something along the lines that "good artists borrow and great artists steal." Whether Picasso said it or not, it was sage advice to me. I borrowed, lifted, and I stole where I could.

For example, in *Breach of Conduct*, there was a character whose light red dress subtly grows deeper red as the movie progresses and her character grows stronger. The audience might not notice, but they would feel the difference. I borrowed this trick from Hitchcock's use of subliminal symbols.

John Ford, Howard Hawks, and Sidney Lumet all had their actors rehearse and rehearse the most dialogue-heavy and tricky scenes first, and then they only needed to shoot a couple of takes. If it worked for them, I knew it was an idea worth emulating.

On *Animal House*, John Landis taught me to never cut the camera. It brings everything to a screeching halt. Just keep filming, and subsequent takes are usually looser and more fun.

Mike Nichols would get the takes he wanted and then ask his cast to blast through the scene once more as fast as they could so he could have a different version to play with in the editing room.

I also learned from a lot of editors turned directors. They always knew best what might be needed in the editing process. Jerry London was one of those directors. After he would get everything the scene called for in the last close-up, he would call to the camera operator, "Pan down to the phone. Hold it." Then he'd ask the actor to pick up the phone and say the first line with the camera following the action so Jerry would always have in the editing room another option to open the scene. He'd often get three or four different cuts like that—just pieces for him to possibly use in postproduction, and the extra options hadn't cost the production anything.

Those who directed me, of course, became the teachers and coaches.

Nobody can compose a scene like Steven Spielberg. Always with complete confidence and mastery of what he was doing (even when the cockpit was on fire). Like most directors, I've studied all of Spielberg's movies. Michael Ritchie once told me to always give your stars and central characters an important filmic entrance to subliminally let the audience know this is someone important, and I marveled at the way Spielberg introduced Golda Meir in *Munich*. The camera pans with a man coming into a conference room with a stack of papers, as he slowly crosses in front of the entire table of seated people. But as the camera follows him, his papers block the lens so you can't see who is seated at the head of the table. When the papers are finally set down, at last the camera reveals Golda Meir in a powerful close-up. (I borrowed this technique for a *Covert Affairs* scene.)

The greatest thing about being a director was breaking down the script and then finding comparable scenes in other films to use as inspiration. Just like when I was a kid, I'd see a particular scene, love it, and meticulously break down how it had been done. I was never happier than when I could spend hours just watching films; it was my job to look at wonderful movies. And now they paid me to do it.

Along the way, I'd also collected a trusted cadre of in-person mentors.

Frank Darabont (*The Shawshank Redemption, The Green Mile, The Walking Dead*) was a guy just getting started in his own directing career when he helmed USA's *Buried Alive*—where Jennifer Jason Leigh and her boyfriend, well, bury me alive. Actually, it was Darabont's first feature-length film, but you'd never guess it. You could just tell this guy was special, and while he and a superb young English producer named Niki Marvin made *Buried Alive* for a nickel, I picked Frank's brain during the film and after on direction advice.

Michael Ritchie (*Fletch*) and Bruce Paltrow (*A Little Sex*) were now personal friends. Blindfolded, they could shoot a scene better than most. They would guide me and answer my questions anytime I asked for help.

Freddie Koenekamp, the cinematographer of films such as *Patton* and *Papillon*, taught me all the easy ways to light something difficult. Bob Ferretti, a great editor I'd met, taught me how to thoughtfully make my shot lists, which are a director's daily bible. Christopher Rouse, who worked with me as the editor on my first TV movie, *Breach of Conduct*, and later won an editing Oscar for *The Bourne Ultimatum*, showed me how if I staged a scene one way, it would take three times longer to shoot and light, but if I blocked it just slightly differently, it would be simpler to execute—saving time, money, staying on schedule, and eliminating heartache for hundreds of people. Anyone can direct a movie with unlimited time and money, but that isn't the job directors are hired for. You are being given the responsibility to stay on schedule and within budget *and* deliver an artistic product that is better than everyone's original expectations.

Sometimes the advice came from unexpected places and with more clarity than Spielberg himself could have given me.

In the language of film, anytime something changes in a story or important information is being given—that's a dramatic *beat*. "I want to kill you!"—*beat*. "Your mother's dead . . ."—beat. First kiss happens—beat. Nailing these is a major key to telling stories visually, and every director is on a constant quest to do them well.

Struggling with a scene one day, I turned to a dolly grip, the guy who literally pushes the dolly that holds the camera in position.

"I'm looking for a way to emphasize a moment here," I said. "Something . . . I don't know, something for the audience to pick up on. You know?"

The dolly grip shrugged. "Every time there's a beat," he said. "Either the actor moves or the camera moves." He went back to work.

I'd never heard it described that simply. Not by any of my fancy director pals. This was just a seasoned film vet who had moved the camera on enough beats to understand why he was doing it.

A pro.

———

In the early 2000s, television movies were no longer staples. This meant that for me to continue directing, the only avenue open was a return to episodic television. After my experience on *St. Elsewhere*, I was understandably tentative. Sure, I had directed numerous TV movies by this time, but that didn't count for anything in the episodic world. Hollywood wants you to stay in your lane as long as it can keep you there. If you want to do something new, you have to press it. No one will make it easy for you—not even the people you're paying a percentage of your salary to. My agents encouraged me to talk to my series producer friends and "perhaps get a shot that way." *(Thanks for the help, agents.)*

Fine. I knew producer Pen Densham (*Robin Hood: Prince of Thieves*, *Backdraft*) from *Breaking News*, the show that never saw the light of day. Pen was doing a revival of *The Twilight Zone* and was willing to give me a shot directing an episode. (I'd been on Rod Serling's *Zone* as a child actor—"A Short Drink from a Certain Fountain," but my short scene was cut.) New shows were half-hour episodes that would be shot in five days. Most episodic TV is eight days, so this schedule was down and dirty. I got the script and went to work.

My episode was about a group of college students who get lost in the woods and seek refuge in a cave where *Twilight Zone* stuff happens. I was fortunate that my episode landed on a split week in the schedule: We'd shoot for two days, have the weekend off, and then come back and finish the remaining three days of filming. In Vancouver, British Columbia, we got the first two days of exterior scenes in as planned, and I was feeling pretty good. But Pen called me after seeing the dailies on Friday night. He asked me to "liven" things up, make the shots more dynamic and irregular, not so static and balanced. Panic set in. No one tells you you're doing good or bad; they usually just give you a note and then never hire you again.

I spent the next two days watching every DVD I could lay my hands on to do with caves, horror movies, and mayhem. With little sleep, I watched everything, completely reworking my plans to shoot the episode. I showed up on Monday with a new concept and a new energy to shoot the interior cave scenes. I had to drag the cinematographer kicking and screaming into this new approach, because he liked the static and balanced style of shooting. I think he was just lazy. I had so much fun in the next three days with the cast and crew, letting go of all restraint and embracing a more visually exciting take on the story.

I didn't hear from Pen Densham again until he saw the director's cut (my assembly of the episode). He told me it was among the best episodes they had done yet. I credited him for shaking things up and giving me permission to go wild! It clearly *had* worked.

And I started to get offers for more episodic directing work.

But I wanted to direct President Bartlet.

———

FOR MORE THAN A YEAR, I'D BEEN LOBBYING JOHN WELLS (A PRO-ducer on *The West Wing*) to let me direct an episode. "Fine," he agreed, but he wasn't letting me into the Oval Office quite yet. "We've got a show in New York you can direct. It's a cop show."

He offered me a complex and demanding episode of *Third Watch* and crossed his fingers. Now I found myself in a tight spot: If my episode of *Third Watch* didn't work, I could kill two careers with one bullet—directing and acting (*The West Wing*). The pressure was on.

It just so happened that the other creator/producer of *Third Watch* was Ed Bernero, a retired Chicago beat cop and a great man with both feet firmly on the ground. Ed was friendly to all, but he did not suffer fools. I worked night and day to get ready for my shoot. Spielberg style, I mapped out every shot, every transition, every montage, and every stunt in extreme detail. When I arrived in New York for preproduction, I had my first meeting with Ed. I started to explain to him everything I was going to do. Before I got forty-five seconds into my description, he held up both hands with a smile. "Okay," he said. "Shoot it the way you want to. Just give me a good episode that looks like *Third Watch*. And, good luck." No micromanaging—ah, the good ol' days.

I worked extremely well with the cinematographer, the stunt coordinator, and the rest of the fantastic crew; I also got on very well with the talented cast and went back home happy. I spent four days cutting the episode, turned it in, and went on to playing Vice President Hoynes on *The West Wing*.

As I'm preparing for a scene with Allison Janney, there came a knock on the dressing-room trailer door. When I opened it, it was John Wells with a big smile. He'd just seen my episode of *Third Watch*. "You knocked it out of the park!" he exclaimed. "I love it. Our other producers love it. Studio loves it. Great job!"

And off he went.

Level up! After the success of the *Third Watch* episode, I was now a bona fide network episodic TV director. Thank you, John Wells and Ed Bernero.

———

AFTER THE *THIRD WATCH* RUN, AND LONG BEFORE MY *WEST WING* return, I'd built enough cred—and sample work—to get a few more jobs. I directed episodes of *Without a Trace, Numb3rs, Killer Instinct, Criminal Minds,* and *Cold Case.*

After my first episode of *Cold Case,* they asked me to join the show as a director/producer mostly because its star, Kathryn Morris, had somehow enjoyed working with me on *Hell Swarm.* Guess she figured if I had her back on that fiasco of a film, I could certainly support her on a hit TV show. Kathryn and the showrunner didn't get along; they were oil and water. By the end of the first season, she was often threatening to quit. The situation was bad. She needed an ally on set. So I joined the team.

Kathryn and I would sit and talk in her trailer for hours, where I'd advise her to think about her career. I stressed the value of a hit show and a steady paycheck. She was a fervent actor with total dedication; she'd done anything we'd asked on *Hell Swarm* as if Francis Ford Coppola were asking her to do it. And on *Cold Case,* she would always settle in and there would be another few episodes before things devolved again.

I'd joined the *Cold Case* team as the Kathryn whisperer.

What it needed, apparently, was a Tim whisperer.

When I started directing, I always thought it was my job to fight to make the best piece of film this show could ever have. At all costs.

I was a purist. Or, maybe, an infant.

It's hard to tell the difference sometimes.

After I was onboard as an executive producer, I was wrapping up a *Cold Case* episode I had directed and I asked editorial for some particular stock footage to use. These are little scenes (random shots of skylines or settings, etc.) that every studio has compiled from *all* its productions so that other productions can make use of the footage. Long gone, at this point, were the days on *Bonanza*, where each season, we had to reshoot the wide shots of us riding left and right. Today, that's stock footage. The request was for an episode I had directed, but I was also an executive producer on the show. I had been asking politely for weeks. Eventually, I got less polite. We needed the episode finished, and I finally laid into the editorial department, half of whom were sitting on yoga balls when I did so.

The call from the showrunner came that same night. "You can't talk to editorial like that!" she warned me. I tried explaining to her how long I'd been waiting for that stock footage, but this wasn't anyone's concern now but mine. In this new role, I needed to learn how either to play politics or to keep my mouth shut. The mouth shutting lasted a few months.

One morning, I found the director of the next episode sitting at my desk in my office on my computer when I came into work.

"What the hell are you doing in here?" I asked.

"I needed your DVD player," he said simply, not even looking up. "You weren't here. No big deal."

"It *is* a big deal," I corrected. "Don't ever just come in my fucking office without my permission." This request didn't seem unreasonable to me. (Plus, I knew he was angling for my job.)

Now he lifted his head, and other words were exchanged. *So much for politics and keeping my mouth shut.*

The executive producers of *Cold Case* asked for a meeting.

For the only time in my career, I'd been fired.

And that pesky director, by the way? Yeah, he got my job.

———

"YOU HAVE SUCH EXPERIENCE DOING COMEDY. IT'S YOUR BRAND. Let's focus on directing comedy shows!" This was my manager making lemonade out of lemons, which is what you're paying them for.

Easier said than done. "You're a cowboy actor—you're not a preppie" is the same thing as "You're a murder cop show director—you're not a comedy director." "You're an episodic and MOW director—you can't do commercials." I needed to find a way (once again) to get the powers that be to see me as I wanted to be seen. Not the way they insisted on seeing me.

Like everyone else, I needed help along the way.

Pen Densham had helped me break the mold into episodic TV. John Wells had given me a chance to get back into network TV, and Bruce Paltrow had let Otter direct Denzel Washington. To help me get into commercials, Generate stepped up.

Generate was my management company, and it had a thriving business doing commercials and branded entertainment projects for Madison Avenue. When it asked if I would direct a commercial for Lipton, I couldn't say yes fast enough. I reminded myself that David Fincher, Ridley Scott, Spike Jonze, Sofia Coppola, Michael Bay, and a dozen other directors started, and learned, making commercials. Advertisements always had enormous Spielbergian budgets and were a great chance to keep working on my craft. I made dozens of commercials with Generate, and my one directing award is for a series of commercials built around the *Mad Men* show for the Unilever brand offerings, including Dove soap, Breyers ice cream, and Hellmann's mayonnaise. This was a turning point for me, and it wouldn't have happened unless I'd been fired off of *Cold Case.*

These commercials were all comedic and helped me break out of crime procedurals so that I could pursue directing comedies. Sometimes I traded acting to build out my directing credentials, but I began to be offered directing-only jobs for the likes of *Psych, Greek, Burn Notice, White Collar,* and *Suits.* And believe me, it's much more fun to go to work and laugh at humorous performances all day than it is to keep adding blood to the murder scenes of crime procedurals.

———

EVERY TV DIRECTOR WANTS TO BE A PILOT DIRECTOR. IT'S LIKE making a movie, but with the chance that it will spawn hundreds of sequels, one a week. When you're hired to direct a TV episode, say Season 4, Episode 406, you are being hired to drive a race car that someone else designed and built. When you direct a pilot, however, you're the designer, mechanic, and driver of a car's first race, and if that car wins, you win, too, for the life of the show.

It had happened very quickly. My agent called and told me I was wanted in Los Angeles for a meeting on a Saturday morning with the producers of a new show for USA called *Covert Affairs.*

Good news—it's a pilot. Bad news—I hadn't even seen the script yet, and I've got less than twenty-four hours to prepare my pitch. What I didn't know was that the studio already had another director who had withdrawn because of a scheduling conflict or maybe a better offer. But Tom Brady didn't care about Drew Bledsoe's getting hurt, so neither did I.

My agent told me that USA was interested because I had proven my ability to handle comedy and action on my episodes of its show *Burn Notice.* That, combined with my experience making longer-form MOWs, and it looked like the stars were finally aligning.

It's Saturday morning, I've crammed all night, and I arrive promptly to meet the producer. It was one of the coldest meetings that I'd ever had. He hardly said a word, and just kept nodding as I outlined my vision: where the jokes should land, how I'd capture the action, everything in great detail. But I got the silent treatment in return. Like I'd done after thousands of auditions and meetings before this, I walked back to my car, took a deep breath, and drove back up the 101 to my family in Santa Barbara thinking, *Well that didn't go well. I shouldn't have told Megan I was finally up for a pilot—now I have to tell her I didn't get it.*

On Sunday morning, the phone rang, and I had the offer to direct *Covert Affairs*. My first pilot! I was overjoyed. I had misread the producer, and he really liked me.

But actually, I hadn't misread anything.

I got the latest draft of the script and dug in, working on it. A week later, I heard from the producer that the USA executives overseeing the show want to have a meeting. He never said anything about the purpose of the meeting or any other details. When we went in for the meeting, it was casual and congenial. The network executives raved about the shows I'd done for them and felt it was perfect that I'd be directing this pilot for them. Then, a bombshell. The network also offered me the role of one of the show's leads: the head of the CIA. USA was especially happy with the *Burn Notice* episode that I had both acted in and directed, so the execs knew I was capable of doing this.

"Wow," I said. "I'm flattered and honored." As I was about to go on, my new producer interrupted and said, "Since this is Tim's first pilot, it's probably best not to put too much on his plate with both directing and acting. Let's just have him direct." I was blindsided. This guy was turning down a job for me without so much as a single conversation regarding the part, the situation, or how I felt about it. I was pissed. And there was zero way he hadn't been part of previous conversations where this was discussed with the network. (In retrospect, he probably protected me from myself and let the directing be the only thing I was focused on.) Shortly after, the meeting ended—awkwardly, thankfully—and we all went our separate ways.

This producer insisted I use *his* cinematographer instead of the ones I'd presented. His seemed like a good choice, but I was nervous that the producer had him in his pocket. But OK, fine. I next chose my frequent film editor Bob Ferretti as our editor. He'd done big action movies and lighter films, and his résumé matched mine for tone and was exactly what the network had said they wanted when it hired me to helm the project. A few days later, I got a call from the producer. He didn't think my editor was right for this show; Bob hadn't done enough comedy. I assured him I knew this man well and he would prove a great fit for the action and could handle the comedy, too. I told him not to worry; this was the right choice for us. He dropped it for a moment, but when I arrived in Toronto to scout locations, the producer approached me again: "I don't want to use your editor. I've got a better one."

It's the director—no one else—who hires the cinematographer and the editor. Cleary, the dynamic between us was shaping up badly. The producer questioned every move I made, every choice I selected, and every crew member I invited onto our team. If the pilot doesn't work—they're going to blame me. I'd given him his choice for cinematographer, and I didn't want to quibble about stuff like this. There was too much work to do and too little time. But the hits kept coming.

The next battle was about our stunt coordinator. My first choice was to bring in the superb stunt coordinator of *Burn Notice*, Artie Malesci. This guy could do everything. Artie and I had a great rapport, and we had also done a feature movie for Fox: *Behind Enemy Lines: Colombia*. If it ain't broke, don't fix it.

The producer argued against bringing in someone from the United States, which would cost more, and I countered with "Let's not step over dollars to save dimes. This is money well spent." Artie could work with our wonderful actor, Piper Perabo, who hadn't yet really done any stunts to speak of—but you knew she'd absolutely nail it with some training. These two would choreograph the action ahead of time and rehearse her through it to keep her safe. Their work would make it easier for her to do the stunts once we got on set. He was the total pro. (This is exactly the way *Burn Notice* was done.)

But to save a few pennies, my new producer wouldn't let Artie stay in Toronto for the entire shoot to work with Piper on her stunt work. His plan was to send Artie back to the States unless we were filming stunts on the set, and a *local* stunt coordinator would help Piper learn Artie's choreography on her weekends off. I hated this compromise, but I was also assured it wasn't up for discussion.

Perhaps predictably, I got a call early one Sunday morning that Piper was in the hospital with a badly sprained, possibly broken ankle, which she had injured when the local stunt guy was training her. I was devastated and furious. First, because our leading lady had been needlessly injured, but also because now she wouldn't be able to do the stunts herself—which she could have done! We had to rechoreograph the remaining stunt scenes with a double, which never looks as good. All because of the choice to cheap out on Artie being there for her. ("Cheap" is expensive!)

It became more and more obvious that this producer didn't trust me, like me, or want me on this project. He basically wanted total control, and that is not how good shows get made. I grew up around producers who took supporting the director as their main objective, second only to safety. The truth is, it's hard to find producers who know that—*and can do it*. Many are merely frustrated directors and want to micromanage everything. That path leads to conflict and chaos.

Despite having a producer who didn't have my back, and despite Piper's injury, the production turned out great. I had everything I needed to put together a great show in the editing room.

Stupid Tim . . .

As we shot the pilot, I kept asking the producer what the final edit time should be. We knew we were making a two-hour pilot. But two hours isn't really 120 minutes. It could be 97 minutes, it could be 100 minutes. In cable, there is some leeway with the commercial times and where they need to land. "Don't worry about it," he said. For two weeks, that was the answer.

"Can we call USA and get a running time locked down?" I asked.

"No."

When I finally showed him my cut, there was dead silence. I leaned back, confused. I knew how good it was, and Piper was terrific.

"It's way too long," he said.

I realized we'd been set up. My editor was fired that same day. The producer hired the editor he'd wanted all along, and they took over the project and ultimately delivered a final cut . . . one suspiciously identical to the one I'd handed in. *Covert Affairs* was ordered to series almost immediately.

———

Months later, USA called to see if I could direct the pilot of *Suits*, a fun show about corporate attorneys. The same guy from *Covert Affairs* was producing, but I swallowed my pride and said, "Sure, let's talk." *Shockingly,* after my network meeting, he chose another director for the pilot. But I took the high road and told him, "If you ever need an *episode* directed, let me know." I got the call during Season 1. Wow! It seemed that *both* of us were taking, or considering, the high road.

During shooting, one of the principal actors pulled me aside on a short break and groused about the producer not letting them push the boundaries of the character. "Here's how I handled it," I smiled warmly. "I'd shoot a version *his* way just to keep him happy and then do two or three more the way *I* wanted. We ended up using my takes . . . 'cause they were better." The actor laughed. "Just trust your gut," I told him. "You know what you're doing."

He smiled proudly and went off to wherever and I turned to find the producer glaring at me from across the set in the video village with all the monitors and technicians. His headset was still on his head and I looked up at the still-open mic dangling three feet above *my* head on set.

He'd heard every word. *Oops. Truth hurts.*

We haven't worked together since.

———

COVERT AFFAIRS WENT ON TO BE A GIANT HIT FOR USA. IT launched me as a pilot director, and I was fortunate enough to be trusted with pilots for multiple networks.

Everything in my professional life was picking up.

My personal life, however, clearly needed a better director.

Empty Chairs

THE VACANT CHAIR STARED BACK AT ME.

"Okay, well, fuck you, then!" I continued. "You don't give a damn what happens to us! Or to Mom. You walked out on us. . . . All you ever think about is yourself!"

Then I imagined words of explanation and defense from my father.

"Don't give me that shit," I said, glaring at the chair. "You've had forty fucking years to do that, and haven't. Not once. This—you and I—that's not something you'll ever get back."

The chair now remained silent and empty in response. A terrible yet peaceful stillness filled the room again.

—

MY MARRIAGE TO MEGAN, NOW IN ITS TWENTY-FOURTH YEAR, needed some help. We'd been a strong couple on the communication front, but things were devolving fast. It was clear to me, to both of us, that we'd become roommates raising children together. While neither of us wanted that, we couldn't break the pattern.

There were, I knew, unresolved things—those classic *childhood* things—I needed to work on to become a better husband and father.

Therapy and counseling seemed, maybe, a reasonable option.

My one year in college, I was technically majoring in psychology. I'd never been to a psychiatrist or therapist, but there was still something about the field that interested me. Maybe the actor in me was interested in motivations; maybe I simply recognized that my childhood hadn't been the best and that some understanding of that through therapy would serve me well.

In 1971, as part of our divorce settlement, I was paying for Jennifer Leak to see a therapist during our requisite separation. She soon wanted me to also talk to him, and like a dutiful soon-to-be ex-husband, I headed into Beverly Hills to some therapist's office. "Well, you know," Dr. Somebody said, "she's really, really caught off guard and upset by all this. Really distraught."

"I understand," I replied carefully.

"And . . . I think maybe you can help her," he told me.

"Of course. Anything," I said.

"If you tell her that you really *do* love her," he told me. "And . . . that there's a chance that you can get back together with her."

"But that's not true," I replied. "It's *never* going to work; I mean, it's over. It's done."

"What could it hurt?" he asked.

Because of this, for years I thought therapists were charlatans and bullshitters. This expert wanted my soon-to-be ex-wife to believe something that wasn't true, which is horrifying. So, despite clearly still having some things to work out, I'd never given too much thought about going myself.

Now I was yelling at empty chairs.

———

"How was that?" I asked, turning to the only other person in the room, psychiatrist to the stars, Dr. Phil Stutz.

In lieu of marriage counseling for two, I'd decided on some "me counseling" for one.

I'd asked two or three people about who I might see, and they all said Phil Stutz. He was twice the cost of other therapists but seemed to be *the* Hollywood whisperer. A lot of big directors and actors were openly seeing this guy. (In 2022, Jonah Hill would make a documentary about him.) Dr. Stutz was a New Yorker who had worked as a psychiatrist at the Rikers Island jail for years before moving his practice to Los Angeles in the early 1980s. The great thing about Stutz was that he believed he could actually resolve issues; one and done, they say. Rather than looking at me or other patients as a weekly annuity he could use to buy a bigger boat, Stutz said in our first meeting, "We're gonna get to the heart of what's going on with you. We're gonna fix it, and then you're not going to see me anymore."

I liked that.

He proved brilliant, and I loved him. When I was having trouble and was going through a period of debilitating nerves during auditions, Stutz was able to work with me to provide prospective, something that I'd lost along the way. He would ask me what I was doing after I had an audition.

"What do you mean?" I replied, confused. "I drive home."

"Nope," he said. "Make a plan for yourself for later in the day. You're going on a hike or gonna go shopping or get a cookie and some coffee over at such-and-such place. Something. Your life doesn't begin and end at that audition. Your life goes on beyond that." It was the same advice Leslie Nielsen had tried giving me thirty years earlier. "This is a job," Stutz reminded me. "You're good at it and you love it, but it's just something we're doing. Life is other things."

I thought about Molly, Emma, Cooper, and Megan back home.

"What are you doing after the audition?" he asked again.

"Spending time with my kids," I said. "Taking my family to dinner."

Perspective on life was one of the great gifts that Stutz gave me, perspective on the good things like my family. He also alerted me to behaviors that I thought were good but had been hurting me for years.

———

I'D GROWN UP IN A HOUSE WITH TWO ALCOHOLICS WHO CONstantly yelled at each other. My survival mode for the sake of myself and my sister was to become the peacemaker. Whatever I *could* do to keep things stable, I *would* do.

Personally and professionally, I'd allowed myself to take second place for years.

My friend Mike and I were great pals. As kids, we'd make up plays and skits, and we'd perform them for our parents. He wanted to be an actor too. He also agreed that Janelle Penny was the hottest girl in my school. He was much-needed family, an older brother to me.

As we entered our twenties, I noticed he was putting me down all the time. Every conversation included "jokes" or comments at my expense: "You get by on your looks." "You're just a reservist, not a real Marine." "You're an okay actor." "You get by with charm, not talent."

When Mike returned from Vietnam, he got in touch with me. I was playing Romeo in San Diego, and he told me, "I'd love to come down and see the play."

I could not have been more excited to have him come. "Great!" I replied. I was renting the top floor of a house with an extra bedroom and invited him to stay with me. I coordinated everything. "See the show, we'll grab dinner after or go to a party somewhere." But during the second half of the performance, the seat he'd been in was now empty. And in the dressing room afterward, he hadn't come back, either. Quick calls to the house went unanswered. My pal was full-on MIA.

Back home, I found the house empty and a note.

"Tim, I wanted to. Just couldn't take it."

It finally hit me. All the put-downs. The notion of watching me on stage was just beyond his pride. We tried talking about it when I got back to L.A. but no apology or understanding came of it.

On that date I had with Janelle Penny, once I'd hit the height requirement, Mike had gotten himself invited as a tagalong. I figured what the hell; it would take some of the pressure and weirdness off of Janelle and me. Mike hit on her all night long. Snaked me from the first hello; any move I'd ever seen him try on a girl was in full effect tonight. In between his efforts, he found ways to mock my career.

Charles, another actor "pal," was apparently from the same camp. Thanks to *1941*, I'd gotten him invited to a party that included folks like Steven Spielberg. In short order, he'd cornered Spielberg and was talking shit about me, heckling my acting and résumé. The one thing he had in common with the director was me, so he took the low road for easy conversation. Steven, thankfully, was just staring at this guy in alarm when I caught my supposed friend red-handed.

These were the relationships Stutz helped open my eyes to, and there's been little interaction with either man, and those of similar ilk, since. And I'm glad of that. (But I *do* miss the friends I once had.)

I HAD ALSO ATTRACTED THESE SORTS OF PEOPLE IN MY PROFESsional life. I ought to have rapidly cut my relationship with my old business partner Dan Grodnik when we'd finished *Blind Fury* together.

Thanks to my work with Stutz, and great counsel from director/ pal Bruce Paltrow, another compassionate member of the church of "Why waste time on people like that?" I was getting better at identifying and avoiding people who hurt me, so that I could learn to spare myself the pain. But I still had to resolve my issues with the guy in the empty chair: my father.

———

IT WAS DARK IN THE ROOM AND VERY COLD WHEN I ENTERED.

Surgical lights tilted down to a man lying on a gurney. Nurses buzzed everywhere attending to him. Several doctors hovered over him. An oxygen cannula was taped to his nose. The man's eyes, filled with fear and surprise, caught mine as I entered, a flicker of recognition despite my surgical cap, mask, and gown. I took his hand in mine and squeezed it reassuringly.

"Hiya, pops. How ya doin'? I'm here for you."

———

WHEN MY PARENTS SPLIT, MOM WAS STILL AROUND TO RECEIVE any anger or distress I needed to dish out. And I doled out the lumps. Dad, however, was three-hundred-plus miles away in Arizona, and all the resentment, betrayal, pain, and rage had grown untended for more than twenty years.

And, as always, I'd kept my mouth shut throughout it all.

I'd learned that for a long time, my father didn't believe my sister and I were his biological children. He and Mom hadn't been able to conceive for years, so when my sister and I finally arrived, he harbored the notion that my mother had, possibly, screwed around on him. The fact that my sister, Sue, and I looked exactly like him wasn't enough proof to verify otherwise. Because of this, he kept all three of us at arm's length.

We were basically strangers by the time I was twenty.

———

I WAS ABOUT TO TURN TWENTY-FIVE WHEN *BONANZA* WAS CAN-celed and my father came to stay with me for two weeks in Los Angeles. I had just lost my job—that was how he saw it. That was how he always saw it.

"Well, what are you gonna do now?" he asked me. He assumed I'd move on to another career, like he had done from the liquor store to the upholstery business to the next one and the next one. I care-fully tried to educate him about the life of an actor. "Another job will come along," I said. "I'm not worried." I explained this while he asked many questions about my life, spending habits, savings, and so on. But he didn't buy it. I think he thought I'd someday come to my senses and get a real job like other people. He wanted to offer advice to me about my life, but we didn't have that kind of relationship. We had two different ways of looking at the world, and from his point of view, he would *never* see mine.

———

As I look at my life now as a parent, I've grown more and more sympathetic to his plight. How could a person who came from the Depression, who chugged soda down because they were afraid it would be their last one—even though his family had owned the store—ever understand my dreams? I remember being angry about it then, but now I look at my kids and I am so proud of them and their careers, but honestly, how can I be expected to understand what they do all day? What I have learned is that I have to love them no matter what they do and I cannot ever let my lack of understanding of what *they* love get in the way.

———

Eventually, as my dad and I glared at one another, I had to be honest and make him stop. "I love you, Dad. I wish that you *had* been there when I was growing up. I wish I'd spent every day with you and gotten to know you better. A history where I could take your advice now. But we *don't* have that history." He nodded, maybe even understood. "We can create something man-to-man starting today," I offered sincerely. "Just start over. But let's not pretend you know me or know what I want to do. Then maybe we can get to a place where we both actually are, not what we were supposed to be."

After that visit, things got a lot smoother and easier between us. I had let go of a lot of my anger, and I hope my doing so gave my father permission to not feel guilty about things from the past.

This was a step in the right direction. Or, at least, a step.

Dad had been living a modest life in Phoenix, working for the Arizona State Liquor Control Department, when something magical happened to him. His sister had introduced him to Gisela, a well-to-do woman who actually lived *on* the Paradise Valley Country Club, and they hit it off. All of a sudden, my father was plucked out of his lonely, meager life in Phoenix and was living sumptuously and traveling around the world first class with "Gi." He'd never traveled anywhere before but now spent summers at her family home in Gloucester, Massachusetts. I figured, at last, maybe Dad would be able to grow past the ghosts of the Depression. But the more time I spent with the two of them, the more I realized Dad was often Gi's caretaker and comforter. They both drank a lot, and it was his job to take care of her when she'd had a few too many. This went on for years. I knew it wasn't a great environment or relationship for my dad, but what could I do? I had as much business lecturing him as he did me.

In the summer of 1979, Dad called with news. The doctor had found something in his lungs. He'd smoked two packs a day my whole life. The finding was a surprise to no one, but it didn't make it any less painful to hear. "I'm sick," he allowed only. "They're checking the lungs and running some kind of scope down there."

"I'll come to you," I said, and flew to the hospital in Tucson. There, all that method acting finally paid off. I was preparing to play a doctor in an adaptation of the best-selling novel *The House of God* and as a result was able to pull some strings and be in the operating room with my father for his procedure. He looked scared. I'd seen him tired, defeated, and even angry but never before scared. A tough thing for a son to see. We held hands as the anesthetic took hold and they slid the bronchoscope down his throat.

I spent the rest of the day with my dad and later drove him from the Tucson hospital back to Paradise Valley and Gi's home. That evening, we talked about everything except lung cancer. I spent the night there and headed to Philadelphia the next day to report for rehearsal on *The House of God*. While filming, I couldn't stop worrying about my father.

A few days later, the biopsy came back. Dad's throat proved fine. His lungs, not so much: He had stage 3 cancer. The prognosis was dim. Perhaps a year? Or perhaps six months? No one knew. He had already lost weight and didn't have his usual energy. And Gisela wasn't proving much help. The core of their relationship had been *him* taking care of *her*. I think my dad did his best to ignore that aspect, but despite all the ups and downs between me and my father, Gisela's inability to help him shattered my heart. She simply wasn't up for the challenge of taking care of him.

After I finished *The House of God*, I went to see him in Arizona. "Why don't you come stay with me?" I found myself saying aloud. "We've got the best doctors in the world in Los Angeles, I'm plugged in at Cedars-Sinai Hospital, the finest cancer hospital this side of the Mississippi, and we would get you the best care possible."

I had a home with plenty of room at the time. "My house is perfect for you. You'll have your own room, and I'll be there to take you to appointments. We'll spend time together and hopefully find a way to beat this cancer." Somewhat surprised these thoughts and offers were coming out of my mouth. Anything that had come before today suddenly no longer mattered. All of that could wait until we got him better.

He listened carefully. He was very quiet. And several weeks later, he got on a plane to come stay with me in Los Angeles. I put a hospital bed in the guestroom, and a nurse would come and stay with him whenever I was gone. He became part of my life again. If I had a party, he'd come out and visit for a bit, then go back and rest.

He was in attendance at smaller dinners and got to know all my friends, too.

For six months, he was back in my life. This was the most normal relationship that we had ever had.

WE TRIED ALL SORTS OF TREATMENTS WITH SOME OF THE BEST SPE-cialists in Los Angeles. We even tried a guy in Dallas who wanted patients to visualize the cancer away, to imagine conquering the cancer and the bad cells being destroyed by chemotherapy. My dad's reaction: "Nah, get me a cigarette."

Always the Depression kid, he would obsess about how much this was costing me. I always had to divide by three and still be lectured about it. If the nurse cost $100 a day, I'd tell him $30 when asked, and he'd erupt: "Jesus Christ!! You're just pissing it away!" Then I'd lie about insurance taking care of it. Anything to ease his worried mind.

HIS HEALTH GREW WORSE. WORDS LIKE "MONTHS LEFT" CAME OUT during appointments. My sister, who'd been preparing to take the bar exam, decided to put the test off until Dad was either healed or gone. "It's not like that," I assured her. "He's got plenty of time; just take your test." It became a heated argument, one of many I've lost to my big sister over the years, and she moved to L.A. to help.

As the cancer spread and he got weaker and weaker, his pain medication got stronger. This made him groggier and more confused. "What can I do to help you?" I asked my dad one night, just the two of us alone. Trying to see if there was somewhere he wanted to see or something he wanted to do that he'd never gotten to do. In the dimly lit room, he lay shrouded in the weight of his illness, a fragile figure, his eyes filled with resignation now more than any fear.

"Just shoot me," he said. He wasn't joking.

"That ain't me, Dad," I replied. "We can fight this if you want, but I'm not the guy to ask for that." The old .22 I kept in the house was locked away.

The moment finally came when it was time to find Dad his own place with full-time care. He needed professionals, not me and my sister. We'd just started the hunt for a good place when his health dropped to a whole new low. My sister had been right about the timing of things. Dad went into hospice, where he hung on for weeks, going in and out of consciousness for days at a time. We'd sit in the room and talk to him as if he could hear us. I'd tell him about my day for the first time ever.

During all the time he stayed with me, he only spoke to Gisela a few times. Since he went into hospice, she had not reached out at all. We reached out to her and let her know of his condition and asked her to call. She did, and he opened his eyes when he heard her voice. He was aware that she was on the phone sending her affection. He was able to mumble a few words to her. After the call, he slumped back into a coma. He died in his sleep the next morning. My sister was with him when he passed, and I got there just after he was gone. We both believed that he wouldn't let go until he heard from Gisela.

I went into his room and sat with him for a while. By sitting with his body, I came to realize that his spirit was no longer there; my father was gone. This was a kind of closure for me. I'd made him a promise during his illness that, no matter what, he would always be in my heart. And he is.

I said my goodbyes and told him I loved him. It was over.

He was cremated, and I soon went to Hawaii with a girl-friend for a trip planned a year before. I needed to be away from that house and family and death for a while. When we got back home, my mom was furious. "How could you leave your father? You just left him!"

His ashes were in an urn in my house.

"There's nothing happening," I told her. "He's gone. Also, you hated him." *Now* she was, for some reason, interested. Not interested enough to come to his final ceremony, however.

I took my dad's ashes out into the Pacific.

"I'll leave you back here," the boat's captain said, and then went forward to the bow to give me some privacy in the back. It suddenly got somber.

On the back of the boat, they had installed a deck closer to the water to make it easier to pour the ashes overboard. I didn't quite know what to do. I thought about all of our recent time together, the few good childhood memories. I told him he would always be with me and that I loved him. I knelt down on the small deck, undid the top of the urn, and slowly reached toward the water to pour the remains of my father into the sea.

"Hey?!"

The boat's captain had returned.

"Yeah?" I asked, looking up with the urn tilted above the Pacific, my dad beginning his final earthly journey.

"You're the guy in *Animal House*, right? What was it like working with Belushi?"

"Just give me a minute, will ya?"

It was another twenty years before I could truly put our troubled relationship to rest. Stutz and his empty chairs were a big part of that.

But would any of it be enough to save the other troubled relationship in my life? I knew my marriage to Megan was in trouble. Things had happened that I had tried hard to ignore.

Now I was the one who looked scared.

Return to Timalot

DING!

"I feel so much more relieved now that I've decided how to deal with the sitch at home."

The cryptic text arrived on my phone at around 6 a.m.

It was from my wife, Megan. I was directing in Los Angeles and was staying in our L.A. place, which was common for me to do, rather than drive home two hours each way every night. She was in New York for some social events and medical appointments, which was common for her to do. It was a little early for her to text, so I groggily looked at the message briefly, glasses off, and assumed she was talking about a "stich" she'd gotten from a dermatologist in New York. *Oh, that's nice,* I thought, and tried to fall back asleep. But something was bothering me. I sat up in bed. *Wait a minute. . . . What was that again?* Grabbing my phone and my glasses, I reread the text. I still didn't quite understand what I was looking at. The word was *sitch,* not *stitch.*

I knew Megan and I were not in a great place. The last year or so had been a constant struggle to try and keep our marriage alive. After staring at the text—rereading it over and over and having a discussion, out loud, with the ceiling fan—I began to realize that *I* might be the "sitch."

I texted back: "That sounds ominous."

I'm in love with someone else began to ring in my ears.

My marriage to Megan ended with a mistakenly sent text message. The text message itself wasn't a mistake; she just didn't mean to send it to me. A sad and ironic end to a twenty-five-year marriage. But there is no good way, or good time, to end a marriage. The abruptness of it was kind of a godsend. The truth was that I had been ignoring hint after hint, for nearly two years, that this marriage was over. This text she meant to send to someone else—someone whom she was intimately confiding in—*finally* got through to me. Those cyber-gods work in mysterious ways.

Alone in the tiny guesthouse, I was in shock. Lost. Spinning. *How much of this is on me?* I'd started dating Megan when she was nineteen, and we'd been married when she was twenty-six. She was pregnant at twenty-seven. Before we were married, I'd promised she would never have to give up her career as a professional ballet dancer. The idea was that we would be fifty-fifty—bicoastal so that she could continue her career. Then almost instantly two wonderful children were born, followed five years later by our amazing son. Then the Lampoon thing happened. Becoming a director happened. Continuing to act happened. I was gone too frequently. My promises to make that 50 percent became 45 percent, then 35 percent, then . . . why bother? I was obsessed with my work, and she went along for the bumpy ride. I *had* made a bunch of mistakes.

There was a pit in my stomach that knew this was the beginning of the end. We had been though some major bumps in the road over the last many months. Bumps that I thought had been overcome through counseling and a recommitment to each other. But now she's sending texts with personal thoughts about me to someone else? GOOD GOD, HOW MANY MORE HINTS WAS I SUPPOSED TO IGNORE THAT THIS MARRIAGE WAS OVER? The next morning, before I went to work, I sadly removed my wedding ring and left it on the bedside table. I stumbled through work directing a TV show until Megan returned from New York to Santa Barbara.

We made some failed attempts at phone discussions over the next several days, which only increased my sense that I was at the top of a roller coaster about to be dropped. As soon as filming was over, I went home to Santa Barbara to confront her. It didn't take more than one look at her face to know that my fears and concerns were well placed. Neither of us had much to say. Finally, I got up the courage to ask the question you only get to ask once.

"Is there someone else?" I asked.

She looked at her hands, then up to my eyes. "Yes."

I FELT LIKE I WAS ON AUTOPILOT AFTER THAT—LIKE I WAS IN A PLAY in a dream, moving through the part emotionless. This was right before Thanksgiving, a huge holiday in our house, when her family would come in from all over. Awkward timing for sure. I packed some things and told Megan that I was moving out, back to my little guesthouse in Los Angeles. We both agreed to protect the children. She didn't want the kids to know that our marriage was over until we could find the right time to tell them. I agreed. Oddly, I told her that we could tell the kids that this was a mutual decision, not the betrayal that it was. *Protect the kids!* She was grateful. We agreed to have Thanksgiving as normal and to tell no one that we were ending our marriage until after the holiday. As Megan walked me to the car with my bags, I tried some levity: "It's usually considered bad form to fire someone before the holidays."

It was official—I'd become Richard Burton's Arthur in *Camelot*. The fallen king of a broken kingdom. The songs from a musical that had stirred my emotions on command for years, a story that had reminded me of my own parents' divorce and the failed family of my childhood. Now it was me in the role of my father and another family botched. My own family. *How were Megan and I any different from my own parents?* Because we'd lasted longer and stayed in a cooling marriage until our kids were older? At the end of the day, I'd slunk off just the same as my father had.

All that mattered to me, now, was how the kids were going to take it. On that, Megan and I were still a united team. I could only hope our three children would take it like Gary Goetzman and I had in *Divorce American Style*. But we'd been fictional characters in a comedy. This was currently *Divorce Secret Style*. As agreed, I hadn't told anyone, and I drove alone back up to Santa Barbara for a "nice" family Thanksgiving. I showed up, playing my part, prepared with smiles and hugs for all.

Arriving, Megan's brother pulled me aside and put his hand on my shoulder. "Tim," he said, "I'm so sorry." This kind of news, apparently, has a way of getting out. Everyone at dinner *but* the kids knew about our forthcoming divorce.

Cheerily passing the stuffing and rolls that year was some of the best acting I've ever done.

———

A few days after Thanksgiving, Megan and the kids came down to L.A., where we'd all have The Talk. The obligatory promises that we were still a family, and always would be, were made to the children when we broke the news to them that we were heading for divorce. There were tears, confusion, and anger. My heart broke over and over and over. I'd watched my father wither away from cancer, watched my mother battle alcoholism and dementia, buried good friends far too soon, and none of it hurt like watching my kids cry that afternoon.

Later, as I sat alone in my little guesthouse, I hoped these weren't empty promises. My girls were in their twenties, young women looking forward to their own lives. It would be my responsibility to build my own bridge with them. Cooper would be harder; he was still at home and would have to live through all this. But I was determined to do better than my father had.

Many months later (*who am I kidding? it was years*), after things settled down and hurt feelings eased, I learned to appreciate and even applaud Megan's midcourse self-discovery and the revamping and reimagining of her life. Nothing is braver and more courageous than continuing to investigate your own heart, embracing and allowing change and growth to occur. I knew it well. It was something that I had done regularly every seven years throughout my own life.

As for me? I retreated to the one place I'd thought of as home for nearly forty years. The longest relationship I've ever had: a few acres in the Hollywood Hills.

A place, poignantly, dubbed Timalot.

———

WHEN I WAS A KID, MY DAD PUT THE REAL ESTATE BUG IN ME. AFTER his and Mom's separation, when he came to visit, he was always driving me around L.A., drifting slowly down streets all over the Los Angeles Basin like a lurking shark, showing me various houses. He would talk about what those places had once cost but how he also knew that whoever bought them was going to lose their shirt when the "next Depression" came along. If he was trying to teach me to fear owning a house, he failed. I saw those houses not as houses but as homes—the thing he couldn't give me and my mom and my sister.

AT NINETEEN, I'D DRIVEN UP A WINDING STREET INTO THE HOLLYwood Hills to pick up Ms. Jennifer Leak for our first official date. Jennifer lived with a roommate in the bottom half of a two-story English Tudor that had been converted into separate apartments.

This was the beginning of a great love affair.

Not with Jennifer Leak; you already know how that one ends.

But with the street I call home.

Lost in a canopy of oak trees more than two hundred years old, with a little creek gurgling through the property, away from everything, and still somehow only ten minutes from half a dozen studios, it was a place where I felt spiritually at home.

While dating Jennifer, I got to know the property owner, a guy named Herman Boden. His family had lived on and developed the property since the early 1940s, and there were now three homes spread over several acres they collectively owned. A guesthouse, the two-story Tudor, plus plenty of acreage to build new or parcel out.

"You ever wanna sell," I told Herman when Jennifer and I moved north to Malibu, "let me know, because we would have loved to live here."

Now divorced from Jennifer, I approached Herman again. "I'm just checking in with you to see, you know, if—"

"Funny you should call today," he said. "Because I'm at my wit's end with my sister-in-law." Herman's brother had recently died, and Herman was already tired of dealing with his in-laws. I made him a lowball offer and was shocked when he accepted.

Financially in over my head, I swiftly turned the Tudor house into a source of income as a rental property and moved into the little guesthouse. My friends thought I was nuts because of how small it was. *Maybe it seemed bigger to me because I'd earned it.* It looked more like a little cabin lost in the woods, a place for Goldilocks to stumble on. I assured them I'd survived in smaller and converted the cottage's attached garage into a bedroom, living there for years until *The Quest* was over.

It took years, but I finally had enough money to no longer need to rent out the bigger Tudor. I moved in and rented out the guesthouse instead. The property next door had three and one-half acres of undeveloped land with a ranch-style house—and I had been carefully keeping an eye on it. One evening after a long day of shooting on *Tucker's Witch*, I came home and discovered a foreclosure sign on the gate next door. I cleaned out what was left in my bank account to buy the ranch house.

My kingdom was growing! I moved down (about three hundred yards) to the new ranch house and rented out the Tudor again.

My pals soon dubbed the new house Timalot.

It became *the* party house. New Year's. Halloween. Super Bowl. Anytime I felt like it was time to cut loose, I had Timalot. My pals and I formed the Fun Club, and this house became our base of operations. I'd eventually added a stained-glass window with knights and another with a painting of a hooded Merlin in the wood—if you're gonna go Timalot, might as well go all the way.

When Megan and I got married, the Fun Club lost its charter, and Megan and I lived in Timalot for a while. Eventually, we put the Hollywood Hills properties up for rent and bought a house on the West Side. From there, our family grew and we wanted to get away from Los Angeles. We relocated to Santa Barbara for more professional peace, great public schools, and sidewalks for our kids to ride a bike on. And for Rob Lowe to steal our nanny.

———

FORTY YEARS LATER, NEWLY DIVORCED FROM MEGAN, AND LIVING as I had back in 1972, my official residence again became the little guesthouse. It was the one constant in my life.

Over the years, I'd looked at a hundred houses here and there, and none had offered me the same spiritual connection as land I'd found picking up Jennifer all those years ago. The trees. The way the russet sunset drips behind the back of the property each evening, and the sound of the small burbling stream.

It was perfect.

The only problem was that I now had it all to myself.

At What Cost?

AND NOW TO MY "HEART ATTACK" AND THE SHOCKING PRESCRIP-
tion: some Pepto-Bismol and "Try to relax more."

Waiting for the elevator outside the doctor's office, bullet dodged
at least for now, I continued my life assessment.

I was single again for the first time in three decades. I had dipped
my toes back into the dating scene but was hopelessly out of my
element.

"So . . . what brought you to Hollywood?"

It was like ninth-grade me all over again. All I needed was Janelle
Penny to tell me she'd date me but only if I was six foot ten. Any
dating skills I'd successfully built in my twenties and early thirties
had atrophied in the ensuing years. I was back to square one and
growing accustomed to spending nights alone in my little Timalot
cottage in the woods.

My work, specifically directing, had thus become a needed distraction. A reprieve from real life. Acting, I could lose myself in for
hours. Directing, however, you could vanish into a project for weeks.
With all the research, the planning, and the execution, I went to
another place—a place where I had some control. (Just like Charles
Laughton had in *Witness for the Prosecution*.)

But directing had changed a lot in the past fifteen years. Producers and writers were now afraid of the actors. Directors and producers were afraid of showrunners. Showrunners were afraid of
whatever celebrity executive producer or network they answered to,

and the networks and studios were afraid of their corporate over-lords, who would ask why they spent $400 on lunch at Mr Chow. Suddenly, there were lots of people in the industry who didn't even know what their jobs were anymore. Whatever hierarchy the studios had in place since the 1930s was mostly gone, replaced with "How cheaply and quickly can we make this thing and get people talking about it on social media?"

It wasn't as much fun. The frustrations were, for the first time, now outweighing the creative thrill. These were headaches and turf wars I didn't need. Still, I took as many directing opportunities as I could get to stay busy (and to pay my alimony): *The Last Ship*, *Person of Interest*, *Lucifer*, *Taken*, *Persons Unknown*, *Criminal Minds*.

When two different studios threatened to sue me, I finally woke to the fact I was maybe too busy. I'd been double-booked to work on two shows at the exact same time. War had been declared on me.

One job was to direct a pilot for USA, and the other was back-to-back acting episodes on *Hart of Dixie*—prior to my becoming a series regular. My acting agent and directing agent worked in the same building, and yet somehow, they didn't talk to each other. They tried sorting it out with the two studios, but neither would budge. Both were threatening to sue me for millions if I didn't make myself exclusive to their show. (Who would have ever imagined I was that much in demand?)

Money was already tight postdivorce; these lawsuits would end me. I was even getting calls from studio VPs with warnings that I would never work at their networks or studios again. *Fifty years in the business, and I didn't know people actually said stuff like that in real life.*

Everything I'd spent a lifetime building was going away.

Family, reputation, security.

I decided to do what I had done during the Universal days after they'd fired me and refused to give me a raise. I'd talk to them myself. So, I picked up the phone and found out that, in reality, only a few days were overlapping. I talked to the producers of *Hart of Dixie* first and asked if they could condense all my scenes on their show into two days, and I would fulfill my commitment to Warner Bros. I also promised that if there were any overages or expenses to make these changes, I'd pay for them out of my own pocket. The producer and studio were taken by surprise. I'd solved *their* timing and budget issue with one phone call.

Next I called 20th Century Fox Studios, to which I was committed to direct their pilot. I assured them that I'd only be missing two days from preparation (shooting wouldn't start for another three weeks) and that I would make it up by working over the weekend after I returned from *Hart of Dixie*. Again, I told them if there were any salaries or expenses for people working extra days, I'd gladly pay for it myself. Tickled pink they were. "Fine by us," they said. Problems solved.

THAT DONE, I'D ALSO STARTED WORKING ON MY HEALTH, JUST LIKE the doctor ordered. Changed my diet, worked out differently. Even tried to tap back into some of those meditation techniques Mike Love of the Beach Boys had once taught me. And in a few weeks, that tightness in my chest relaxed. In a few months, I felt pretty good.

Only then did my big sister tell me that she *knew* the cause of my earlier cardiac saga. "A broken heart," she reckoned.

(Two years later, I'd learn that—even if my sister was only partly right—it *had* been an actual damn heart attack! Indigestion, my ass. "Did you have a heart attack about two years ago?" a new, better doctor asked. This guy had an EKG that said as much, showing the earlier damage. Evidently, I'd just healed myself over the next few months.)

But I didn't know any of that yet.

All I knew was that this guy was telling me to take some antacids and a little break, to get away from Hollywood for a while. And I want to tell him that I've been doing this for a long while and that—unless you're Daniel Day-Lewis or Stanley Kubrick—breaks often lead to the end of careers. "You need to take care of yourself," the first doctor had warned.

I think of my mom working two jobs and sleeping on our couch so my sister and I have a bedroom. I think of Grandma Sadie, barely half recovered from a car wreck, asking to be driven to her job.

I don't have time, or interest, to take care of myself.

I don't have time, or interest, for love.

So, healthy enough to get around again, I did the only thing I knew I was good at: working.

I "moved" full-time to Bluebell, Alabama.

As luck would have it, that's where Elizabeth was.

Always Wear a Tux to Work

(or, in Virgin River, a Parka)

EXT. BLUEBELL, ALABAMA—DAY

DOCTOR BRICK BREELAND is dressed in a tux, like Agent 007
playing baccarat, and he looks pretty damn good for a guy who
could have died six months earlier from a heart attack. He
is also directing the season finale of *Hart of Dixie*, including
nearly a hundred extras in a wedding sequence. It's a Hillbilly
version of *The Godfather*.

IF I WERE LOOKING TO SCORE, I COULDN'T HAVE PICKED A BETTER
day.

Just about every skill I'd managed to collect over the past, ahem,
six decades was on full display. Actor, director, and a guy who still
cleaned up nice when sculpted in full professional makeup and a
quality tux.

My biggest advantage, however, was that I wasn't looking to
score. When directing, all else goes away. (This isn't some brag; it's
survival. There's only so much a guy can focus on. Add acting to

directing, and you're doing two twelve-hour jobs in an eight-hour day.) So I didn't care when one of the producers asked if I would mind if she brought a guest onto the set of *Hart of Dixie* to shadow our production—a rookie script supervisor looking to get into the business.

"Yeah, sure," I said.

I was introduced to the rookie script supervisor: Elizabeth Marighetto.

"Good to meet you," I said and promptly went back to the universe of Bluebell, Alabama. Sure, I'd noticed the quick, easy smile and the eyes that reminded me of the Mediterranean at sunset, but there was work to do.

When she returned to the video village the second day, I found myself slightly less distracted with work. Now I slowed down enough to fully take in the glint of amusement and brainpower behind that Mediterranean hue. The conversation and questions in a deep, warm tone—I still thought about after I'd left the set.

Professionally, we'd exchanged numbers. But I was hesitant. There was an off-balance professional power dynamic (the "veteran" actor and director, and the rookie script supervisor) that could be perceived wrong by any number of people, including her. And, enough of an age gap (twenty-plus years) that I didn't want to be pegged a cliché new divorcé. With two grown daughters of my own, I didn't want to be *that* guy.

But I couldn't get her out of my mind. I finally called to ask her out for an afternoon coffee. Throughout, I was careful to give this woman every possible escape route. But an afternoon coffee turned into an easy-to-say-no-to dinner offer. After dinner, I'd gotten out of the car to walk her to the door—you can take the boy out of the 1950s, but you can't take the 1950s out of the man—and Lizzie (we'd gone informal at this point) stopped me halfway to her door. "You're not coming in," she said. "This is a PG date."

And so it was, and the next few after that.

I'd called to ask Lizzie out on a Wednesday night. Trying to play casual.

"Nah," she told me. "I ain't your Wednesday."

"How about Saturday, then?"

"I'll see you then."

She helped guide me back into dating and out of whatever postdivorce world I'd entered. There was no rush or timeline, no agenda. We were simply dating. Meanwhile, she worked on her own career. She had master's degrees in urban planning and criminology and was in her own reinvention phase, having followed a now ex-husband, a visual effects artist, to Hollywood. Now she was starting from scratch again, trying to get a toehold in a business famous for eating and quickly spitting out newcomers.

"I'm getting nowhere," she'd tell me. "I can't make it."

"This will pass," I'd assure her, knowing from too many years of direct experience. Somehow, I convinced her to just take things a day at a time.

And to her, I'd confess my own trust issues and pains as I recovered from my own failed relationship lessons.

"This will pass," *she'd* assure *me* and somehow convinced me to just take things a week at a time. I didn't want to merely fall into something again like twentysomething Tim would have. And she wouldn't let me. "You gotta make sure," she taught me. I was supposed to be the one with all the experience, but it was Lizzie's strength and insight I admired and grew from. As François Truffaut observed, "Women are truly the professionals in love."

Weeks became months, and months became years. One night, while cooking dinner for Elizabeth—don't be too impressed; it was one of those prepared kits and, even more embarrassing, a prepared kit for *tacos*—yes, something this Angeleno should have been able to handle, but she had Italian parents and I needed all the culinary help I could get. We were listening to a country playlist for music to potentially use in the next *Hart of Dixie* episode I was directing and the Train duet with Martina McBride, "Marry Me," began to play.

I looked across the tacos at this captivating woman who had stolen my heart. As one-half of my mind began to form the words that would change the rest of my life, the other half was asking, *Are you really going to do this over poorly constructed tacos?* We looked into each other's eyes as the song played on.

"*Would* you marry me?" I asked.

She would.

In March 2018, we married in a small ceremony with close friends and family. Whatever heartbreak had led me to that doctor's office, Elizabeth had healed.

—

My agent had passed along the script for a new show.

Dr. Vernon "Doc" Mullins, Virgin River's local medical practitioner who discovers that he is going to have to share his quaint town's general practice with a spunky outsider named Mel Monroe—a situation that annoys him greatly.

Sitting on the couch, I thought about the last character and series I'd had a regular part in: Dr. Bertram "Brick" Breeland, Bluebell's local medical practitioner who discovers he is going to have to share his quaint town's general practice with a spunky outsider named Zoe Hart—a situation that annoys him greatly.

Sitting on the couch, I thought about the last series Robert Young (my original *Window on Main Street* hero with the cool fake fireplace) had a regular part in: Dr. Marcus "Crossfire" Welby, Santa Monica's local medical practitioner who discovers he is going to have to share his general practice with a spunky outsider named James Brolin—a situation that Welby seems just fine with.

Okay, fine. So there are some timeless storylines we can always go back to. And yes, *Virgin River* had some similarities to *Hart of Dixie*. Even my agent had figured out that the new Tim's-a-young-cowboy phase of my career had become the Tim's-a-curmudgeonly-doctor phase.

And this wasn't a pilot. In this new streaming world, you got to make a whole *season* of a show regardless of whether it worked in testing or not. Interesting. Also, I genuinely enjoyed the script and characters and was rooting for the show even though I probably wouldn't be in it. I figured there was no way they would want me for this after eighty episodes of me playing a very similar character on the WB. While typecasting often works, I'd too often heard, "Oh, we've seen him play that before; we want something . . . *fresh*."

Boy, was I wrong. The business had changed. Netflix, through their technology, knew audiences *wanted* to see Tim as a curmudgeonly doctor.

Give the people what they want. I said yes and packed for the north.

———

THOUGH THE FICTIONAL TOWN OF VIRGIN RIVER IS SET IN NORTHern California, all of the episodes are shot in Vancouver and surrounding British Columbia. The symphony of lush greens. The salmon-filled rivers. Bald eagles soaring on a salty breeze over towering spruces. Here, the woods breathe with the scent of pine, spruce, and cedar—woods lush and alive with secrets of centuries past. A story waiting to be discovered by those who venture into its depths, where the wild and the sublime are woven together.

I headed up to Vancouver to shoot my first scenes and meet the producers and the rest of the cast. Still a thousand miles from the sets, I ran into someone I've been running into my whole life.

In the airport, also awaiting her flight, was actor Annette O'Toole.

Annette loped across the terminal to give me a big hug. She was playing Hope McCrea, the mayor of Virgin River and Doc's long-standing nemesis to banter with and (spoiler) love interest. There are certain people the universe clearly wants to you spend time with, and Annette and I were undoubtedly put on some list long ago.

We'd first met on *Almost Summer*, the high school drama I'd been in with Bruno Kirby; she was living with Bruno at the time. We all hung out together for weeks. Only months later, we starred together as a married couple in an episode of *What Really Happened to the Class of '65?*—an anthology series chronicling, as you'd assume, the tenth-year check-in on the 1965 class of fictional Bret Harte High School. The script was an intense emotional story, and working with Annette made it one of my favorite acting experiences. There was a special connection between us as actors and as characters—it was the kind of rhythm you're always looking for but don't find as much as you wish you would.

Four years later—post *1941* and *Animal House* and *To Be or Not to Be*—we were paired again for *The Best Legs in the Eighth Grade*, a made-for-television play where an eighth-grade crush almost drives a wedge between me and Annette. Working with her proved effortless again and an absolute pleasure.

Had nearly *forty years* really passed since then? We'd been in our thirties when last passing scripted barbs and kisses. We boarded the plane together and spent the flight laughing about the old times and what would come next.

We landed in Canada and followed a production assistant to a minivan to head deeper into the Canadian wilderness to meet the rest of our new team. Most were younger—younger by *my* perspective—actors I'd not worked with before: series leads Alexandra Breckenridge (my new medical colleague); Martin Henderson (local stud Jack Sheridan); and Colin Lawrence as John "Preacher" Middleton, a close Marine friend of Jack's, who now works at Jack's

Bar. And a dozen more new names to learn, none of us knowing we'd be doing this for years.

Annette and I had many scenes together in the first season, and the shorthand and comfort we had developed decades before came right back. It made acting with her fun and gave extra credence to our TV marriage. We shot from December 3, 2018, until March 26, 2019. It was a lovely time and one of the most unique in my career. For all of my experience, I'd never made a show for a streaming service, and it was a bizarre, at the time, stretch for me. The process of production was the same, but everything else was odd. In all the shows I'd made over the years as an actor, a producer, a director, a guest star, you name it, I was never in a vacuum. Even if I was shooting away from Hollywood, everyone always knew what else was going on with the show. You had people on the set talking about the ratings, you had billboards of your show you'd drive by on the way to work, and you had network executives buzzing around, pressuring the creatives. Everyone was always on edge to see if you would get picked up for more episodes. None of this happened in *Virgin River*.

This was the land of streaming. The show wouldn't be shown for months, so all of that clamor wasn't a factor. On top of our idyllic location and idyllic make-believe world, this was actor's paradise. We made all our episodes for our first season and went home. We became a family and hoped maybe we would see each other again in a year or so.

Two weeks later, we all got told we'd been picked up for another season—but no one in the world even knew our show existed yet. (At least Netflix, obviously, liked the show.) This was mind-blowing to me and a totally new way of doing things. By the end of that same summer, we were already all back shooting Season 2 of *Virgin River*.

Season 1 still hadn't come out yet. We had no ratings, no feedback from audiences, no long critical reviews in *The New Yorker*. Nothing to build on, nothing to learn from. And one week before we wrapped Season 2, on December 6, 2019, our entire first season was released by Netflix. We had no idea what to expect.

That same week, several patients in Wuhan, China, shared symptoms of an atypical pneumonia-like illness.

Three months later, the world shut down.

And while we all set to protecting, healing, praying, and, in many cases, fearing and mourning, many people braced in their homes found this town called Virgin River. The kind of place, perhaps, we all wanted to be in 2020.

We found our audience.

Big-time.

Audiences were devouring Season 1. Netflix had Season 2 in the can, but despite the concerns we all had for production during a pandemic, Netflix got us all safely back to *Virgin River* in the summer of 2020 to start Season 3. In a career that spanned sixty-five years and over two hundred films and TV shows, I'd never experienced anything like a Covid production. We were back to work before the vaccines were widely available, and what was traditionally the extended family of a filming set was now broken carefully into zones, with masked people being forced away from each other rather than together. Despite it all, we pulled together—Virgin River is a special place, after all—and we shot another season.

On the last day of production, the whole cast was together filming a memorial service for a character, Lily, who had passed away. And for the first time, we began to receive news of how our show was being received by audiences. Word began to spread that *Virgin River* was the number one show in the United States and Canada and in almost every other country in the world on Netflix. No one saw this coming. It was surprising and exhilarating. By Season 4, the show had garnered more than 105.4 million hours viewed worldwide, surpassing *Stranger Things* by some 30 million hours. First-time subscribers, said Netflix, were "heading straight" to *Virgin River* after signing up for the streaming service.

Not since VP Hoynes or Otter had random people so connected me to a character. I'd been Doctor "Brick" Breeland in *Hart of Dixie* for four years, but within two years, people were shouting out "Doc Mullins!" at the grocery store or while I was out on a jog.

———

Virgin River *IS* a special place.

Enough to even live up to the audience fantasies. A fictional town like the ones on the big screen I once wanted to vanish into as a child. A place where you can count on those you love. A place that exists safely protected outside the real world.

Much of the crew builds their entire schedule around staying part of the *Virgin River* team. Other jobs—which everyone, from catering to sound and production assistants, needs to stay afloat—come second.

Whether it was our surviving the pandemic together, the success of the series, our being on location in Canada together, or the heart of the show, the cast and crew are a real family.

When I arrived in Virgin River, "Doc" and Tim had a great deal in common. I was the older, experienced actor, the director-producer who had stood toe to toe with Lucille Ball as a teenager and had seen it all, over the years. Doc was much the same, the old stalwart of the town who had seen it all and was watching the world change before his eyes. It has been a great pleasure to once again be surrounded by great, dedicated actors and craftspeople looking to perfect what they do.

Alexandra Breckenridge and Martin Henderson are the talented actors that *Virgin River* flows through—pun intended. It is their characters' love story and interactions that not only keep our audience coming back but also provide a storytelling anchor for all of us who live in Virgin River.

I've watched Alex from the first episodes as she made the character of Mel real and honest. When I'm acting in a scene with her, it somehow reminds me of my friend John Spencer and the hours we once spent together on *The West Wing*. Alexandra and John, not the combo you'd maybe expect. But Alex has the same gift for making people better as an actor and as a character, just as John did.

And Martin Henderson is following the path of Michael Landon. Everything this guy does looks natural and simple. He's more than just an actor on the show and a totally committed and devoted leader on the set. As I write this, he's stepped into the director's chair in our sixth season, the logical next step for this talented creator.

Maybe someday, he'll mention working with me in *his* memoir.

Fade Out

It's late.

My eyes wander again to the figure napping on the couch across the room, a thick woolen blanket draped over Lizzie's legs, a recently started book open across her chest. The setting sun casts a rosy hue across the surrounding trees and then peeks into our home. There, a crackling stone fireplace fills the room in its own warm, flickering light, casting graceful shadows along the walls like an old movie projector. The book barely rising and falling as my wife sleeps, her thin smile now captured forever.

Just past the couch is a stack of board games we'd picked up for when family stops by. In the corner is a Pack 'n Play, bought for when Molly and Emma visit with our grandchildren. It will stand there proudly waiting for them to brighten the room again.

Meanwhile, there's still work to be done. There's a new project with Gary, one of my oldest, dearest friends. There are notes to take and research to dig into and—*how is it?*—miles to go before I sleep. It's almost as if my career is only starting.

Almost.

I've been lucky. I know that. I've always found a place to tell a story, and I like to believe that somewhere there's a kid clicking into their own version of *Witness for the Prosecution* and having their creative fire ignited.

But the work can wait for now.

The fire pops and I turn to watch its dance of flames again, flames telling stories of their own. A tendril of smoke escapes and curls away from the fireplace, carrying the scent of burning maple.

I reach out to touch the fireplace.

It is smooth, hard stone. And warm to the touch.

But this time it is all real.

I can't imagine a more perfect place to be.

Appendix

TIM'S FILMS EVERYONE SHOULD SEE

Lawrence of Arabia

His Girl Friday

Dr. Strangelove or: How I Learned to Stop Worrying and Love the Bomb

The Godfather and *The Godfather Part II*

Psycho (or any Hitchcock film)

Star Wars

Do the Right Thing

Chinatown

The French Connection

M*A*S*H

Young Frankenstein

Unforgiven

Raging Bull (or any Scorsese film)

Schindler's List (or any Spielberg film)

Pulp Fiction (or any Tarantino film)

The Matrix

1917

TIM'S FAVORITE EARLY FOREIGN FILMS

Day for Night

The 400 Blows

Persona (or any Bergman film)

The Seven Samurai

Zatoichi

Yojimbo

8½

La Dolce Vita

The Umbrellas of Cherbourg

Breathless

The Killer

Cinema Paradiso

Malena

TIM'S FAVORITE CONTEMPORARY FOREIGN FILMS

The Host

Roma

City of God

Parasite

In the Mood for Love

Amélie

Oldboy

Crouching Tiger, Hidden Dragon

The Girl with the Dragon Tattoo

Slumdog Millionaire

Talk to Her

TIM'S TOP EARLY AMERICAN FILMS

Gone with the Wind

Witness for the Prosecution

The Wizard of Oz

Singin' in the Rain

It's a Wonderful Life

His Girl Friday

Bringing Up Baby

Casablanca

Some Like It Hot

High Noon

On the Waterfront

The Searchers

The Manchurian Candidate

TIM'S CONTEMPORARY GENIUSES WE SHOULD ALL APPRECIATE

Christopher Nolan

Quentin Tarantino

James Cameron

Guillermo del Toro

Alejandro Iñárritu

John Hughes

The Coen Brothers

Ang Lee

Paul Thomas Anderson

Wes Anderson

Bong Joon Ho

Steven Spielberg

FILM BOOKS TO READ

An Actor Prepares by Konstantin Stanislavski

The Empty Space by Peter Brook

Adventures in the Screen Trade by William Goldman

Hawks on Hawks by Howard Hawks

Rebel Without a Crew by Robert Rodriguez

Making Movies by Sidney Lumet

Cassavetes on Cassavetes by John Cassavetes

Easy Riders, Raging Bulls by Peter Biskind

Hitchcock/Truffaut by François Truffaut

Who the Devil Made It? by Peter Bogdanovich

End Credits

BEFORE ALL ELSE . . . TO MY THREE WONDERFUL CHILDREN: MOLLY, Emma, and Cooper.

You are the most monumental part of my life and have given me my greatest joys and happiness. My life can be divided into halves: before you and after. You centered and saved my life. You matured me. You taught me to be responsible, more patient, caring, and moderate. Through you, I've discovered the meaning of unconditional love.

Since you were born, I have kept your lives as private as possible. Your mother and I constantly shielded you from being photographed or put on public display. We wanted you to have as normal and private an upbringing as possible. I seldom discussed details of your lives in the press or publications, for I chose to keep my career separate from our family life. In this book, I have followed this example again, mostly choosing not to make your lives, as children *or* adults, public. Your own stories, trials, triumphs, and journeys could fill another book, but those are your stories to tell.

My deepest satisfaction comes from the appreciation and admiration that I have for you as human beings. I love the powerful choices that you've made and are making in the lives that you lead. I love you and my grandchildren!

—

To the strong women in my life who led by example: my grandmother Sadie Embry, my mother Sarah Elizabeth, my sister Sue Ellen, my aunt Ellen Estelle, and, of course, my dear and beloved wife Elizabeth.

There are a handful of other people who are the constants in my life. They all have several things in common, too: These are the ones who've been there over the decades, and they also have kept me laughing:

Jared Hoffman: The man for all seasons! First my agent, then my manager, and then my business partner . . . and always my friend. He never let one role overshadow or usurp the other. There with counsel and support through success, pain, growth, and change. And, he has also been there through the lengthy creation and writing of this memoir, helping me to tell the truth, admit my mistakes, and even hold others accountable when warranted.

Gary Goetzman: My oldest pal and "movie brother," who I thank for often bailing me out of tight situations, or trying to, and reminding me that "it's supposed to be fun!" I've watched Gary grow from a precocious kid actor to a sage and seasoned Hollywood producer at Playtone Pictures, partnered with Tom Hanks. And in all of that time, that mischievous thirteen-year-old still rules!

Ron Tanous: My high school friend who always gave me unvarnished truth and approval whenever it was needed. (And still does!) He pointed to the exit doors from bad situations and urged me toward the doors opening in front of me, which I sometimes didn't see. And he's Captain Hook's son!

Bruce McGill: You learn something about someone when you've been in a fight beside them. Bruce probably saved my ass in our SAE run-in during *Animal House*. But he also taught me about blues music, golf, and being a good travel mate. Always a fine actor, he inspired me to be better and to keep growing.

John Gaines: My first important agent, who embraced me for whatever I was and wasn't, and who became a sage adviser and friend when no one else believed in me.

Michelle Minch: A wonderful woman whom I met on a set in Utah. I offered a helping hand when she needed it, and she has always kept hold of that hand, becoming a dearest friend, a sister, and a beacon of truth in my life. Our hands are still linked.

Bruce Paltrow: A producer/director who became a friend and mentor, both in work and in life. He demanded the best from me as an actor but also wanted the best for me as a man. And he taught me to demand good wines and better friends.

Jennifer Leak: An important part of my life: my first love and my first life partner. Though our marriage lasted only a short while, her heart was a flaming ember that always glowed with strength, humor, and decency. Her second husband, James D'Auria, and she were married for forty-seven years, and I'm so pleased that she found the perfect mate to match her wonderful spirit. Sadly, Jennifer passed just a few weeks after I completed this book. Jennifer's ashes were returned to the graveyard of her childhood church in Rumney, Wales.

Mike Liotta: Master public relations guru! He helped me find the balance between my public and private selves, staying true to my work and keeping my feet firmly on the ground. He also afforded me the honor of officiating at the wedding for him and his lovely wife, Erin Ross.

Bill Jacobson: My legal adviser and friend for thirty-plus years. Always a protector and counselor who has, from the beginning, guarded me from the occasional less-than-honest person and offer. Many thanks, Bill.

To Bob Gersh, Bobby Myerow, Nate Steadman, and all my friends at the Gersh Agency for your help and good counsel.

To Geoffrey Girard for your tireless work, guidance, and making my life legible! (Also, an apology to his family for all of the delayed dog walks or cold dinners.)

Thanks to Peter McGuigan and Joanna Rasheed at Ultra Literary for their infinite efforts and encouragement in the creation of this book, the collection of photos, and all the labor involved therein.

To Joe's Falafel in Hollywood, California, who catered many of our work sessions throughout the book-making process. Thank you, Joe!!

A special final note of deep gratitude to the Hachette Book Group: Ben Schafer, my fabulous editor who was always positive and encouraging; Mary Ann Naples, who shepherded our team gently through the maze of work—aided by a superlative team of Publishing Director Michelle Aielli, Creative Director Amanda Kain, Senior Production Editor Sean Moreau, Marketing Director Michael Barrs, Sharon Kunz for all things about publicity, and Carrie Napolitano for finding a way against all odds to clear all of the photos.

Additional thanks to the team at Grand Central Publishing: Ben Sevier, President and Publisher, and Tiffany Porcelli, Associate Director of Marketing.